Understandings of Democracy

Understandings of Democracy

Understandings of Democracy

Origins and Consequences beyond Western Democracies

JIE LU AND YUN-HAN CHU

OXFORD
UNIVERSITY PRESS

Oxford University Press is a department of the University of Oxford. It furthers
the University's objective of excellence in research, scholarship, and education
by publishing worldwide. Oxford is a registered trade mark of Oxford University
Press in the UK and certain other countries.

Published in the United States of America by Oxford University Press
198 Madison Avenue, New York, NY 10016, United States of America.

© Oxford University Press 2022

All rights reserved. No part of this publication may be reproduced, stored in
a retrieval system, or transmitted, in any form or by any means, without the
prior permission in writing of Oxford University Press, or as expressly permitted
by law, by license, or under terms agreed with the appropriate reproduction
rights organization. Inquiries concerning reproduction outside the scope of the
above should be sent to the Rights Department, Oxford University Press, at the
address above.

You must not circulate this work in any other form
and you must impose this same condition on any acquirer.

Library of Congress Cataloging-in-Publication Data
Names: Lu, Jie, 1977– author. | Chu, Yun-han, author.
Title: Understandings of democracy : origins and consequences beyond
western democracies / Jie Lu and Yun-han Chu.
Description: New York, NY : Oxford University Press, 2022. |
Includes bibliographical references and index.
Identifiers: LCCN 2021023468 (print) | LCCN 2021023469 (ebook) |
ISBN 9780197570401 (hardback) | ISBN 9780197570432 | ISBN 9780197570418 |
ISBN 9780197570425 (epub)
Subjects: LCSH: Democracy—Public opinion. |
Democracy—Cross-cultural studies.
Classification: LCC JC423 .L754 2021 (print) | LCC JC423 (ebook) |
DDC 321.8—dc23
LC record available at https://lccn.loc.gov/2021023468
LC ebook record available at https://lccn.loc.gov/2021023469

DOI: 10.1093/oso/9780197570401.001.0001

1 3 5 7 9 8 6 4 2

Printed by Integrated Books International, United States of America

Contents

Acknowledgments   vii

1. Crisis of Democracy and Democratic Conceptions   1
2. New Instruments for Popular Understandings of Democracy   23
3. Varying Understandings of Democracy in the Contemporary World   47
4. Origins of Varying Understandings of Democracy   73
5. Democratic Assessment Colored by Understandings of Democracy   103
6. Political Participation and Varying Understandings of Democracy   133
7. Conclusions   169

Notes   189
References   199
Index   213

Acknowledgments

The academic journey that led to the publication of this book almost parallels the development of the enterprise of regional barometer surveys, including the Asian Barometer Survey (ABS). As survey researchers gathered together and discussed their findings on popular views of democracy in different regions in the late 1990s, they soon realized the significance of distinct popular understandings of the meaning of democracy. The initial response to such varying democratic conceptions was quite technical; that is, appropriate survey tools (e.g., anchoring vignettes) should be adopted to make respondents' views, assessments, and attitudes comparable across regions and societies. How to effectively ensure the functional and measurement equivalence of related survey instruments for valid comparative studies was the central issue. Nevertheless, as more comparative survey data were collected, thanks to the growing enterprise of regional barometer surveys, scholars gradually realized the theoretical significance of different democratic conceptions for understanding the dynamics of democracy in the world. Accordingly, the literature of popular understandings of democracy grew quickly.

Our initial interest in popular understandings of democracy was triggered by our long-term involvement in the ABS. Yun-han Chu is the founding director of the ABS project, and Jie Lu joined the ABS in 2003 as a research assistant (when he was a graduate student at Duke University) to Tianjian Shi (who was the coordinator of the survey team in mainland China). As we compared popular views of democracy between mainland China and Taiwan using data from the first wave of the ABS, we found fascinating similarities and differences in how people conceptualized democracy in these two Chinese societies. Furthermore, such varying understandings were closely associated with their assessment of democratic practices in the two societies. In subsequent ABS surveys, similar patterns and dynamics have been repeatedly identified. Later, at numerous workshops, seminars, and conferences, the significance of varying democratic conceptions has also been mentioned and addressed by survey researchers affiliated with other regional barometer surveys, including the Latinobarómetro, Afrobarometer, South Asian

Barometer, Arab Barometer, and Eurasia Barometer. We soon realized that popular understandings of democracy might offer a critical lens to examine the dynamics of democratic changes not just in the Greater China region but also around the world. As a result, we launched a comparative study on popular understandings of democracy covering seventy-two societies.

This project would not have been possible without those who helped us with data collection. We deeply appreciate the contribution of all anonymous survey respondents who provided the key information for our empirical exercise. They have been and will continue to be the drivers of democracy's future, and their views and behaviors will shape the world's future political development. Hopefully, our book has contributed to a better understanding of the role played by these people in democratic practices around the world. Large-scale comparative survey projects like the Global Barometer Surveys would not have been possible without the industrious and creative efforts of survey researchers. Many of them had to work in unfriendly and even hostile environments to collect high-quality survey data, risking their health and security. We are particularly grateful to Marta Lagos of Latinobarómetro, E. Gyimah-Boadi, Boniface Dulani, Carolyn Logan, and Robert Mattes of Afrobarometer, Suhas Palshikar and Sandeep Shastri of South Asian Barometer, Michael Robins, Mark Tessler, and Amaney Jamal of Arab Barometer, and Christian Haerpfer of Eurasia Barometer. Special thanks are due to our colleagues at the ABS headquarters, including Yu-tzung Chang, Min-hua Huang, Kai-ping Huang, Chia-yin Wei, Chia-lin Hsu, and Pei-ju Chao.

Each regional barometer has received substantial and long-term financial support from various donors and funding agencies. For example, the Institute of Political Science at Academia Sinica and Hu Fu Center for East Asia Democratic Studies at National Taiwan University have co-hosted the regional headquarters of the ABS and the Secretariat of Global Barometer Surveys for more than a decade. The ABS has received generous multi-year funding support from Taiwan's Ministry of Education and Ministry of Science and Technology, as well as the Henry Luce Foundation in the United States. Individual Asian teams have received support from national funding agencies as well as international donors. These institutional and financial supports were crucial in completing this project.

The Renmin University of China offered teaching release for Jie Lu in Fall 2020, which greatly facilitated his work on the book manuscript. This was supported by the Fundamental Research Funds for the Central Universities and the Research Funds of Renmin University of China (20XNQ003).

At various stages of the project, conversations with (in alphabetical order) John Aldrich, Daniel Bell, Michael Bratton, Joseph Chan, Russell Dalton, Larry Diamond, Bruce Dickson, Min-hua Huang, Bob Mattes, Andrew Nathan, Chih-yu Shih, Doh Chull Shin, Wenfang Tang, and Guangbin Yang were very valuable. We were also fortunate to receive excellent and detailed comments on the entire manuscript from two anonymous referees, who have pushed us to sharpen our theoretical arguments and better connect our research to the broader literature on democracy, public opinion, and political behavior. We also would like to thank our editor at Oxford University Press, Angela Chnapko, for her interest in this project. Mark Weatherall and Audrey Guerra provided excellent editorial assistance at the last stage of this project, which significantly improved the presentation of this book.

We are very grateful for having the opportunity to work with prominent scholars in the enterprise of regional barometer surveys. The whole industry has benefited from their continued efforts and contribution. It is very unfortunate that two leading scholars in the field, Professor Fu Hu and Professor Tianjian Shi, have left us unexpectedly; both were pioneers in the field and played a critical role in the development of this enterprise. Their passing greatly saddened us but also encouraged us to carry on the ongoing research projects and to keep pushing forward our understanding of democratic practices around the world. Therefore, we dedicate this book to our mentors and friends, Professor Fu Hu and Professor Tianjian Shi.

1
Crisis of Democracy and Democratic Conceptions

As a leading scholar of democracy has acknowledged: "democracy is in crisis" (Diamond 2019). In Western democracies, the rise of authoritarian populism (Norris and Inglehart 2018) poses critical challenges to the practices of liberal democracy (whose supremacy has been almost taken for granted since the end of World War II). These challenges have been further exacerbated by the declining popular confidence in democracy among citizens (especially younger cohorts) of Western democracies (Mounk 2018), which may be the harbinger of a deconsolidation of established democracies (Foa and Mounk 2016, 2017; Howe 2017).[1] Beyond Western democracies, the long expected democratic transitions in authoritarian regimes and consolidation of new democracies (thanks to economic modernization, new information technologies, the intentional promotion of democracy advocates, etc.) (Inglehart 2018; Norris and Inglehart 2009; Boix 2011) have come to a halt or even been reversed, partly due to authoritarian or populist leaders' calculated preemptive strikes against opposition mobilization, by soliciting and responding to their citizens' needs more effectively (Tang 2016; Dickson 2016; Manion 2016), smart use of new information technologies (King et al. 2013, 2017), and strategic institutional engineering (Boix and Svolik 2013; Gandhi and Lust-Okar 2009; Truex 2016).

Meanwhile, democracy still enjoys its supremacy in contemporary political discourse, with limited meaningful challenges from alternatives. In the United States, despite his provocative Twitter messages and threats to lock up political opponents, President Trump still had to negotiate with rather than dictate to members of the Democratic Party on various political issues. In Russia, President Putin has never been shy of using all necessary means (including but not limited to arresting his opponents) to secure his political control and power; but he still competes in presidential elections (albeit manipulated in his favor) to earn political legitimacy and did observe Russia's presidential term limits by stepping aside in 2008 (then resuming the presidency in 2012).[2] In Philippines, President Duterte de facto legalized the killing of, and encouraged Filipinos to kill, drug dealers and addicts without observing due process rights when he assumed the presidency, yet he also publicly ordered the military to shoot him if he ever tried to stay on for a second term. Similarly, few of today's authoritarian leaders publicly denounce democracy; instead, they are more inclined to present their regimes as democracies (with varying adjectives attached of course). Furthermore, ordinary people appreciate democracy, widely and deeply: several rounds of large-scale public opinion surveys have established its popularity, even in societies with limited practice of democracy (Cho 2015; Dalton et al. 2007; Shin 2017). Democracy is still the "only game" in contemporary political discourse.

Given the popularity and supremacy of democracy in contemporary political discourse, the hotly debated and discussed crisis of democracy is puzzling. Basically, if most people love democracy and politicians (whether they like it or not) have to live with democracy, how can democracy be in trouble? More specifically, if people love democracy, should they not despise authoritarian leaders and regimes, or even join the advocates of democracy to rebel against authoritarian leaders and regimes? Should not they vote against populist leaders who have blatantly violated democratic institutions, procedures, or norms?

To comprehensively address these questions, we need to examine both supply-side (i.e., evolving political practices and institutional engineering led by political elites) and demand-side (i.e., transformative opinions and behaviors among the masses) dynamics. Intellectual exercises on supply-side dynamics have received a lot of attention from students of democratization and democracy-promoting institutions. Meanwhile, in practical terms, advice and assistance have been offered to emerging democracies in all areas including constitutional design, choices of electoral systems, best practice for enhancing electoral integrity, rule of law, transparency, the protection of minorities' rights, and capacity building in legislative and judicial branches (Diamond and Morlino 2005; Carothers 2015).[3] In contrast, demand-side dynamics have been given scanty attention so far. Therefore, in this book, we focus on some key micro-dynamics that have driven related mass attitudes and behaviors, all of which are centered on how people understand democracy in different ways.[4]

More specifically, we argue that (1) people hold distinct understandings of democracy; (2) popular conceptions of democracy are significantly shaped by socioeconomic and political contexts; (3) such varying conceptions generate different baselines for people to assess democratic practices and to establish their views of democracy; and (4) such distinct conceptions also drive political participation in different ways. Overall, popular understandings of democracy have critically shaped how citizens respond to authoritarian or populist practices in contemporary politics. This book tries to theorize and demonstrate that, as a critical but under-appreciated component of demand-side dynamics, varying conceptions of democracy offer significant explanatory power for understanding why democracy is in trouble in today's world, even when most people profess to love democracy.

1.1 The value of democratic conceptions for understanding the crisis of democracy

There is no lack of research on the crisis of democracy. Nevertheless, there is a noticeable division among the scholars regarding their preferred explanatory variables (depending on their subjects of interest). For those who are interested in possible deconsolidation in democracies (e.g., the rise of populism and extreme parties, increasing political polarization, growing pessimistic views of democracy, etc.), certain macro socioeconomic and political changes over recent decades (e.g., increasing inequality, spread of social media and new information technologies, economic stagnation, increasing salience of identity politics) (Mounk 2018), the cultural backlash against the progressive values that have developed in industrial democracies (a backlash which has been further exacerbated by declining existential security) (Inglehart 2018; Norris and Inglehart 2018; Inglehart and Norris 2017), as well as the compelling inducements and constraints emanating from the international environment (sometimes in a very dramatic way, like a seismic rearrangement of power in the geopolitical arena) (Huntington 1991; Whitehead 2001; Kagan 2015), are the variables of interest.

For those who are interested in the stagnation or recession in democratic transitions in authoritarian regimes, as well as such regimes' resilience against the pressure for democratic changes, authoritarian leaders' strategic institutional engineering (for power-sharing, coopting dissidents, training and disciplining rank and file members, collecting information, regulating and censoring media, etc.) is the focus for analysis (Svolik 2012; Kim and Gandhi 2010; Truex 2016; Koss 2018; Pepinsky 2013; Gandhi and Lust-Okar

2009). Clearly, research on these subjects has greatly improved our understanding of the crisis of democracy in today's world. But we still are left wondering whether there is something shared in common among societies with distinct political regimes that might have contributed to the crisis of democracy. Put another way, can we identify some commonly shared feature or factor that might enable us to establish a coherent framework to explain the crisis of democracy in distinct political settings?

To effectively understand the crisis of democracy, it is important to acknowledge two empirically established facts. First, despite its challenges and problems, democracy still enjoys supremacy in contemporary political discourse. Few politicians are willing to publicly denounce democracy, and most people express a love for democracy (as least, according to existing public opinion surveys) (Dalton et al. 2007; Shin 2017). Second, people hold various expectations of democracy. Some people see democracy as a way of securing their dignity as a human being by ensuring their basic rights and liberty; while others see democracy as a way of facilitating economic prosperity, improving living standards, and delivering quality governance (Shin and Kim 2018; Bratton and Mattes 2001; Lu 2013; Lu and Shi 2015). Basically, democracy is widely appreciated; but people appreciate the type of democracy tailored to their respective personal preferences. This generates highly significant psychological, cognitive, and behavioral dynamics for understanding the prospects for democracy in today's world.

On the one hand, people embracing distinct conceptions of democracy may assess their political regime's performance and democratic nature, respond to political activists' and politicians' mobilization, and engage in various participatory activities in different ways. On the other hand, politicians and political activists may also have strong incentives to shape how people understand democracy and present their way or proposed way of governing as genuinely democratic, given their power in setting the agenda for political discussion, priming specific emotional responses, and framing political discourse. These mass- and elite-dynamics have been carefully documented in both democracies (Carey et al. 2019) and authoritarian regimes (Lu and Shi 2015; Lu et al. 2014).

Consequently, such dynamics can explain why some citizens of democracies have been led astray by populist politicians, ignored these politicians' blatant violations of core democratic institutions, procedures, and norms, and even actively engaged in radical political activities exacerbating political polarization and gridlock. At the same time, such dynamics can also explain why some citizens of authoritarian societies have been incapable of seeing through the democratic disguise of authoritarian leaders, have willingly endorsed the rule of such leaders as some form of democracy (as long as they can deliver quality governance), and have tended to remain silent when democracy advocates mobilize against the authoritarian regime. In sum, by focusing on how people conceptualize democracy in different ways, as well as such varying understandings' attitudinal and behavioral consequences, we can establish a coherent framework (i.e., covering societies with distinct political settings) to shed light on the micro-foundations of democracy's contemporary crisis.[5]

Hence, we strongly believe that knowing how ordinary people define democracy and why they conceptualize democracy in specific ways provides a critical lens through which we can examine and answer many critical questions raised in the aforementioned debates and discussions on the prospects for democracy in today's world. For instance, why do we observe declining enthusiasm for democracy in the trilateral democracies (especially among their younger citizens), as documented by recent surveys (Foa and Mounk 2017, 2016; Inglehart 2016)? Despite the repeatedly demonstrated relationship between economic growth and democracy (Przeworski et al. 2000; Barro 1999), as well as the cogent arguments from different versions of modernization theory (Welzel 2013; Inglehart and Welzel 2005; Eisenstadt 1966; Tipps 1973), why have the expected transitions to democracy in some authoritarian societies (including China and Vietnam as prominent cases) not been achieved, even after decades of continuous economic growth? Furthermore, if we really want to address some of the major deficiencies and problems in existing democratic institutions, thus boosting popular enthusiasm for democracy and improving its prospects, what should be our priorities?

Compared to the aforementioned societal-level socioeconomic, institutional, and cultural features, democratic conceptions (as an individual feature) have many more specific and concrete implications for mass opinions and behaviors, thus enabling us to more effectively uncover and demonstrate the micro-foundations of democracy's contemporary crisis. Compared to certain deep-rooted values (e.g., self-expressive or emancipative values) internalized by individuals through long-term socialization and consolidated via generational replacement, popular conceptions of democracy not only offer more satisfying middle-range explanations (with clearly specified causal mechanisms) for related political attitudes and behaviors but also provide greater opportunities to examine the political dimension of democracy's contemporary crisis. For example, what is the role of strategic political competition in shaping popular understandings of democracy (which, in turn, affect how people view their regime's political practices in distinct ways and push for political changes in their preferred but different directions).

1.2 Why do popular understandings of democracy matter?

It is nothing new to argue that people hold different views on many critical things, including democracy. For students of political science, this lack of consensus is no accident, since they cannot even agree among themselves (i.e., the so-called experts on political issues) on what democracy means (Schmitter and Karl 1991) or on the effective measures of democracy for empirical analysis (Treier and Jackman 2008). However, the belief in the superiority of democracy as a political regime (as least, in comparison to all other regimes that have been tried in history, as Winston Churchill famously argued) in promoting people's collective welfare and ensuring their dignity via institutionalized protection of rights and liberty has been widespread since the end of World War II, despite some recent scholarly reflections and debates on these issues (Fukuyama 2014, 2016).[6] Furthermore, thanks to the dominance of the liberal democracy discourse that has been successfully established since its Third Wave (Huntington 1991), "democracy" has become the only discursive game in town, if not the only political one (Dalton et al. 2007; Shin 2017).

As a consequence, most people associate "democracy" with many desirable things, although many may just throw up their hands when probed for its meaning (Cho 2014, 2015). Even those who can attach substantive meanings to the D-word do not necessarily share a common understanding of the term. Likewise, most politicians rarely denounce democracy in public and have tried to present their behaviors, policymaking, and even power maneuvers as democratic, even though their blatant and outrageous violations of certain fundamental principles of democracy have been documented by journalists and scholars.[7] In particular, for many authoritarian leaders, democracy is a necessary and convenient political fig leaf that can be adapted for and tailored to their political rule and survival. Moreover, such suitably tailored discourses on democracy have been systematically cultivated and promoted, especially in non-democracies (Lu and Shi 2015; Lu et al. 2014; Kirsch and Welzel 2019; Kruse et al. 2019). It should not be difficult for students of political science to see through politicians' manipulation of discourses on democracy and related propaganda. However, it would be a mistake to downplay the significance of such manipulation and propaganda or simply brush them aside as cynical political maneuvers.

Existing scholarship on the influence of elite discourse on public opinion (Zaller 1992; Druckman 2004; Druckman et al. 2013) strongly suggests that political leaders can collect concrete benefits by engaging in such discourse manipulation and propaganda (Geddes and Zaller 1989; Stockmann 2013; Lu et al. 2014), in particular, by shaping how their people understand democracy (besides using democracy as a garb for their power maneuvers). Therefore, the crux of our argument is that popular understandings of democracy provide the benchmark against which people assess their existing political regimes and evaluate possible alternatives, by shaping their expectations on what a "good" regime should look like. Such understandings and related assessments may further shape how people participate in politics. All these have significant implications for political dynamics in societies with different political regimes and varying experiences of democratic politics.

In established democracies, as Crow (2010) argues, people are inclined to assign different weights to various aspects of democracy. For instance, US youth have differing views on whether individual rights or equality should be emphasized more as defining features of democracy (Flanagan et al. 2005). The differences among European adults in their conceptions of democracy are no smaller, with some highlighting the significance of social justice and others prioritizing liberty and free elections (Ferrin and Kriesi 2016).[8] Likewise, in Latin American and African democracies, people differ in their democratic conceptions regarding whether more weight should be placed on the protection of political rights or on sound socioeconomic performance (Canache 2012; Mattes and Bratton 2007; Gillman 2018; Baviskar and Malone 2004; Camp 2001).

Theoretically, for citizens of established democracies who prioritize quality governance (including but not limited to clean and efficient politics as well as effective social welfare systems that contain and even rebalance escalating inequality) as defining features of democracy, their evaluations of democratic governments with lackluster performance in these regards are unlikely to be flattering. The resulting unfavorable views of democratic governments and political authorities, in turn, could erode these citizens' enthusiasm for democracy. Moreover, a sustained fermentation of such unfavorable views, if not effectively addressed and rectified in a timely manner, may further lead to widespread apathy toward democracy. This could be part of the reason why recent survey data show an alarming crisis in popular support for democracy in many established democracies (Foa and Mounk 2016, 2017). It may also explain why students of democracy have been calling for more effort on ensuring good governance in democracies to confront the challenges posed by declining popular support for democracy (Diamond and Plattner 2015; Fukuyama 2016; Rotberg 2014). Furthermore, as such apathy grows, people in democracies might become less sensitive to politicians' abuse of power, less able to act against their violations of fundamental democratic principles, and more attracted to their populist appeals. These factors favor the rise of populist authoritarian leaders in democracies (Moffitt 2016; Mudde and Rovira Kaltwasser 2012; Norris and Inglehart 2018), clearly damage the health of democracy, and significantly contribute to the deconsolidation or even death of democracy (Levitsky and Ziblatt 2018).

In authoritarian societies or new democracies, the political implications of varying popular understandings of democracy are at least as serious as, if not more serious than, those in established democracies given the high stakes associated with potential regime change and institutional rearrangement (Lu and Shi 2015; Lu et al. 2014). Existing studies on democratization and regime change generally assume that popular demand for democracy exclusively follows the institutional prescriptions (i.e., highlighting competitive and fair elections, institutionalized protection of liberty and rights, division of power, checks and balances, the rule of law secured by independent judiciary, etc.) that are widely shared and promoted by the advocates of democracy in these societies. Therefore, whenever democracy movements appear, average citizens are expected to naturally and effectively align their demands with those of democracy advocates and, thus, to collectively push to replace non-democratic regimes with democratic ones.

However, in today's world, almost all authoritarian leaders have tried to present their political practice as some form of democracy. These leaders are also keen on using the mass media and education system to indoctrinate their citizens with such manipulated discourses on democracy that work to their advantage (Reuter and Szakonyi 2015; Stockmann 2013; Kirsch and Welzel 2019; Kruse et al. 2019). For citizens of authoritarian societies or new democracies who prioritize effective governance (including but not limited to sustained social stability, reliable access to basic needs, steady economic growth, etc.) as a defining characteristic of democracy, a competent and efficient authoritarian government may not necessarily be less democratic than a dysfunctional democratic one (e.g., entrapped in partisan gridlock, paralyzed by ethnic conflicts, or crippled by corrupt and inefficient bureaucrats). Thus, in authoritarian societies, democracy advocates' call to overthrow the regime and replace it with a genuine democracy might fall on deaf ears, especially when the regime can rule effectively and govern competently.[9] The prevalence of such understandings in new democracies also creates a favorable environment for shrewd and ambitious politicians, who might take advantage of their citizens' growing dissatisfaction with newly elected governments, offer them attractive promises and short-term benefits, and eventually engineer possible backsliding to authoritarianism to fulfill their desire for unchecked power.[10]

Overall, it should be fair to argue that examining the origins, dynamics, and consequences of popular conceptions of democracy offers critical information for understanding public opinion and political behavior in both democracies and authoritarian regimes. Furthermore, such nuanced micro-level dynamics can also help us understand significant political changes in the contemporary world by providing an often ignored but critical piece to the puzzle. The main point is that, without effectively integrating popular understandings of democracy into theory building, it is very difficult to provide solid and meaningful micro-foundations for explaining the aforementioned macro-political phenomena, such as declining support for democracy and rising populism in democracies, as well as the existence of widespread support for democracy but without sufficient collective mobilization for political changes in autocracies.

1.3 Critical but missing dynamics

We further argue that the salient trade-offs between democratic principles and instrumental gains (both of which are desirable to most people in any society) are central to the theorization, operationalization, and measurement of popular conceptions of democracy.[11] Unfortunately, despite the widely acknowledged value of incorporating popular understandings of democracy, until now, pertinent scholarship has not sufficiently theorized the salience of popular willingness to trade off democratic principles for instrumental gains and has not effectively developed appropriate empirical instruments to capture these critical dynamics.[12]

Existing scholarship on democratic transition and consolidation has carefully documented the widespread anxiety over such trade-offs among the masses (Pop-Eleches and Tucker 2014, 2017; Houle 2009; Howe 2017) and the elites' strategic weighing of such trade-offs in their political maneuvers (Acemoglu and Robinson 2006; Boix 2003). Even in established democracies, such trade-offs might be highlighted and even mobilized to the center of partisan politics under favorable contexts. As Wolf (2017, 2019) has vividly demonstrated in his widely-read *Financial Times* reports, the 2008–2009 global financial crisis and the ensuing Great Recession have created exactly the context that enhances the salience of such trade-offs.

Given the worsening fiscal imbalance and threatened viability of entitlement programs in advanced industrial democracies, the economic insecurity and associated anxiety of the middle and working class have been aggravated. These mature democracies have also witnessed exacerbated distributive conflicts between the winners and losers of economic globalization, as well as inflamed popular resentment regarding their glaring income and wealth inequality. Altogether, these have contributed to the rise of the radical anti-globalization movement of the far left and the ultra-nationalistic populist movement of the far right in North America and Europe (Mudde and Rovira Kaltwasser 2012; Webb 2013; Moffitt 2016; Bonikowski and Gidron 2016). What has further surprised most students of democracy is how citizens in these democracies have responded to populist politicians' blatant violations of fundamental democratic principles. Rather than punishing these populist politicians with their ballots, electorates in many cases have even rewarded them at the ballot box. These are glaring reminders of the threats to key democratic principles and institutions. In other words, people living under different regime types (including autocracies, new democracies, and established democracies) do recognize and evaluate such potential trade-offs. And, when necessary, they do make meaningful and consequential choices between key democratic principles/institutions and something else (depending on how they conceptualized democracy).

For us, the contrast between the following two conceptions of democracy is critical and central. The first understanding emphasizes the instrumental values of democracy in delivering socioeconomic and political goods. Thus, democracy is primarily conceptualized as a way of governance and is expected to be competent in satisfying its people's demands via effective public policies. The second understanding of democracy prioritizes the intrinsic values of democracy in ensuring a decent way of life for everyone. Therefore, democracy is mainly conceptualized as a way of life and is expected to realize the principle of popular sovereignty and ensuring its people's dignity, as well as their inalienable rights and liberty, via established institutions and procedures. Overall, the contrast between the two conceptions of democracy hinges upon the willingness to trade off democratic principles for instrumental gains.[13]

Theoretically, the prevalence of such willingness in an authoritarian society substantially raises the bar for its transition to democracy. Such barriers can be further exacerbated when the authoritarian regime is competent in satisfying their citizens' material needs, effective in driving liberal democratic ideas out of their mass media and education system (including repressing advocates of such ideas), and skillful in shaping their people's hearts and minds via indoctrination and propaganda. Similarly, in a democracy, the prevalence of such willingness also raises popular expectations and demands for elected leaders to deliver short-term material benefits, creates space for various populist sentiments and extreme parties, and generates leeway for ambitious politicians to ignore or violate key democratic principles in the name of satisfying popular needs. All these pose significant challenges to the consolidation and health of democracy. Conversely, when citizens are less willing to trade off key democratic principles for instrumental gains, political mobilization for democratic transition in authoritarian societies can be greatly eased by targeting the regimes' under-provision or lack of democratic institutions and procedures, thus orienting popular dissatisfaction and collective efforts against the Achilles heel of authoritarian regimes. Similarly, by controlling and inhibiting such willingness, democracies can improve their consolidation and resilience by aligning regime support with people's identification with key democratic principles, thus making popular support for democracy more diffuse (Easton 1965, 1975) and less susceptible to short-term vicissitudes in governance.

It is important to emphasize that we do not argue that there are some inherent and unavoidable trade-offs between key democratic principles/procedures and good governance. A positive correlation between democratic institutions and procedures, on the one hand, and good governance, on another hand, has been theoretically defended and empirically established in the literature (Przeworski et al. 2000; Treisman 2000; Olken 2010; Deacon 2009). What we have tried to argue is that, when socioeconomic and political conditions highlight the tensions between the intrinsic and instrumental aspects of democracy, people's willingness to trade off the former for the latter has critical implications for democracy. The continuing ramifications of the 2008–2009 global financial crisis, as well as the ongoing COVID-19 pandemic, have created exactly such a context around the world.

Besides its theoretical and academic significance for pertinent comparative research, this contrast is also of high salience in today's world, given the growing tensions between the world's two largest economies, China and the United States. Both countries, at least according to their respective official discourse, are "great democracies."[14] Nevertheless, these two countries boast distinct political regimes and rely on different models of governance and growth and equally actively engage in global campaigns to, explicitly or implicitly, defend and promote their respective ways of governance.

Politically, since the Cold War (1947–1991), the United States has been closely associated with the model of liberal democracy in global political discourse, although there are growing concerns over the deteriorating quality of US liberal democracy over the past decades (Fukuyama 2006; Gilens 2005; Mounk 2018; Diamond 2019), especially in the Trump era (Inglehart and Norris 2017). Economically, the United States has pioneered and been leading the world's technological innovations since the 1970s, especially in information technology, artificial intelligence, and biotechnology. The *2019 Global Technology Innovation Report* still identifies it as the most promising market for innovation and technology breakthroughs, endorsed by 23% of those surveyed.[15] The US economy is recovering from the lingering impact of the 2008–2009 global financial crisis triggered by its subprime mortgage market crisis. Its GDP growth rate has bounced back from negative growth of about 2.5% in 2009 to positive growth of about 2.3% in 2019, performing much better than most other established democracies. Overall, the defining features of US democracy are embodied within its constitution, which promotes checks and balances, division of power, rule of law, and institutionalized protection of people's inalienable rights and liberty. This model has had a long and lasting impact on many people's understandings of democracy. It has also guided the designs of constitutions in many new democracies. Meanwhile, it is undeniable that US society, like that of most advanced industrial democracies, is challenged by increasing inequality, polarization, and partisan gridlock as well as shrinking social mobility. The unexpected success of Donald Trump in the 2016 presidential election and the rising anti-establishment and populist sentiment among the US public are indubitable indicators of such problems (Mounk 2018; Norris and Inglehart 2018). It should be reasonable to argue that, despite its obvious advantages, US democracy also shows major deficiencies.

China's market-oriented reforms and state-led industrialization since the late 1970s have not only prevented the collapse of its economy but also transformed it into "the world's factory," contributing to around 30% of global economic growth in 2018. Meanwhile, China also has moved up the global value chain by restructuring its economy via government-sponsored technological innovations. The same report on global technology innovation in 2019 ranks China as the second most promising market for innovation and technology breakthroughs, endorsed by 17% of those surveyed and outperforming the UK (endorsed by 9% and ranked third), Japan (ranked fourth), and India and Singapore (tied for fifth). Although the Chinese economy similarly suffered from the 2008–2009 global financial crisis and was further burdened by various domestic issues, it still managed to secure impressive growth rates of 6.6% and 9.4% in 2008 and 2009 respectively, while accommodating the "new normal" with corresponding adjustments in its economy. Furthermore, according to recent statistics from the International Labor Organization,[16] China has managed to ensure a real salary growth faster than that of all G20 countries and most other economies in the world following the 2008–2009 global financial crisis and the ensuing Great Recession. In other words, the Chinese way of promoting economic growth has done a much better job in riding the tide lifting all boats. As Fukuyama publicly claimed at the beginning of 2016: "an historic contest is underway, largely hidden from public view, over competing Chinese and Western strategies to promote economic growth. The outcome of this struggle will determine the fate of much of Eurasia in the decades to come."[17]

It is no wonder that many developing and even developed countries are stunned by China's outstanding performance in achieving economic growth, despite increasing concerns over its sustainability and wild speculations about its forthcoming economic crisis or even collapse. Politically, Communism mixed with some Confucian components remains the official ideology endorsed by the Chinese Communist Party (CCP). Since the late 1970s, the CCP has moved away from its earlier totalitarian model of governance under Mao (Naughton 2007; Fewsmith 2013), promoted some institutionalization in its selection and management of cadres and leaders (Li 2012; Nathan 2003), and expanded its domestic channels for participation (Wang 2006, 2008; Tsai 2015; Chen 2012; Tang 2016). Nevertheless, China still is today's largest one-party regime, with sophisticated and effective control over its society and people (Shirk 2007; Shambaugh 2008; Dickson 2016) and limited meaningful competition in its domestic politics (Shambaugh 2016). Meanwhile, the CCP is fully aware of the dominance of democracy in contemporary political discourse and therefore seeks to present itself as a "genuine democracy," though of course with Chinese characteristics (or socialist democracy), to both domestic and international audiences (Lu et al. 2014; Lu and Shi 2015; Shi and Lu 2010; Hu 2020). This new "democracy cocktail" mixing economic growth, social stability, and political monopoly by a disciplined and competent ruling party has become increasingly attractive for many developing societies, especially those trapped in poverty and violence and lacking normal political life. Therefore, for some students of democracy, the China model has posed a serious and meaningful challenge to the prospects for liberal democracy in today's world (Diamond and Plattner 2015; Plattner 2017; Öniş 2017; Diamond 2019).

The book's main goal is to understand how popular conceptions of democracy may affect the prospects for democracy in the twenty-first century. Our comprehensive review of the pertinent literature, careful observation of major socioeconomic and political changes in today's world, the growing salience of the rivalry between China and the United States in promoting their respective ways of governance, and the widely shared acknowledgment of democracy as the most attractive and politically correct veneer for politicians to present their regimes all suggest the necessity of incorporating popular understandings of democracy in our analysis of the prospects of democracy. Furthermore, popular willingness to trade off democratic principles for instrumental gains should be central to the theorization, operationalization, and measurement of democratic conceptions.

1.4 Research design and data

To effectively address our research questions, we need two sources of data for empirical analysis. First, we need detailed information about how people conceptualize democracy, as well as associated demographic, sociopsychological, cognitive, behavioral, and other attitudinal features. These will enable us to examine individual-level cognitive, psychological, attitudinal, and behavioral dynamics centered around popular understandings of democracy. Second, we need detailed information about the socioeconomic, political, and cultural contexts in which people are embedded. These will enable us to examine some societal-level macro-mechanisms, as well as possible macro-micro interactions, that might shape and moderate the aforementioned individual-level dynamics centered around democratic conceptions. For the first, sampling surveys provide the more effective tools for data collection. For the second, international organizations like the World Bank, IMF, and Freedom House, as well as various academic sources, have complied relevant datasets. Methodologically, we mostly rely on mixed-effect models (Gelman and Hill 2007; Luke 2004; Snijders and Bosker 2012) to integrate these two sources of data for effective statistical analysis and efficient estimation.

Despite rapid growth, there are still only a limited number of large-scale comparative studies (i.e., covering multiple regions with varying political and cultural traditions) on popular understandings of democracy, primarily due to the challenges and difficulties in gathering appropriate data.[18] The World Values Survey (WVS) and regional barometer survey projects (e.g., Latinobarómetro, Afrobarometer, Asian Barometer, etc.) provide the key empirical data for existing large-scale comparative studies. In one of the earliest comparative analyses of different conceptions of democracy, Dalton et al. (2007) examine popular responses from forty-nine societies, with survey data collected from various sources during the late 1990s and early 2000s. Cho (2015) extends this line of research using the 2005–2008 WVS data from fifty societies for analysis. The most recent scholarship on "authoritarian notions of democracy" by Kirsch and Welzel (2019) relies on 2010–2014 WVS data from sixty societies for analysis; while Zagrebina (2020) broadens the geographical coverage of her examination of popular preferences over visible-vs.-invisible attributes of democracy by combining 2005–2014 WVS data from seventy-five societies. Table 1.1 provides detailed information on the geographical coverage of these studies.

Different from the aforementioned comparative research on popular understandings of democracy, this book examines the 2010–2013 Global Barometer Surveys (GBS II) data from seventy-one societies. GBS II offers the only large-scale comparative survey data with the appropriate instruments that capture the critical trade-off dynamics in how people conceptualize democracy, and also enables us to extend this line of research with an extensive, but more focused geographical coverage.[19]

The GBS is a collaborative research project consisting of six regional barometers. It is the first comprehensive effort to measure, at a mass level, the current social, political, and economic climate around the world. It provides an independent, non-partisan, scientific, and multidisciplinary view of

Table 1.1 Geographic Coverage of Related Large-Scale Comparative Studies

	Dalton et al. 2007	Cho 2015	Kirsh and Welzel 2019	Zagrebina 2020	This Book
North America	1	2	1	2	1
Oceania		1	2	2	
Western Europe	2	10	5	11	
Eastern Europe	7	9	13	17	
Latin America	17	7	9	9	18
East and Southeast Asia	9	8	9	9	13
South Asia		1	2	2	5
Sub-Saharan Africa	12	6	7	10	30
North Africa		2	2	4	5
Middle East	1	4	10	9	
Total	49	50	60	75	72

Notes: The number of covered societies in a region is shown in cells. The cells with dark grey shading show the number of covered societies in the regions of high concern for this book.

public opinion on a range of policy-relevant issues. Currently, the GBS network covers 70% of the world's population and is still expanding. It now covers six regions, including Africa (Afrobarometer), East and Southeast Asia (Asian Barometer), South Asia (South Asia Barometer), Central and South America (Latinobarómetro), the Middle East (Arab Barometer), and countries of the former Soviet Union (Eurasia Barometer). To ensure a meaningful benchmark case for related comparisons, this book also includes a national representative survey of the United States in 2017. Altogether, this book examines representative survey data from seventy-two societies.[20]

As shown in Table 1.1, the seventy-one cases in GBS II exclusively come from societies outside of Western democracies. Furthermore, we have more societies from Asia (including East, Southeast, and South Asia) and Africa (including both sub-Saharan and North Africa).[21] This not only dramatically expands the related literature's geographical coverage (thus, making related empirical analysis more comprehensive and corresponding conclusions more general) but also offers additional opportunities to scrutinize the contextualized dynamics in the evolution of popular conceptions of democracy, as well as how such varying understandings shape people's assessment of democratic practices and engagement in distinct participatory activities.

This is of particular significance for our understanding of democracy's contemporary crisis, especially beyond the context of Western democracies. For instance, many new democracies established in Africa and Latin America since the Third Wave have to fight for their consolidation and against the push-back of authoritarian forces, especially when their economic performance and governance quality become worrisome. Despite their much longer history of democratic practices, South Asian democracies are still confronted with the challenges posed by religious and ethnic conflicts, as well as the mounting pressure of satisfying the demands of their large, low-income population. East and Southeast Asian democracies have also faced challenges over recent years as the engine of their economic growth has switched to a lower gear, a challenge further exacerbated by various social and political problems like inequality, ethnic intolerance, and corruption. Meanwhile, some authoritarian regimes in East Asia (including China, Vietnam, and Singapore) and Africa (including Angola, Cameroon, and Uganda) have been quite resilient against the pressures of democratization. Incorporating these cases into our empirical analysis will dramatically enrich the variation in the socioeconomic, political, and cultural contexts wherein popular conceptions of democracy are shaped, popular assessment of democratic practices are established, and various participatory activities are initiated and sustained. As a consequence, we shall be in a much better position to empirically test the aforementioned theoretical conjectures on why democracy is in trouble nowadays.

1.5 Overview of the book

There are seven chapters in this book. This chapter summarizes our core theoretical arguments and presents the main research framework of this book. Figure 1.1 summarizes the key empirical relationships examined in the book and provides the roadmap for the organization of subsequent chapters.

As illustrated in Figure 1.1, the center of our theorization and empirical analysis is popular understandings of democracy. This also is the key issue for Chapters 2 and 3. In Chapter 2, we review pertinent research on varying understandings of democracy to assess the empirical challenges in studying this elusive concept and to propose some new survey instruments (i.e., to measure popular understandings of democracy, the PUD instruments), with theoretical justification. In particular, we emphasize the tensions and critical

18 UNDERSTANDINGS OF DEMOCRACY

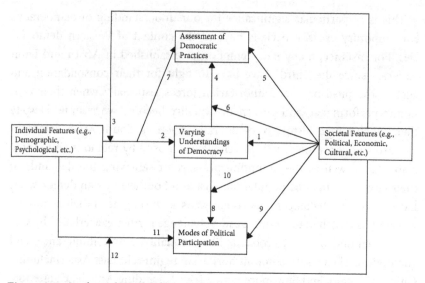

Figure 1.1 Analytical Model of the Book

trade-offs that confront people as they view and assess democracy and bring such tensions and trade-offs to the center of instrument selection. We further examine the validity and reliability of the PUD instruments using both survey experiments and different psychometric models to establish a solid methodological foundation for subsequent empirical analysis.

Chapter 3 presents systematic descriptive evidence on the status of popular conceptions of democracy in today's world, using GBS II data from seventy-one societies. To make the descriptive analysis more informative, we have included comparable information from the United States and relied on different psychometric models to uncover the latent characteristics that shape people's responses to the PUD instruments. Regardless of how we measure and assess popular conceptions of democracy (as either a continuous latent variable or discrete latent categories), we have consistently found that the PUD instruments are sufficiently sensitive to the socioeconomic and political environment, thus revealing significant and substantial variation in popular conceptions of democracies across regions, between societies, and among individuals. To ensure that the variation documented in the PUD instruments is not something transient or idiosyncratic (given the cross-sectional nature of the GBS II data under examination), we further explore the longitudinal dynamics of this critical attitude using the ABS twowave, rolling-cross-sectional surveys from thirteen East Asian societies. The results suggest a high level of longitudinal stability in how East Asians conceptualize democracy.

Having established the validity and reliability of the PUD instruments as a proxy of popular understandings of democracy, as well as the global patterns of varying conceptions, in Chapters 2 and 3, we move on to explore such popular understandings' origins and implications for critical political attitudes and behaviors in Chapters 4, 5, and 6. Chapter 4 uses mixed-effect models to examine the origins of varying conceptions of democracy (i.e., Diagram Paths 1, 2, and 3 in Figure 1.1). Due to data limitations, we are only able to account for some key individual demographic, cognitive, and psychological features as we explore the impact of surrounding economic, political, and cultural contexts. Overall, our findings demonstrate the salience of surrounding economic, political, and cultural contexts in shaping popular conceptions of democracy. Short-term fluctuations (like economic growth vs. recession), mid-term changes (like democratic practices gauged by Freedom House ratings and economic development measured by per capita GDP), and long-term evolutions (like the history of personal dictatorships and Confucian political traditions) all play important roles in this regard.

Chapter 5 examines the attitudinal consequences of popular understandings of democracy. In particular, we focus on the influence of this critical mass opinion on how citizens assess democratic practices in both foreign countries and their own societies (i.e., Diagram Paths 4, 5, 6, and 7 in Figure 1.1). On average in almost all GBS II societies (including China), people offer a higher rating of democratic practice in the United States than in China. Meanwhile, there is noticeable variation in such evaluations, with much more variation in how people assess China's democratic practice. Mixed-effect regressions confirm that, *ceteris paribus*, people who have embraced the procedural understanding of democracy by prioritizing its institutions and procedures in protecting basic rights and liberty are more critical of China's democratic practice but more favorable to that in the United States. We further examine how such varying conceptions of democracy affect popular views of democratic practices in respondents' own societies. Similar mixed-effect regressions reveal that, again, people's different understandings of democracy significantly shape how they assess their own societies' democratic practices. On average, people who prioritize the intrinsic values of democracy (compared to their fellow citizens who emphasize democracy's instrumental values) are less satisfied with their regime's democratic practices and more critical in assessing its democratic nature. A more nuanced but critical finding is that this impact is significantly stronger among citizens of autocracies but much weaker among those of democracies. We also find that, although people differ in their conceptions of democracy, younger cohorts with a higher level of education are generally more critical of their own societies' democratic practices. Furthermore, even a full democracy still needs to deliver (i.e., delivering good governance through better economic and political performance) to win over people's hearts and minds, therefore fostering its popular support.

Chapter 6 focuses on the implications of popular conceptions of democracy for political behavior, that is, the attitude-to-behavior connections (i.e., Diagram Paths 8, 9, 10, 11, and 12 in Figure 1.1), in particular, conventional and unconventional political participation. Overall, we have found that, compared to their fellow citizens who emphasize the instrumental values of democracy, people embracing the procedural understanding of democracy are significantly more likely to cast ballots, help with electoral campaigns, contact political and government agencies or agents, join a demonstration, march in a protest, or use violence for a political cause. Meanwhile, the impact of popular understandings of democracy on political participation varies significantly, depending on the features of the regime in a society: it is much stronger in authoritarian regimes than in democracies. In some cases, the impact even reverses as we move from autocracies to democracies. For instance, people embracing the procedural understanding of democracy are significantly more likely to engage in protests and demonstrations or use violence for a political cause under authoritarian regimes. However, they are significantly less likely to engage in such activities in democracies. We further argue that such patterns are primarily driven by the expressive values served by political participation, which people embracing the procedural conception of democracy are more attracted and sensitive to.

Chapter 7 summarizes the empirical findings, revisits our theoretical framework for understanding democracy's contemporary crisis by focusing on popular conceptions of democracy, highlights our theoretical and empirical contributions to pertinent literature, and draws some conclusions and suggestions for future research.

Appendix

Table A1.1 Geographical Distribution of GBS II Societies

North America	Latin America	East and South East Asia	South Asia	Sub-Saharan Africa	North Africa
1	18	3	5	30	5
USA (2017)	Argentina (2013)	Japan (2011)	Bangladesh (2013)	Benin (2011)	Algeria (2013)
	Bolivia (2013)	Hong Kong (2012)	India (2013)	Botswana (2012)	Egypt (2013)
	Brazil (2013)	South Korea (2011)	Nepal (2013)	Burkina Faso (2012)	Morocco (2013)
	Chile (2013)	Mainland China (2011)	Pakistan (2013)	Cape Verde (2011)	Sudan (2013)
	Colombia (2013)	Mongolia (2010)	Sri Lanka (2013)	Ghana (2012)	Tunisia (2013)
	Costa Rica (2013)	Philippines (2010)		Kenya (2011)	
	Dominican Republic (2013)	Taiwan (2010)		Lesotho (2012)	
	Ecuador (2013)	Thailand (2010)		Liberia (2012)	
	El Salvador (2013)	Indonesia (2011)		Madagascar (2013)	
	Guatemala (2013)	Singapore (2010)		Malawi (2012)	
	Honduras (2013)	Vietnam (2010)		Mali (2012)	
	Mexico (2013)	Cambodia (2012)		Mozambique (2012)	
	Nicaragua (2013)	Malaysia (2011)		Namibia (2012)	
	Panama (2013)			Nigeria (2012)	
	Paraguay (2013)			Senegal (2013)	
	Peru (2013)			South Africa (2011)	
	Uruguay (2013)			Tanzania (2012)	
	Venezuela (2013)			Uganda (2012)	

Continued

Table A1.1 Continued

North America	Latin America	East and South East Asia	South Asia	Sub-Saharan Africa	North Africa
1	18	3	5	30	5
				Zambia (2013)	
				Zimbabwe (2012)	
				Mauritius (2012)	
				Sierra Leone (2012)	
				Niger (2013)	
				Togo (2012)	
				Burundi (2012)	
				Cameroon (2013)	
				Cote d'Ivoire (2013)	
				Guinea (2013)	
				Ethiopia (2013)	
				Swaziland (2013)	

2
New Instruments for Popular Understandings of Democracy

As discussed in Chapter 1, popular understandings of democracy provide the benchmark against which people assess their existing political regimes and evaluate possible alternatives, by shaping their expectations on what a "good" regime should look like. Such understandings and related assessments may further shape how people participate in politics. All these have significant implications for the political dynamics in societies with different political regimes and varying experience of democratic politics. Furthermore, we have argued that people's willingness to trade off democratic principles for instrumental gains should be central to our theorization of democratic conceptions and related empirical exercise.

In this chapter, we review existing literature on varying understandings of democracy to assess the challenges in studying this elusive concept and to introduce some new survey instruments with theoretical justification. We further examine the validity and reliability of the new instruments using both survey experiments and different psychometric models to establish a solid methodological foundation for subsequent empirical analysis.

2.1 How to capture the elusive concept?

Despite the widely acknowledged value of incorporating popular understandings of democracy in democracy research, until now, its application in existing scholarship has suffered from a thorny issue of measurement: how to effectively capture the theoretical construct in empirical analysis covering different societies and regimes? This poses a significant challenge for contemporary research on popular understandings of democracy, constrains fruitful dialogues among researchers, and impedes accumulative comparative research to develop and test general theories.[1]

The most obvious approach (and also the one with the longest tradition) is to ask people directly what democracy means to them (i.e., an open-ended question administered via surveys). Some of the earliest and most recent comparative research on how people understand democracy uses exactly this method to explore distinct meanings attached to democracy by people with varying socioeconomic, political, and cultural backgrounds (Dalton et al. 2007; Shi 2015; Shi and Lu 2010; Crow 2010; Canache 2012; Gillman 2018; Baviskar and Malone 2004). This might still be the only valid and meaningful approach for research in regions or societies where pertinent information is not available or has never been collected (Schaffer 1998). Nevertheless, besides its high costs of data collection and processing, there also are significant challenges in identifying theoretically meaningful and comparable themes for comparative analysis from thousands of ambiguous words, fragmented sentences, or incomplete statements. For instance, the choice of coding schemes and specific coding of ambiguous words have a noticeable influence on the findings and conclusions (Schaffer 2014).[2]

To overcome the aforementioned deficiencies in using open-ended survey questions to measure popular understandings of democracy, researchers have developed a variety of closed-ended survey instruments to capture this elusive concept. Some have adopted rating scales by asking respondents to assess the respective salience or significance of certain pre-specified aspects of democracy. Some have used forced-choice questions by asking respondents to identify their perceived most important or critical aspect among some pre-specified understandings of democracy. Such closed-ended survey instruments are more cost-effective in data collection and processing and can provide meaningful comparisons across regions and societies for analysis. Thus, an increasing number of recent studies have followed this approach (Mattes and Bratton 2007; Lu 2013; Lu et al. 2014; Lu and Shi 2015; Huang et al. 2013; Ferrin and Kriesi 2016). Nevertheless, it is exactly because of the closed-format and pre-specified nature of such survey instruments that related findings and conclusions might be significantly conditional on which aspects of democracy are included or listed for respondents' evaluations. For instance, asking people to assess how important A, B, and C respectively are to democracy has implicitly excluded the possible salience of D in popular conceptions of democracy. Similarly, for the same group of people, asking them to choose between A, B, and C for the most crucial feature of democracy may produce a different answer than if they had been asked to choose between A, B, and D.

Furthermore, even among the scholars favoring closed-ended survey instruments for analysis, there still is no consensus on the best design of such instruments. Should we ask respondents to evaluate the respective salience, significance, or essentialness of various socioeconomic and political aspects of democracy in their related understandings one after another (i.e., in a parallel and independent style) (Kriesi and Morlino 2016; Bratton et al. 2005; Mattes and Bratton 2007; Heyne 2019)? Alternatively, should we ask them to evaluate the relative salience, significance, or essentialness of the socioeconomic and political aspects of democracy by juxtaposing the features for contrast and comparison (Lu 2013; Lu et al. 2014; Lu and Shi 2015; Huang et al. 2013)?

Besides well-documented methodological trade-offs on using rating versus ranking designs (Groves et al. 2009; Tourangeau et al. 2000; Alwin and Krosnick 1985), there is a more critical theoretical question: how to deal with people who believe that "all good things should go together" (Schedler and Sarsfield 2007)? For rating instruments, this is a perfectly legitimate scenario since each specified socioeconomic or political aspect of democracy is rated independently. Nevertheless, the power of empirical analysis might be severely compromised if a significant portion of respondents regard the specified socioeconomic and political aspects as equally or similarly salient, significant, or essential for a democracy (thus, shrinking the empirical variation for analysis). For ranking instruments, the empirical challenges in dealing with this scenario are effectively avoided, since respondents are forced to assess all specified socioeconomic and political aspects of democracy simultaneously for comparison and ranking. However, the findings based on the ranking data might miss an interesting component of the underlying dynamics, especially regarding those who do believe that all good things come together in a democracy and even see democracy as the "end of history" (Fukuyama 1992). We do not think empirical evaluations alone will be able to effectively address the aforementioned debates on how to measure this elusive but critical concept, that is, popular conceptions of democracy.

As students of political science have recognized, conceptualizations, operationalization strategies, and measurements should serve specific theoretical purposes (Gerring 2012; Sartori 1970; Collier and Mahoney 1993). Our overarching research question is: How do popular understandings of democracy affect the prospects for democracy as the world gradually recovers from the 2008–2009 global financial crisis (i.e., the worst financial crisis since the Great Depression of the 1930s)? More specifically, we want to understand: How are varying understandings of democracy cultivated and sustained in distinct socioeconomic, political, and cultural contexts, especially in societies located at the periphery or outside of the conventionally conceptualized Western civilization zone (e.g., societies in Asia, Latin America, and Africa)? How have such varying conceptions of democracy moderated the dynamics of democratic transition in authoritarian societies? How have such different views of democracy conditioned the dynamics of consolidation/deconsolidation or even the breakdown of democracies?

To effectively examine these questions, we cannot simply assume that "all good things go together" with democracies; otherwise, our research questions (especially the last two) could be meaningless. We argue that it is critical to fully recognize and theorize the salient trade-offs between various desirable socioeconomic and political goals that people cherish in any society. We further argue that the contrast and trade-offs between the following two conceptions of democracy are critical and central. The first understanding emphasizes the instrumental values of democracy in delivering socioeconomic and political goods. For this understanding, democracy is primarily conceptualized as a way of governance and is expected to be competent in satisfying its people's demands via effective public policies. We identify this conception as a substantive understanding of democracy. The second understanding of democracy prioritizes the intrinsic values of democracy in ensuring a decent way of life for everyone. For this understanding, democracy is mainly conceptualized as a way of life and is expected to realize the principle of popular sovereignty and ensuring its people's dignity, as well as their inalienable rights and liberty, via established institutions and procedures. We identify this conception as a procedural understanding of democracy.

As discussed in detail in Chapter 1, the contrast between the substantive and procedural understandings of democracy are not only of theoretical and academic significance for related research, but also resonate with the increasing rivalry between China and the United States as two competing models of governance. Both China and the United States call themselves "great democracies" and each has attracted a large audience for possible institutional learning or even transplanting. Capturing the distinction between a substantive understanding of democracy as a way of governance (emphasizing its instrumental gains) and a procedural understanding of democracy as a way of life (prioritizing its intrinsic values embodied in key democratic principles) should be central to our theorization, operationalization, and measurement of popular understandings of democracy. The corresponding instruments, therefore, should focus on and be able to effectively capture the relative priorities that people assign to democracy's key principles versus its instrumental gains.

2.2 New ranking instruments in GBS II

Methodologically speaking, asking people to rank critical features of democracy (i.e., making choices when the trade-offs between such features are highlighted), rather than asking for their respective ratings of such critical features or probing for their free responses using an open-ended survey question, should be the most effective empirical strategy to serve our theoretical goals. But what critical features of democracy should be included for ranking? Theoretically, a significantly large number of features of democracy could be included. However, these are not necessarily of equal salience for ordinary people. To maximize the empirical leverage of our survey instruments, we should focus on the features that are of high salience to ordinary people when they assess democracy.

The scholarship using open-ended survey questions to examine how people understand democracy has provided rich information in this regard (Dalton et al. 2007; Shi 2015; Shi and Lu 2010; Crow 2010; Canache 2012; Gillman 2018; Baviskar and Malone 2004). Instead of priming or constraining respondents with pre-specified features of democracy, open-ended survey questions provide sufficient opportunities and unique leverage to tap the most salient features of democracy that ordinary people may spontaneously recall when probed for related responses. Since earlier waves of regional barometer surveys (including all members of the GBS) have used open-ended survey questions on understandings of democracy, such information can provide rich and solid empirical foundations for an appropriate and effective design of our closed-ended survey instruments. Put otherwise, we can use the most commonly and widely reported features of democracy (i.e., substantiated via open-ended survey questions in earlier waves of regional barometer surveys) as pre-specified aspects of democracy for respondents' assessment, thus maximizing the empirical validity and leverage of the instruments.

In earlier waves of the GBS, the conventional open-ended survey question was used to collect varying popular understandings of democracy around the world.[3] Then GBS researchers conducted extensive and independent content analysis and further cross-validated their findings and coding schemes to identify some key components in popular responses to the open-ended question. More specifically, qualitative analysis of the earlier waves of GBS data shows that people around the world have regularly and repeatedly mentioned the following four key aspects of democracy: (1) social equity, (2) good government, (3) norms and procedures, and (4) freedom and liberty. To minimize the possible influence of measurement errors on post-survey inferences, the GBS II has intentionally included four sets of indicators for each component (i.e., trying to tap the same latent component from distinct perspectives) in the new survey instruments. The crafting of all indicators is also based on popular responses to the open-ended survey question collected in earlier waves of the GBS.[4]

For instance, to tap a social-equity-based understanding of democracy, the following set of four indicators are used: (1a) "Government narrows the gap between the rich and the poor," (1b) "Basic necessities, like food, clothes and shelter, are provided for all," (1c) "Government ensures job opportunities for all," and (1d) "People receive state aid if they are unemployed." To tap a good-government-centered understanding of democracy, the following set of four indicators are used: (2a) "Government does not waste any public money," (2b) "Government provides people with quality public services," (2c) "Government ensures law and order," and (2d) "Politics is clean and free of corruption." Similarly, another two sets of indicators are used to tap the norms-and-procedures-based (i.e., 3a–3d) and freedom-and-liberty-centered (i.e., 4a–4d) conceptions of democracy respectively: (3a) "People choose government leaders in free and fair elections," (3b) "The legislature has oversight over the government," (3c) "Multiple parties compete fairly in the election," (3d) "The court protects the ordinary people from the abuse of government power," (4a) "People are free to express their political views openly," (4b) "People are free to organize political groups," (4c) "Media is free to criticize the things government does," and (4d) "People have the freedom to take part in protests and demonstrations." The upper section of Table 2.1 presents all indicators and their corresponding components.

For respondents' effective ranking of the distinct features of democracy, the GBS II selected one indicator from each of the four sets, presented the four indicators collectively as a ranking set, and asked respondents to select one as the most essential characteristic of democracy with the following probe: "Many things may be desirable, but not all of them are essential

POPULAR UNDERSTANDINGS OF DEMOCRACY 29

Table 2.1 Detailed Wording of GBS II New Ranking Instruments

Social equity	
1a	Government narrows the gap between the rich and the poor.
1b	Basic necessities, like food, clothes, and shelter, are provided for all.
1c	Government ensures job opportunities for all.
1d	People receive state aid if they are unemployed.
Good government	
2a	Government does not waste any public money.
2b	Government provides people with quality public services.
2c	Government ensures law and order.
2d	Politics is clean and free of corruption.
Norms and procedures	
3a	People choose government leaders in free and fair elections.
3b	The legislature has oversight over the government.
3c	Multiple parties compete fairly in the election.
3d	The court protects the ordinary people from the abuse of government power.
Freedom and liberty	
4a	People are free to express their political views openly.
4b	People are free to organize political groups.
4c	Media is free to criticize the things government does.
4d	People have the freedom to take part in protests and demonstrations.

	Ranking Set 1	Ranking Set 2	Ranking Set 3	Ranking Set 4
Item1	1a	3b	2c	4d
Item2	3a	1b	4c	2d
Item3	2a	4b	1c	3d
Item4	4a	2b	3c	1d

characteristics of democracy. If you have to choose only one from each four sets of statements that I am going to read, which one would you choose as the most essential characteristic of a democracy?" To minimize the possible question order effect, the GBS II further rotated the order of the four components in each of the four ranking sets, as shown in the lower section of Table 2.1. Basically, the GBS II ranking instruments asked respondents to identify the most essential characteristic of democracy when confronted with the trade-offs between (1) social equity, (2) good government, (3) norms and procedures, and (4) freedom and liberty. They were asked to do the ranking four times with distinct indicators for each of the four components. Moreover, each time, they were confronted with the trade-offs presented in a different order. In our subsequent discussion, we referred to the four sets of indicators for ranking as the instruments for popular understandings of democracy (PUD).

As discussed earlier, one deficiency with all ranking instruments is that the results might, to some extent, be conditional upon how different indicators are grouped for comparison. Basically, the result of ranking between A, B, and C could be different from that of the ranking between A, B, and D. To fully address this deficiency, the only technical solution is for researchers to completely randomize the assignment of different indicators for comparisons across respondents, similar to the design of conjoint experiments (Hainmueller et al. 2014; Sniderman 2018). To achieve this, computer-assisted personal interviewing (CAPI) systems (via smartphones or tablets) should be used. Unfortunately, given the technical infrastructure of GBS, most survey teams cannot afford CAPI systems and have to rely on the traditional paper-and-pencil interviewing (PAPI) technique for data collection. Thus, the GBS II opted for a compromise between the ideal design and practical constraints. Basically, the GBS II crafted a pool of four indicators for each of the four key aspects of democracy (i.e., social equity, good government, norms and procedures, and freedom and liberty). Then it randomly selected one indicator from each pool to compile one ranking set. The four ranking sets displayed in Table 2.1 were the result of three such random draws. Although this is far from perfect, by taking such random draws, the GBS II did try its best to minimize the design effect of the PUD instruments. Furthermore, the key issue here is not which specific indicator is selected, but which aspects (as latent features captured by the indicators) are more likely to be prioritized when their trade-offs are highlighted. To some extent, like dealing with measurement errors, appropriate psychometric modeling (e.g., factor or latent class analysis) can take the unique features of each ranking set into consideration and more effectively focus on the trade-offs between the latent aspects. The subsequent sections of this chapter address exactly this.

2.3 Performance of the PUD instruments

In order to assess the validity and reliability of the PUD instruments, we follow a two-step strategy for assessment. The first step relates to the possible question order effect in the PUD instruments and is more technical. If the

PUD instruments fail the first step of assessment (which indicates a strong question order effect), we cannot rely on the PUD instruments for meaningful and valid empirical tests. The second step relates to the influence of differing operationalization of the latent construct that the PUD instruments are designed to capture on the key results and is more theoretical. The latent construct (i.e., varying conceptions of democracy) could be operationalized in different ways (e.g., an ordinal vs. nominal construct) depending on related theorization. If our key results based on the PUD instruments are highly sensitive to how the latent construct is operationalized, we cannot rely on the PUD instruments for robust and reliable empirical tests.

Question order effect: First of all, we want to make sure that the PUD instruments do not suffer from serious question order effect. Ideally, we should randomly assign the order of different indicators in the same ranking set for each respondent (i.e., full randomization that can be easily accommodated in a CPAI system) to minimize possible question order effect. However, as discussed earlier, full randomization is not feasible for the GBS II due to the dominance of the PAPI technique in data collection. Therefore, we need to make sure that the GBS II design of the PUD instruments does effectively mimic the result of full randomization. For this assessment, we ran two empirical tests using observational in one and experimental data in the other.

According to accumulated knowledge and research in survey methodology, responses to survey questions are likely to be affected by recency or primacy effect, depending on the mode of data collection (Groves et al. 2009; Bishop 1987). Survey respondents are inclined to choose the first (most likely in surveys dominated by visual stimuli) or the last (most likely in surveys dominated by auditory stimuli) answer category in their responses. Although the GBS II has intentionally rotated the order of different indicators to minimize possible question order effect, its reliance on the PAPI technique with show-cards for the PUD instruments (i.e., the dominance of auditory stimuli) may still trigger some recency effect (if there is any documented question order effect).

Figure 2.1 uses violin plots to demonstrate the distributions of endorsement rates for each of the four answer categories in each ranking set of the PUD instruments in GBS II. The solid lines in the violin plots indicate the median of endorsement propensities. Since we focus exclusively here on the existence of possible recency or primacy effect, we do not differentiate between various indicators but simply the order of these indicators in each ranking set.

32 UNDERSTANDINGS OF DEMOCRACY

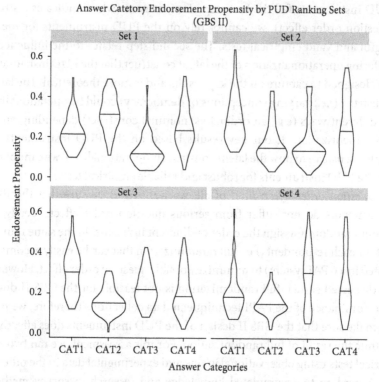

Figure 2.1 Question Order Effect in the GBS II PUD Instruments

If recency or primacy effect is highly salient in responses to the PUD instruments, we should expect a much higher endorsement rate for the first or the last answer category in most ranking sets. However, as shown in Figure 2.1, there is no consistent pattern in which answer categories (CATs) have the highest endorsement rate. In ranking sets 2 and 3, answer CAT1 was endorsed by the largest percentage of the GBS II respondents, while, for ranking sets 1 and 4, the largest percentage of respondents endorsed CAT2 and CAT3 respectively. It seems that there is minimum primacy effect and a lack of recency effect in responses to the PUD instruments in GBS II. Given the data collection mode of GBS II (i.e., the PAPI technique), the dominance of auditory stimuli in survey responses, and the evidence presented in Figure 2.1, it should be reasonable to argue that there is negligible question order effect in the PUD instruments in GBS II.

A more direct assessment of the influence of possible recency or primacy effect on the PUD instruments is to use a survey experiment. Put otherwise, we can randomly assign a group of respondents to the PUD instruments with the original GBS II design (i.e., with a pre-fixed order of answer categories) and another group of respondents to the same PUD instruments but with fully randomized order of answer categories. Then we can compare the responses from the two groups to see if there are statistically and substantively meaningful differences. Since the random assignment makes the two groups of respondents identical (on average, of course) in all other aspects, any differences in their responses to the PUD instruments should be attributed to the distinction between the original GBS II design and the full randomization design. We did this survey experiment (using Qualtrics) via the M-Turk online recruitment platform in the fall of 2017 with American adults as experimental subjects.[5] The results are presented in Figure 2.2.

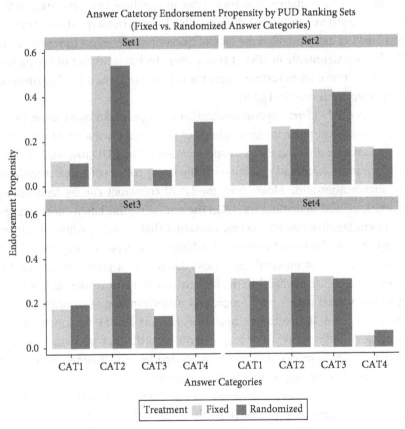

Figure 2.2 American Survey Experiment on the Question Order Effect in the PUD Instruments

Figure 2.2 displays the average endorsement rate for each of the four answer categories in each ranking set for the two experimental groups respectively. Light grey bars represent the experimental group assigned to the PUD instruments with the original GBS II design; dark grey bars represent the experimental group assigned to the same PUD instruments but with fully randomized order of answer categories. As clearly shown in Figure 2.2, regardless of which ranking set is examined, there is no significant difference between the two experimental groups in their average responses. All between-group differences are statistically insignificant, with corresponding p-values (based on Chi-square tests) ranging between 0.4 and 0.7. In other words, there are no meaningful differences in popular responses to the PUD instruments with pre-fixed or fully randomized order of answer categories. Basically, there is little recency or primacy effect in popular responses to the PUD instruments. It is reasonable to conclude that responses to the PUD instruments in GBS II do not suffer from serious question order effect. Having demonstrated the lack of question order effect in responses to the PUD instruments in GBS II (i.e., a more technical aspect of the instrument), we move on to further assess the performance the PUD instruments in serving our theoretical goals.

Influence of different operationalization strategies: Like many other political attitudes, popular understandings of democracy are a latent construct that cannot be directly observed and measured. The PUD instruments only capture some empirical reflections of the latent construct when stimulated by survey questions. Meanwhile, the latent construct can be legitimately operationalized in distinct ways. On the one hand, this latent construct can be operationalized as an interval construct that covers a whole spectrum ranging from the lowest end of full willingness to trade off key democratic principles for instrumental gains (associated with a pure substantive understanding of democracy) to the highest end of a lack of any such willingness (associated with a pure procedural understanding of democracy). On the other hand, it also can be operationalized as a nominal construct that consists of different types of respondents with distinct understandings of democracy, thus incorporating varying categories of willingness to trade off key democratic principles for instrumental gains.

Theoretically, cogent arguments can be made for both strategies of operationalization. Empirically, the validity of the former operationalization should be assessed with confirmatory factor analysis (CFA) as a conventional measurement modeling technique (Long 1983; Reise et al. 1993).[6]

The validity of the latter operationalization should be assessed with latent class analysis (LCA) as an unconventional but increasingly popular measurement modeling technique (Collins and Lanza 2010; Vermunt and Magidson 2002). If the PUD instruments are valid in serving our theoretical goals, that is, the four ranking sets with four groups of indicators do effectively capture the critical but latent trade-off dynamics in how people conceptualize democracy, the CFA and LCA models should uncover similar patterns in the GBS II data. Then, our related findings and conclusions based on the PUD instruments are unlikely to be driven by the specific operationalization and corresponding statistical models used for analysis.[7] Thus, the confidence in the validity and robustness of our findings should be greatly enhanced.

Theoretically, the indicators of (1) social equity and (2) good government are expected to capture the substantive understanding of democracy, while the indicators of (3) norms and procedures and (4) freedom and liberty are expected to capture the procedural understanding of democracy. Respondents' endorsing the indicators of either social equity or good government, even when contrasted with the indicators of norms, procedures, freedom, and liberty, suggests some willingness to trade off the latter (i.e., key democratic principles) for the former (i.e., possible instrumental gains) when necessary. Thus, for effective CFA analysis, we recoded the original four-point scale of the ranking sets into a binary: 0 for the endorsement of (1) social equity or (2) good government as the most essential characteristic of democracy and 1 for the endorsement of (3) norms and procedures or (4) freedom and liberty as the most essential characteristic of democracy. Put otherwise, we dichotomized the ranking sets to zoom in on the distinction between the substantive and procedural understandings of democracy and to focus on the critical trade-off dynamics involved. In this way, we operationalized the latent construct of popular understandings of democracy as a continuous spectrum ranging from the lowest end indicating the highest propensity to prioritize democracy's instrumental values to the highest end suggesting the highest propensity to emphasize democracy's intrinsic values.

Furthermore, to ensure meaningful comparisons across societies, we followed best practice in pertinent research, pooling the survey data from the seventy-two societies together, weighting them proportionally to their respective sample size, and imposing a one-factor CFA model for analysis. With this model specification, we can secure the same baseline for comparing the latent factor scores uncovered by the pooled CFA model. Table 2.2 summarizes the results of a series of one-factor CFA models with identical

Table 2.2 One-Factor CFA Models for the PUD Instruments

	East Asia	South Asia	Sub-Saharan Africa	North Africa	Latin America	USA	GBS II + USA
Factor loadings							
Intrinsic 1	0.456 (0.017)***	0.393 (0.022)***	0.586 (0.010)***	0.612 (0.026)***	0.419 (0.016)***	0.670 (0.071)***	0.535 (0.006)***
Intrinsic 2	0.538 (0.018)***	0.553 (0.023)***	0.631 (0.010)***	0.538 (0.026)***	0.647 (0.018)***	0.747 (0.077)***	0.644 (0.006)***
Intrinsic 3	0.563 (0.018)***	0.605 (0.024)***	0.613 (0.010)***	0.684 (0.029)***	0.477 (0.016)***	0.711 (0.061)***	0.617 (0.006)***
Intrinsic 4	0.483 (0.017)***	0.485 (0.022)***	0.354 (0.010)***	0.356 (0.027)***	0.466 (0.017)***	0.628 (0.073)***	0.494 (0.006)***
Model fit indexes							
Chi-2	0.407 (2)	4.079 (2)	289.276 (2)***	16.622 (2)***	138.063 (2)***	4.517 (2)	343.183 (2)***
CFI	1.000	0.998	0.965	0.986	0.941	0.990	0.984
TIL	1.000	0.995	0.896	0.958	0.823	0.969	0.951
RMSEA	0.000 [0.000, 0.009]	0.011 [0.000, 0.026]	0.056 [0.050, 0.061]	0.035 [0.021, 0.052]	0.060 [0.051, 0.068]	0.036 [0.000, 0.080]	0.042 [0.038, 0.045]
Data information							
Societies	13	5	30	5	18	1	72
Used-N	17,922	8,760	46,333	5,825	19,110	998	98,948
Total-N	19,436	10,617	47,985	6,006	20,204	1,000	105,248

Source: GBS II + USA ($N = 105,248$).

Notes:

Weighting and stratification information is incorporated for analysis.

Robust standard errors in parentheses; 95% confidence intervals in brackets.

* $p < 0.1$ ** $p < 0.05$ *** $p < 0.01$.

specification but varying scopes of pooled data (i.e., different clusters of societies with similar geographical features and cultural backgrounds).

Following CFA analysis best practice, RMSEA, CFI, and TLI are key model-fit statistics and thus our focus for assessing the CFA models. Generally, CFA models with RMSEAs less than 0.08, CFIs larger than 0.9, or TLIs larger than 0.9 are accepted as valid (Bentler 2000; Hoyle 1995; Browne and Cudeck 1993). As shown in Table 2.2, regardless of the regions under examination, the one-factor CFA model fits the data consistently well: RMSEAs are less than 0.08, and CFIs and TLIs are larger than 0.9. Meanwhile, all item factor loadings are statistically significant, which suggests that the four ranking sets of PUD instruments have indeed effectively captured one shared latent construct. Furthermore, although the CFA has been specified and tested using data from regions with distinct socioeconomic, political, and cultural environments (i.e., East Asia, South Asia, Sub-Saharan Africa, North Africa, Latin America, and the United States), we have secured highly consistent results. Therefore, it should be fair to argue that the performance of the PUD instruments is not context specific and should enable meaningful cross-society comparisons.

It is also worth noting that, although the PUD instruments were originally designed based on the information collected via open-ended survey questions administered mostly in new democracies and non-democracies in Asia, Africa, and Latin America, their performance is highly satisfying (statistically speaking) even in the textbook case of mature liberal democracy, that is, the United States. As shown in the sixth column of Table 2.2, besides a small RMSEA and large CFI and TLI (all indicating very good performance of the specified model), the one-factor CFA model shows an insignificant Chi-square statistic when fitted to the 2017 US survey data. Put otherwise, the model has effectively uncovered the data-generating process that shapes the American public's responses to the PUD instruments. In subsequent analysis, we will use the information collected from the United States as the benchmark to assess popular understandings of democracy, given the widely shared acknowledgement of the United States' long and rich tradition of liberal democracy (which is expected to orient the majority of the American public toward a procedural understanding of democracy, thus making the American public much less likely to trade off democratic principles for instrumental gains).

The last column of Table 2.2 presents the information of the one-factor CFA model fitted to the pooled responses from around one hundred thousand respondents living in seventy-two societies with varying socioeconomic, cultural, and political environments. When applied to the pooled data from all seventy-two societies (i.e., imposing the same latent structure on these societies), the overall one-factor CFA model reports highly satisfying model-fit statistics, with a RMSEA of 0.042, a CFI of 0.984, and a TLI of 0.951. Overall, when popular conceptions of democracy are operationalized as a continuous latent construct, the PUD instruments do effectively capture the varying priorities in related understandings as people are confronted with potential trade-offs between the instrumental and intrinsic values of democracy.[8]

This CFA analysis faces two potential challenges. First, dichotomizing the four ranking sets simply ignores the influence of item non-response (i.e., "don't know," "don't understand the question," "no answer," etc.). As some recent research has suggested (Shin 2017; Cho 2015; Shin and Kim 2018), popular ignorance of democracy (despite its serious implications for democratic practice) might have been underestimated in the existing literature; and this is primarily driven by the insufficient attention paid to item non-response in survey data. Second, the dichotomous coding might have overlooked some significant differences between various indicators. For instance, the indicators of (1) social equity and (2) good government were coded (i.e., forced) to be functionally equivalent, that is, both were coded as indicators of a substantive understanding of democracy. Similarly, the indicators of (3) norms and procedures and (4) freedom and liberty were also coded as functionally equivalent. To what extent is this assumption of functional equivalence justifiable? We need more empirical evidence in this regard. Fortunately, LCA models allow us to address these two issues effectively, thus providing some robustness checks for this CFA analysis. Furthermore, the LCA models enable us to move away from the continuous operationalization of the latent construct of popular understandings of democracy and engage in a nominal operationalization (i.e., different types of people with distinct conceptions).

Figure 2.3 presents information on item non-response rates of the PUD instruments, again using violin plots. Across the four ranking sets, the median of item non-response rates falls consistently below 10%, which is normal compared to the situation of item non-response rates in other major comparative survey projects. Nevertheless, there are still a number of societies showing some high item non-response rates in the four ranking sets (as high as 50%), which means that we do need to take the Don't know (DKs)

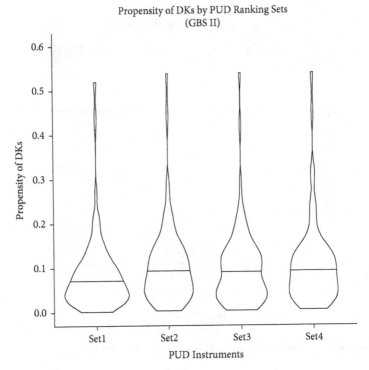

Figure 2.3 Item Non-Response Rates of the PUD Instrument

seriously and systematically incorporate them into our theorization and analysis.[9] Therefore, we adopted the following five-point coding scheme for subsequent LCA analysis both to deal with the issue of item non-response and to minimize the influence of artificial coding.

Basically, we coded responses to each ranking set using a five-point nominal scale: 1 for social equity, 2 for good government, 3 for norms and procedures, 4 for freedom and liberty, and 5 for non-response. Then we ran a series of LCA models to compare their performance in fitting the data, revealing the number of latent types of respondents with distinct conceptions of democracy. For theoretical reasons stated earlier, we focus on the comparisons between LCA models with two, three, and four distinct latent types.[10] As with the CFA analyses, we ran a series of LCA models for each of the seventy-two societies, then used Akaike Information Criterion (AICs) and adjusted-Bayesian Information Criterion (BICs) to choose the LCA models showing the most satisfying performance. The findings

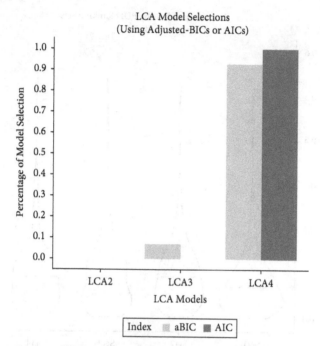

Figure 2.4 LCA Model Comparisons in Seventy-Two Societies

are summarized in Figure 2.4. As displayed in Figure 2.4, regardless of the model-comparison statistics used, the LCA with four distinct latent types consistently outperforms its counterparts with either two or three distinct latent types. More specifically, comparisons of AICs suggest that the four-class LCA model outperforms two- and three-class LCA models in all cases, while comparisons of adjusted-BICs suggest that the four-class LCA model outperforms two- and three-class LCAs in around 94% of all cases. Put otherwise, as theoretically expected, the LCA analyses suggest that the PUD instruments have effectively uncovered four distinct groups of people with varying understandings of democracy.

Further analysis of the data reveals that, among the four distinct groups, one is dominated by respondents with non-responses (e.g., DKs) to three or more ranking sets, who are thus labeled Agnostics. Another group is dominated by respondents mostly identifying indicators of (1) social equity or (2) good government as essential characteristics of democracy; those we label Benefit-Seekers. A third group dominated by respondents mostly identifying indicators of (3) norms and procedures or (4) freedom and liberty as essential characteristics of democracy are labeled Principle-Holders. And the last group dominated by respondents identifying a bag of mixed indicators as essential characteristics of democracy are labeled Fence-Sitters. As the LCA results suggest, Principle-Holders are rarely willing to sacrifice key democratic principles for instrumental gains, while Benefit-Seekers are always ready to trade off such democratic principles for concrete socioeconomic and political benefits when they are forced to choose. Fence-Sitters do not respond to such trade-offs in a consistent way: whether they are willing to trade off democratic principles might be conditional upon the nature of the instrumental gains under examination. With possible measurement errors considered (e.g., random choices from respondents who know nothing about democracy), the Agnostics not only make perfect sense statistically, but also resonate quite well with the findings of recent research on ignorance about democracy among a significant percentage of people around the world (Shin 2017; Cho 2015).[11]

How do the results of LCA align with those of CFA, despite their distinct operationalization of the same latent construct under examination? Statistically, the one-factor CFA model with dichotomous indicators (as reported in Table 2.2) is equivalent to a two-parameter Item Response Theory (IRT) model. Our subsequent analyses focus on the uncovered IRT scores (i.e., latent factor scores that summarize individuals' willingness to trade off key democratic principles for instrumental gains). Giving our coding of the PUD instruments, a larger value of the IRT score indicates a higher propensity to prioritize democracy's intrinsic values and a lower willingness to trade off key democratic principles for instrumental gains; while a lower value of the IRT score indicates a higher propensity to emphasize democracy's instrumental values and a higher willingness to secure instrumental gains even at the cost of key democratic principles.[12]

To examine how the CFA and LCA results are related, we have presented the distributions of IRT scores (based on the one-factor CFA model) for each latent group identified by the four-class LCA model with violin plots in Figure 2.5. The solid line in each violin plot stands for the median value of the related distribution of IRT scores.

As illustrated in Figure 2.5, the differences between Agnostics, Fence-Sitters, Benefit-Seekers, and Principle-Holders regarding their respective willingness to trade off key democratic principles for instrumental gains are quite obvious and highly significant. On average, Principle-Holders report the lowest willingness to engage in such trade-offs, by emphasizing

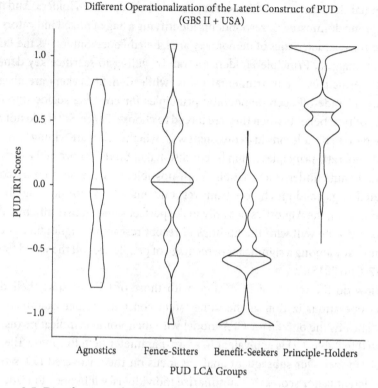

Figure 2.5 Distributions of PUD IRT Scores for Different PUD LCA Groups

democracy's intrinsic values. Benefit-Seekers, as expected, report the highest willingness to engage in such trade-offs, by prioritizing democracy's instrumental values. Furthermore, while Principle-Holders and Benefit-Seekers cluster toward the respective ends of the spectrum, Fence-Sitters and Agnostics both show a much larger variation in their willingness to engage in such trade-offs, and they, on average, are quite moderate in this regard. It is worth noting that Agnostics show the highest variation in their willingness to engage in such trade-offs. This is partly driven by the significant influence of randomness in their responses to the PUD instruments, which results in the high uncertainty in related IRT scores.[13]

This high consistency in how the CFA and LCA models have differentiated between the varying conceptions of democracy significantly boosts our confidence in the validity and robustness of the PUD instruments, as well as its value in serving our theoretical goals. Regardless of how latent constructs of interest are operationalized, people's distinct styles of engaging in the trade-offs between key democratic principles and instrumental gains are always highly salient and consistently captured. In subsequent chapters, we will use the PUD instruments to examine the distribution, origins, and consequences of varying popular understandings of democracy in the contemporary world.

2.4 Conclusions

Like students of political science who cannot agree upon what democracy means, ordinary people hold distinct understandings of democracy, as systematically documented by existing scholarship. For us, examining popular conceptions of democracy (including its patterns, origins, and attitudinal and behavioral consequences) provides a critical bottom-up and a complementary demand-side perspective for understanding democracy's contemporary crisis.

The variety of popular conceptions of democracy has significant implications for its prospects in the contemporary world. In democracies, popular understandings of democracy may shape people's expectations on how democracy should perform and, thus, provide the benchmark against which they assess their democratic regime and extend their critical support. In non-democracies, popular understandings of democracy might color people's assessments of their authoritarian regime or dictatorship and, in turn, moderate their responses to mobilization for democratic transition. Therefore, uncovering popular understandings of democracy is indispensable for both diagnosing the challenges posed by rising populist sentiment and even popular disbelief in democracy (which might lead to democratic decay or deconsolidation) in today's democracies, as well as scrutinizing the obstacles raised by authoritarian leaders' increasing sophistication in disguising the non-democratic nature of their rule via propaganda and indoctrination against mobilization for democratic transition. Furthermore, our comprehensive review of the pertinent literature and close following of major socioeconomic and political changes in today's world suggest that the salient trade-offs between various desirable socioeconomic and political goals that people cherish in any society are central to the theorization, operationalization, and measurement of popular conceptions of democracy.

The instruments adopted by existing studies to capture and measure popular understandings of democracy have various limitations and deficiencies. Open-ended survey questions do provide sufficient flexibility, with little unwanted intervention or imposed structure from researchers, for tapping various understandings of democracy. However, these instruments are difficult to use for large-scale comparative research, and they completely ignore critical trade-offs confronting citizens in both democracies and non-democracies as they assess democracy. Closed-ended survey questions are much friendlier for large-scale comparative research. In particular, asking people to rank different aspects of democracy effectively captures the critical trade-off dynamic involved in popular assessment of democracy. Nevertheless, due to the question structure and pre-specified answer categories imposed by researchers, such instruments might bias the empirical findings. We propose to examine the patterns, origins, and consequences of varying popular understandings of democracy using the new ranking instruments (PUD) designed by the GBS II.

Taking advantage of the open-ended instruments used in its earlier waves of surveys, GBS II has identified four key aspects of democracy that have been widely and consistently reported as essential characteristics of democracy by ordinary people around the world: (1) social equity, (2) good government, (3) norms and procedures, and (4) freedom and liberty. The former two effectively capture what we define as the substantive understanding of democracy that focuses on the instrumental values of democracy in delivering quality governance; while the latter two tap into what we define as the procedural understanding of democracy that emphasizes the intrinsic values of democracy as a way of life that ensures people's dignity and inalienable rights. For the PUD instruments, GBS II has identified four indicators for each of the four key aspects, organized four ranking sets with four different indicators (i.e., one for each of the four key aspects with rotated order), and presented the ranking sets to respondents to choose the most essential characteristic of democracy, thus, tapping into their respective conceptions of democracy when trade-off dynamics are highlighted.

Our empirical examination of the survey and experimental data collected from seventy-two societies (i.e., those covered by the GBS II and the United States) shows that there is little recency or primacy effect in responses to the PUD instruments. Our survey experiment in the United States further confirms that the PUD instruments with the GBS II design closely mimic the performance of the PUD instruments with fully randomized order of answer categories. Thus, the PUD instruments do not suffer from significant design deficiencies.

Meanwhile, both CFA and LCA analyses confirm that the PUD instruments do effectively differentiate between distinct understandings of democracy, despite these models' different operationalization strategies, statistical modeling assumptions, and techniques in dealing with item nonresponse. While the CFA results reveal people's latent willingness to trade off key democratic principles for instrumental gains, which falls on a continuous spectrum, the LCA results uncover four distinct latent groups of people (i.e., Principle-Holders, Benefit-Seekers, Fence-Sitters, and Agnostics) making varying choices when the trade-offs between democracy's intrinsic and instrumental values are highlighted. The CFA and LCA results align with each other quite well. This has greatly boosted our confidence in the validity and reliability of the PUD instruments in capturing our key variable of interest.

Overall, the GBS II new ranking instruments should enable us to effectively capture distinct conceptions of democracy, to zoom in on the contrast and trade-offs between democracy's intrinsic and instrumental values, and to scrutinize how such varying conceptions of democracy may shape the prospects for democracy in today's world.

Appendix

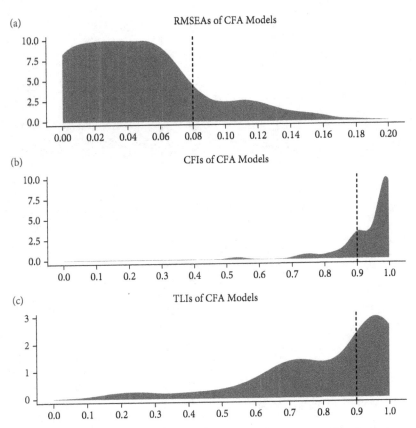

Figure A2.1 One-Factor CFA Model-Fit-Statistics for Seventy-Two Societies

3
Varying Understandings of Democracy in the Contemporary World

Using survey experiments and different psychometrical modeling strategies, Chapter 2 has demonstrated the validity and reliability of the GBS battery (i.e., the PUD instruments) in capturing various understandings of democracy. Although the PAPI technique GBS relied on for data collection prevented it from adopting an ideal design with full randomization of indicators for ranking, our analysis of both related observational and experimental data suggests that, in its current design, the PUD instruments is not significantly affected by possible question order effect. Furthermore, both CFA and LCA analyses confirm that the PUD instruments can effectively differentiate between people holding varying conceptions of democracy and in particular, distinguish between those who emphasize the instrumental values of democracy in delivering socioeconomic and political goods and those who prioritize the intrinsic values of democracy in ensuring individuals' dignity and inalienable rights through appropriate institutions and procedures. We have further argued that such a distinction is of particular value for our overarching research question (i.e., How do popular understandings of democracy shape critical political attitudes and behaviors, which, in turn, affect the political dynamics in both democracies and authoritarian societies?) by highlighting how people make choices when confronted with the trade-offs between key democratic principles and instrumental gains.

In this chapter, we use the information collected via the PUD instruments to demonstrate the cross-sectional variation in popular understandings of democracy around the world (i.e., seventy-one Asian, African, and Latin American societies covered by the GBS II and the United States), as well as the longitudinal features of this critical political attitude in Asia (i.e., thirteen Asian societies covered by the ABS III and IV). We examine the following questions in particular: How do popular understandings of democracy vary across societies? Will we get consistent or distinct patterns using different psychometrical modeling strategies? Is the variation in democratic conceptions revealed by the PUD instruments mainly driven by some idiosyncratic factors associated with the GBS II survey (given its cross-sectional nature)? Is it justifiable to use understandings of democracy to examine mid-range or long-term political dynamics in different societies? For distributions of popular conceptions of democracy within different regions and societies, we rely on the GBS II data (collected between 2010 and 2013 and covering seventy-one societies), together with a national representative online survey from the United States in 2017. For the longitudinal features of popular understandings of democracy, we rely on the third and fourth waves of the Asian Barometer Survey (ABS) data collected from thirteen Asian societies between 2010 and 2015.

Furthermore, as discussed in Chapter 2, theoretically, the PUD instruments are reflective indicators of the latent construct that we are interested in, that is, people's willingness to trade off key democratic principles for instrumental gains as they conceptualize democracy. Hence, the raw scores of the PUD instruments are not the ideal subject for examination, given the influence of various measurement errors.[1] The latent factor scores (i.e., the IRT scores) extracted via the CFA modeling, or the latent groups uncovered via the LCA modeling, should be more appropriate for our analysis, since the measurement errors have been effectively accounted for via appropriate statistical procedures. In subsequent analyses, we will focus on these latent features (either as continuous factor scores or discrete groups).

3.1 Popular understandings of democracy as a continuous latent spectrum

One reasonable and justifiable strategy is to operationalize democratic conceptions as a continuous latent propensity that covers a whole spectrum ranging from the lowest end of full willingness to trade off key democratic principles for instrumental gains (associated with a pure substantive understanding of democracy) to the highest end of a lack of any such willingness (associated with a pure procedural understanding of democracy). As previously shown in Table 2.2, a series of one-factor CFA models have successfully uncovered a similar continuous latent spectrum. This latent spectrum ranges from its lowest end of a pure substantive understanding of democracy to its highest end of a pure procedural understanding, with mixed conceptions falling in between.

It is worth emphasizing that for this operational strategy, we coded the original four-point scale of the ranking sets into a binary: 0 for endorsing the indicators of (1) social equity or (2) good government as the most essential characteristic of democracy (i.e., the substantive understanding of democracy emphasizing its instrumental values) and 1 for endorsing the indicators of (3) norms and procedures or (4) freedom and liberty as the most essential characteristic of democracy (i.e., the procedural understanding of democracy prioritizing its intrinsic values). Statistically, the one-factor CFA model with dichotomous indicators is equivalent to a two-parameter IRT model. Therefore, our examination here focuses on the uncovered continuous IRT scores (i.e., latent factor scores that summarize individuals' varying willingness to trade off key democratic principles for instrumental gains). Given our coding of the PUD instruments, a larger value of the IRT scores indicates a higher inclination toward a procedural understanding of democracy and thus a lower willingness to trade off key democratic principles for instrumental gains. Conversely, a lower value of the IRT scores indicates a higher inclination toward a substantive understanding of democracy and thus a higher willingness to engage in such trade-offs. Using boxplots, we have plotted the distributions of the IRT scores for each of the regions under examination and ranked their regional means in an ascending order in Figure 3.1. Dark solid segments indicate the median of the IRT scores for each region.

Compatible with our expectation and also consistent with the conventional wisdom on the popularity of liberal democracy in the United States and Latin America, the box-plots in Figure 3.1 show that, on average, people in the United States and Latin America are more inclined to prioritize the intrinsic values of democracy in ensuring individuals' dignity and inalienable rights through appropriate institutions and procedures.[2] In contrast, their counterparts in East Asia and North Africa are, on average, far more inclined to emphasize the instrumental values of democracy in delivering socioeconomic and political goods.[3] Meanwhile, the average popular conceptions of democracy in South Asia and sub-Saharan Africa fall in between, but leaning more toward the substantive understanding.[4] For us, that Americans outperform their counterparts in other societies in prioritizing the intrinsic values of democracy as they conceptualize the D-word provides a comforting and critical piece of evidence reconfirming the validity of the PUD instruments. Despite documented problems and issues with US democracy (Foa and Mounk 2017; Mounk 2018; Inglehart and Norris 2017), at least as reported by the GBS II data, Americans, on average, are much less likely to trade off

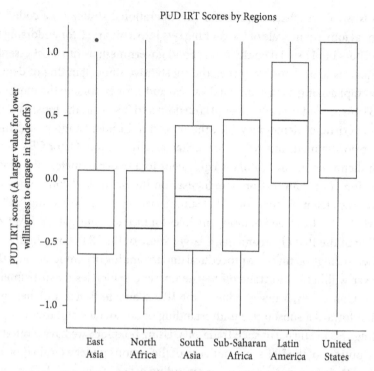

Figure 3.1 Regional Distribution of PUD Instruments' IRT Scores

key democratic principles for instrumental gains than their counterparts in Latin America, Africa, and Asia. It seems that the long practice and tradition of liberal democracy have, to some extent, insulated US democracy against possible challenges and attacks. Hopefully, the US public's relatively lower willingness to trade off key democratic principles for instrumental gains will ensure the resilience of US democracy against the backlash of populism and increasingly polarized partisan politics.[5]

It is also clearly illustrated in Figure 3.1 that, within each region, there is still significant variation in how people conceptualize democracy. For instance, in East Asia, despite the strong and lingering influence of Confucianism (which prioritizes good governance over institutions and procedures as defining features of an ideal government) (Shin 2012; Shi 2015), large numbers of people have embraced the procedural understanding of democracy. In the United States, despite the rich and long tradition of liberal democracy (which aims to check the operation of power via democratic institutions and procedures), a large number of people have endorsed the substantive understanding of democracy. Therefore, for a more effective examination of the spatial variation in popular understandings of democracy, it might be more useful to further deconstruct the regions and examine each of the seventy-two societies.

In Figure 3.2, we have plotted the weighted mean IRT scores of popular understandings of democracy for each of the seventy-two societies on a world map using different shades of grey.[6] A darker color indicates a higher popular inclination toward the procedural understanding of democracy, and thus a lower willingness to trade off key democratic principles for instrumental gains. Similar to the patterns revealed in Figure 3.1, on average, the color of the United States and Latin America is much darker than that of Africa and Asia. Basically, the procedural understanding of democracy is much more popular in the continents of North and South America. Meanwhile, in Africa and Asia, the substantive understanding of democracy has effectively won the hearts and minds of the majority of the people. In other words, citizens of the United States and Latin American societies are much less willing to trade off key democratic principles for instrumental gains, while their African and Asian counterparts are more willing to engage in such trade-offs when necessary.

However, there are noteworthy outliers in the map, which run against the general pattern across the continents. For meaningful interpretations and comparisons, we use the United States as the benchmark for evaluations: the mean IRT score in the United States is about 0.42, indicating the prevalence of the procedural understanding of democracy. In Ecuador, Nicaragua, Guatemala, and Paraguay, the mean IRT scores range between 0.19 and 0.27.[7] Put otherwise, despite the prevalence of popular views that prioritize

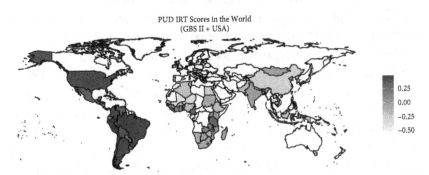

Figure 3.2 Variation in IRT Scores of Democratic Conceptions

the intrinsic values of democracy in Latin America, the citizens of Ecuador, Nicaragua, Guatemala, and Paraguay, on average, are actually less inclined to embrace this procedural understanding of democracy.

Similarly, in Asia, most people emphasize the instrumental values of democracy in their views, thus pushing the regional mean IRT score down and close to −0.4.[8] However, the citizens of Mongolia, Cambodia, India, and Philippines are comparatively more inclined to prioritize the intrinsic values of democracy. More specifically, the mean IRT scores in Mongolia, Cambodia, India, and Philippines range between −0.01 and −0.05, indicating a somewhat balanced mix of citizens endorsing the procedural or substantive conception of democracy.

Africans are more heterogeneous compared to their Asian and Latin American counterparts. At one extreme, in societies like Morocco (−0.55), Swaziland (−0.42), Mali (−0.40), and Niger (−0.38), the majority of their citizens emphasizes the instrumental values of democracy in their related understandings, pretty much like their East Asian counterparts in Japan or Vietnam. At the other extreme, in societies like Tanzania (0.30) and Cameroon (0.24), the prevalence of the procedural understanding of democracy makes these African societies look like Mexico or the Dominican Republic in Latin America. Meanwhile, there also are societies like Kenya (−0.01), Burundi (−0.01), and Mozambique (0.01) with a somewhat balanced mix of citizens oriented toward the procedural or substantive conception of democracy.[9]

It is quite obvious that the variation in popular understandings of democracy within each continent seems no less significant than that between the continents. Put otherwise, society-specific socioeconomic, cultural, and political contexts might have played an equally, if not greater, influential role in shaping popular understandings of democracy than those of conventionally conceptualized cultural zones (which align quite well with different continents). We will visit this point more systematically in Chapter 4.

There is one caveat regarding these interpretations based on the IRT scores: they all are relative numbers with a meaningless zero point that is anchored to the sample features under examination. Using the IRT scores, it is perfectly fine to argue that, compared to how Americans conceptualize democracy, on average, Japanese and Moroccans place more emphasis on the instrumental values of democracy, while Brazilians and Peruvians are equally or even more likely to prioritize the intrinsic values of democracy. Nevertheless, we still are not quite sure about the situation in each of the seventy-two societies, that is, the nature of their citizens' varying understandings of democracy. This is where LCA models can provide more empirical leverage by operationalizing varying democratic conceptions as distinct latent groups.

3.2 Popular understandings of democracy as distinct latent groups

As demonstrated in Chapter 2, the results of a series of LCA models suggest that we are able to identify four distinct groups of people based on their responses to the PUD instruments. One group is dominated by respondents who did not respond to three or more ranking sets (i.e., coded as DKs), thus labeled Agnostics. A second group is dominated by respondents who mostly identified the indicators of (1) social equity or (2) good government as essential characteristics of democracy, thus labeled Benefit-Seekers (who are always ready to trade off key democratic principles for instrumental gains). A third group is dominated by respondents who mainly identified the indicators of (3) norms and procedures or (4) freedom and liberty as essential characteristics of democracy, thus labeled Principle-Holders (who are rarely willing to sacrifice key democratic principles for instrumental gains). The last group is dominated by respondents who identified a mixed bag of indicators as essential characteristics of democracy, and are thus labeled Fence-Sitters (whose willingness to engage in such trade-offs might be conditional upon the nature of the instrumental gains under examination). Following the same logic of using the United States as the baseline for CFA analysis, we pooled the GBS II and 2017 US national survey data together, specified a four-class LCA model, and plotted the weighted percentages of the four groups of people for different regions in Figure 3.3.

To ease comparisons against the CFA results reported in Figure 3.1, we examined the same six regions and ranked them in an ascending order of their respective percentages of Principle-Holders (i.e., citizens embracing a procedural understanding of democracy who are rarely willing to trade off key democratic principles for instrumental gains). Quite consistent with the pattern displayed in Figure 3.1, the United States outperforms the other regions by having the largest percentage of Principle-Holders (about 47%). The United States also has the smallest percentage of Agnostics (around 0.7%). Latin America, again, closely follows the United States, by boasting the

54 UNDERSTANDINGS OF DEMOCRACY

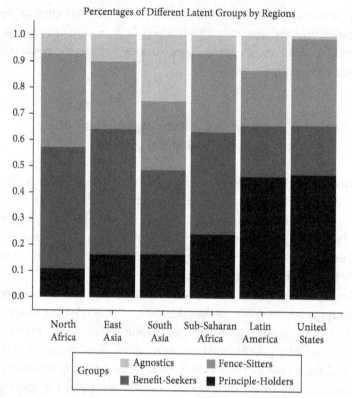

Figure 3.3 Reginal Distribution of PUD Instruments' Latent Groups

second largest percentage of Principle-Holders (about 46%). In this regard, North Africa, East Asia, and South Asia perform much worse, with about 11%, 16%, and 17% of their respective populations classified as Principle-Holders; sub-Saharan Africa (around 24%) falls in between.

If we focus on the percentages of Benefit-Seekers who emphasize the instrumental values of democracy and are always ready to sacrifice key democratic principles for instrumental gains, the order of the regions is simply reversed. This should not be surprising given the mutual exclusion of the four latent groups. East Asia and North Africa perform much better than other regions, with around 47% and 46% of their respective people classified as Benefit-Seekers. Latin American and the United States both show a much smaller percentage in this regard, namely, 19% and 18% respectively. Sub-Saharan Africa and South Asia fall in between, with about 39% and 32% of their respective people classified as Benefit-Seekers.

Besides what we have already learned from Figure 3.1, Figure 3.3 also reveals some nuanced features of popular conceptions of democracy, especially the prevalence of Fence-Sitters. Their responses to the PUD instruments are not consistent. For different ranking sets, their endorsement of the essential features of democracy may change back and forth between democracy's intrinsic and instrumental values, although the two are consistently presented as potential trade-offs. Overall, these people's conceptions of democracy mix both procedural and substantive components; and their willingness to trade off key democratic principles might be conditional upon the nature of the instrumental gains under examination. In this regard, North Africa outperforms the other regions, showing the largest percentage of Fence-Sitters (around 35%). Surprisingly, the United States is ranked second, with about 33% of its people reporting inconsistent conceptions of democracy. Meanwhile, Latin America has the lowest percentage of Fence-Sitters, namely, about 21%. Sub-Saharan Africa (about 29%), South Asia (about 26%), and East Asia (about 26%) fall in between. Different from the significant cross-regional variation in the percentages of Principle-Holders or Benefit-Seekers, there is a surprising consistency in the percentages of Fence-Sitters across regions, at roughly one-third. We will further explore the implications of such mixed conceptions of democracy in later chapters.

Figure 3.2 reveals substantive variation in popular conceptions of democracy (measured with the IRT scores) even within a region. Will we get similar patterns as we differentiate between the four groups of people holding distinct understandings of democracy? We have calculated the respective weighted percentages of Principle-Holders, Benefit-Seekers, Fence-Sitters, and Agnostics for each of the seventy-two societies. Again, we have presented this data on a world map using varying shades of grey, with darker color indicating a higher percentage of citizens classified into a specific latent group.[10]

As illustrated in Figure 3.4a, the United States and Latin American countries are much darker than the rest of the map, indicating a larger percentage of their citizens prioritizing the intrinsic values of democracy (classified as Principle-Holders). Latin American countries are quite homogenous in this regard: the percentage of Principle-Holders ranges from a low of around 36% (Ecuador) to a high of about 56% (Peru). Furthermore, countries like Peru (56%), Columbia (54%), Panama (52%), Argentina (52%), and Brazil (51%) outperform the United States (around 47%) in this regard, with more than 50% of their citizens rarely willing to trade off key democratic principles for instrumental gains. Asian societies also are quite homogeneous in this

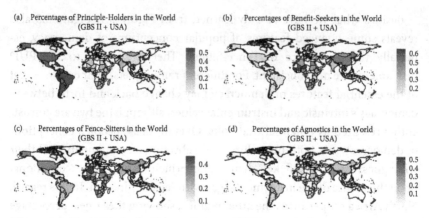

Figure 3.4 Variation in the Latent Groups of Democratic Conceptions

regard, but with a much lower percentage of their citizens adhering to democratic principles. The percentage of Principle-Holders in Asia ranges from about 2% (Vietnam) to around 28% (Cambodia). Less than or around 10% of the citizens of Vietnam (2%), mainland China (8%), Bangladesh (11%), Thailand (12%), Japan (12%), Pakistan (14%), and Taiwan (14%) are classified as Principle-Holders.[11] Comparatively speaking, African countries demonstrate more heterogeneity in this regard. On this continent, there are societies like Morocco (6%), Egypt (7%), Mali (8%), Niger (8%), and Tunisia (9%) where less than 10% of citizens prioritize the intrinsic values of democracy. But there also are countries like Tanzania (41%), Cape Verde (39%), Zambia (39%), Ghana (33%), Ivory Coast (31%), Cameroon (31%), and Madagascar (31%) with around 30% or more of their citizens classified as Principle-Holders.

As we examine the percentages of Benefit-Seekers (Figure 3.4b) who emphasize democracy's instrumental values and are generally willing to trade off key democratic principles for instrumental gains, Latin American countries, again, are quite homogenous in boasting a low percentage of Benefit-Seekers, just like their North American neighbor (i.e., about 19% in the United States). This group ranges from less than 15% of the population (El Salvador, Peru, Bolivia, and Brazil) to around 25% (Nicaragua, Paraguay, Guatemala, and Ecuador). Both African and Asian societies show much more heterogeneity regarding the prevalence of Benefit-Seekers among their respective citizens. Among African countries, the percentage ranges from around 20% (Tanzania and Cameroon) to more than 50% (Swaziland, Niger, Mali,

Morocco, Tunisia, Malawi, and Senegal). Similarly, among Asian societies, the percentage jumps from about 25% (India, Vietnam, and Bangladesh) to more than 50% (Japan, Thailand, Taiwan, Singapore, and mainland China).

Comparatively, as illustrated in Figure 3.4c, the percentage of citizens holding somewhat mixed understandings of democracy (i.e., classified as Fence-Sitters) shows more heterogeneity among African countries. It ranges from a low of around 10% (Swaziland, Mozambique, and Madagascar) to a high of about 45% (Liberia, Algeria, Sierra Leone, Egypt, and Benin). Among Latin American countries, this percentage ranges between around 15% (Chile, Colombia, Peru, and Honduras) and 30% (El Salvador and Ecuador). In Asia, the percentage runs between around 10% (Nepal) to about 35% (Pakistan, Bangladesh, and Singapore). It is worth noting that, among the US public, about 33% have embraced somewhat mixed understandings of democracy, without clearly prioritizing either its intrinsic or instrumental values. These Americans might be tempted into trading off key democratic principles when the expected return of instrumental gains is highly attractive. This resonates with rising populism in the United States (Bonikowski and Gidron 2016; Norris and Inglehart 2018), as well as some recent findings on how partisan political concerns could undermine democratic values among the US public (Graham and Svolik 2020; Svolik 2019).

Figure 3.4d presents the percentages of Agnostics (i.e., people who cannot provide meaningful responses to three or more ranking sets of the PUD instruments). In the United States, only around 0.7% of its citizens might have a hard time coming up with a meaningful response when confronted with the trade-offs between key democratic principles and instrumental gains. Basically, almost all Americans (more than 99%) have some knowledge of democracy and can make a choice when confronted with such trade-offs. Again, this should not be surprising given the status of the United States as a textbook case of liberal democracy with a long tradition of democratic practice. The highest within-continent variation in the percentages of Agnostics is found in Asia: between less than 1% (Philippines and Cambodia) and a surprisingly high of around 50% (Nepal and Vietnam). In Africa, this percentage runs between less than 1% (Benin and Namibia) to around 20% (Mozambique and Madagascar), with most African societies reporting close to or less than 10% of Agnostics among their citizens. Latin America shows more homogeneity in this regard, with the percentage of Agnostics hovering around 10% in most societies. It is only in Chile and Bolivia that this percentage jumps to around 20%. As discussed in Chapter 2, there are various reasons for having Agnostics in a society. Some people just may not have enough information or knowledge about democracy to give a meaningful response. Some people who do have related information and knowledge may not feel comfortable in making a choice when confronted with the trade-offs between key democratic principles and instrumental gains. Some people may just want to minimize their efforts in completing the survey, thus skipping complicated questions (like the PUD instruments) by using "I don't know" as an easy way out. Or, some issues with survey administration might have created unwanted challenges or unnecessary burdens for respondents to provide meaningful responses. Therefore, it is very difficult to fully assess the dynamics of Agnostics without access to related survey paradata for in-depth analysis.[12] In Chapter 4, we will try to explore some of the cognitive dynamics involved and offer some preliminary assessment of Agnostics.

It should be fair to argue that, given this evidence, there is significant variation in how people understand democracy and many are willing and able to choose when key democratic principles and instrumental gains are presented as trade-offs. Using the United States as a meaningful benchmark, both relative assessments (i.e., using the IRT scores) and absolute evaluations (i.e., using the LCA latent groups) agree that Latin American countries, on average, look more like their North American neighbor than societies in Africa and Asia; on average, there is a more salient presence of the procedural understanding of democracy (i.e., Principle-Holders) in Latin American societies. Societies in Asia and North Africa, on average, show a more salient presence of the substantive understanding of democracy (i.e., Benefit-Seekers). In other words, the US public and counterparts in Latin America, on average, are less willing to trade off key democratic principles for instrumental gains than the citizens of Asian and North African societies, while the willingness of those in sub-Saharan Africa to engage in such trade-offs falls somewhere in between.

Our analyses based on the LCA models have established even more interesting findings that have been conventionally ignored in related research: in all seventy-two societies a significant portion of citizens do not clearly prioritize the intrinsic or instrumental values of democracy when they conceptualize the D-word, thus holding somewhat mixed understandings of democracy (i.e., Fence-Sitters). As a consequence, their willingness to trade off key democratic principles could be conditional upon the nature of the instrumental gains under examination. These Fence-Sitters are willing to sell, but only when the expected return of instrumental gains is sufficiently attractive. We will dig deeper to understand the origins and consequences of the documented variations in popular understandings of democracy in subsequent chapters.

However, before we move on, it is critical to be fully aware of the limitations of the analyses just presented, and related findings, given the cross-sectional nature of the GBS II data. More specifically, do the PUD instruments mainly capture something that is transient and sensitive to idiosyncratic and short-term fluctuations, or something that boasts sufficient inertia and primarily responds to slow-moving dynamics and systematic transformations? Answers to this question have critical implications for the validity of using the PUD instruments to address our overarching research question (i.e., how do popular understandings of democracy affect the prospects for democracy in today's world?). Without knowing the longitudinal performance of the PUD instruments, our interpretations of related empirical data might be misguided. To secure a more solid empirical foundation for subsequent analyses, we explore the PUD instruments' longitudinal features, using two waves of rolling cross-sectional surveys conducted in thirteen East Asian societies.

3.3 Longitudinal stability in popular understandings of democracy

Ideally, to effectively examine the longitudinal features of popular understandings of democracy, we should collect related information using the same instruments to survey the same group of people repeatedly over an extended period of time. Basically, we need panel survey data. Unfortunately, it can be prohibitively expensive to operate and maintain panel surveys for comparative survey projects like the GBS. And the high erosion rate (i.e., respondents dropping out during the course) may also significantly compromise the effectiveness of panel surveys. A second-best approach would be to use rolling cross-sectional surveys in a number of societies: that is, using different representative samples for surveys in the same group of societies over time. Although not ideal, such rolling cross-sectional survey data still allow us to assess the longitudinal features of attitudes and behaviors at the aggregate level, given the relatively stable underlying population.[13]

In ABS III & IV surveys (conducted between 2010 and 2015), the PUD instruments have been consistently administered in thirteen East Asian societies. Therefore, for each of the thirteen societies, we have two opportunities (separated by three to four years) to measure and document how their people conceptualize democracy. As we pool the two waves of survey data together and impose the same CFA and LCA models for analysis (which ensures the same baseline for scoring or grouping respondents), we can legitimately compare the resultant IRT scores or uncovered percentages of distinct latent groups in the thirteen societies over time. This enables us to effectively assess the longitudinal features of popular conceptions of democracy. To ensure the robustness of our findings, we have followed the same approach adopted in earlier analyses, namely, using both CFA and LCA models for cross-validation.

Figure 3.5 presents our CFA results based on the pooled data of the ABS III and IV surveys. We have followed the same coding rule used for earlier analyses; therefore, a larger IRT score suggests a higher inclination toward prioritizing the intrinsic values of democracy as one conceptualizes democracy (thus, lower willingness to trade off key democratic principles for instrumental gains). Figure 3.5a presents the boxplots for the IRT scores of popular conceptions of democracy in each of the fourteen societies for both waves of the ABS survey.[14] Dark solid segments indicate the median of the IRT scores for each society at a specific wave. Across the board, the medians in twelve East Asian societies, other than mainland China, do not change sign between the two waves of surveys. In other words, our conclusions on the overall pattern in any of the twelve societies regarding their respective prevalent conceptions of democracy (i.e., the substantive vs. procedural understanding) do not change, regardless of which wave of the survey is under examination.

More specifically, in societies like Japan, Hong Kong, Taiwan, Thailand, Indonesia, Singapore, and Vietnam, citizens, on average, are more inclined to embrace the substantive understanding of democracy, emphasizing its instrumental values. Meanwhile, in societies like South Korea, Mongolia, Philippines, Cambodia, and Malaysia, citizens, on average, are more inclined to prioritize the intrinsic values of democracy, thus embracing the procedural understanding. The outlier is mainland China. The 2011 national survey from mainland China suggested the prevalence of the substantive understanding of democracy among its people, while the 2015 national survey suggested a significant move, with an increasing number of Chinese oriented toward the procedural understanding of democracy. Despite the fact that we do not have enough data to figure out what has driven such a noteworthy change in mainland China, if the modernization and cosmopolitan theories

VARYING UNDERSTANDINGS OF DEMOCRACY   61

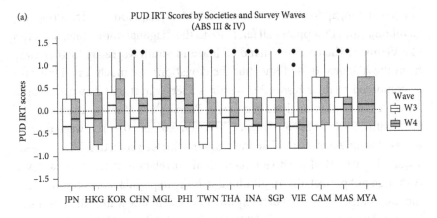

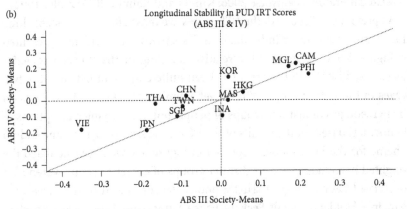

Figure 3.5   Longitudinal Features of CFA IRT Scores

of democracy (Welzel 2013; Welzel and Alvarez 2014; Norris and Inglehart 2009; Inglehart and Welzel 2005, 2010; Inglehart 2018) are right, China's continuous economic growth over the past decades and the Chinese people's increasing access to the practice of liberal democracies via the internet or international travels might have pushed Chinese society in a direction of transformation that is compatible with the change displayed in Figure 3.5a.

Figure 3.5b presents the thirteen societies' respective weighted means of the IRT scores for both waves using black dots. The diagonal dotted line suggests how the black dots should have behaved had the thirteen societies' weighted means been identical between the two waves of surveys. The closer the black dots fall along the dotted line, the greater the longitudinal stability of the popular conceptions of democracy (as operationalized by the PUD instruments' IRT scores). As illustrated in Figure 3.5b, societies like Japan, Singapore, Taiwan, Indonesia, Malaysia, Hong Kong, Mongolia, Cambodia, and Philippines all fall close to the diagonal dotted line. Societies like Vietnam, Thailand, mainland China, and South Korea are further away from the diagonal dotted line, but the deviations are much less significant as compared to their respective within-society variation (shown in Figure 3.5a). A correlation analysis suggests a Pearson's correlation coefficient of 0.87 (with a 95% confidence interval between 0.62 and 0.96) between the two waves of weighted mean IRT scores from the thirteen societies. This suggests a quite high level of positive longitudinal correlation at the societal level. Although not perfect, the longitudinal stability in popular conceptions of democracy outperforms that of many other critical political attitudes examined in related literature (Converse 2006; Kinder and Kalmoe 2017; Zaller 1992).

As previously discussed, the IRT scores are most effective in establishing the relative ranking of individuals and societies. The evidence presented in Figure 3.5 suggests that the relative standing of the thirteen societies (as assessed by the IRT scores) has been quite consistent between the two waves of the ABS surveys. Will we get a similar conclusion if we focus on the percentages of distinct groups of people holding varying conceptions of democracy, based on the results of the LCA models? Using the same coding scheme for the LCA models reported in Figure 3.3, we have calculated the weighted percentages of four distinct groups of citizens (as uncovered by a four-class LCA model applied to the pooled data of ABS III and IV surveys)—Principle-Holders, Benefit-Seekers, Fence-Sitters, and Agnostics—in each of the fourteen societies. Related findings are presented in Figure 3.6.

The upper panel of Figure 3.6 presents the information for ABS III (with thirteen societies) and the lower panel presents the information for ABS IV (with fourteen societies). To examine longitudinal stability, we focused on the thirteen societies with comparable data from both waves. As shown in Figure 3.6, except for Vietnam, in the other twelve societies, there is no highly dramatic shift in the distribution of their respective citizens between the four groups over time. There are some noticeable changes in societies like Thailand. More specifically, between the two waves of ABS surveys in Thailand, there was little change in the percentage of Principle-Holders among its citizens (i.e., about 14% in Wave III and around 15% in Wave IV). However, there was some significant move between the groups of Benefit-Seekers (i.e., dropping from about 59% in Wave III to about 39% in Wave IV) and Fence-Sitters (i.e., increasing from about 18% in Wave III to around 32% in Wave IV). Given the political turbulence in Thailand since the late 2000s

VARYING UNDERSTANDINGS OF DEMOCRACY   63

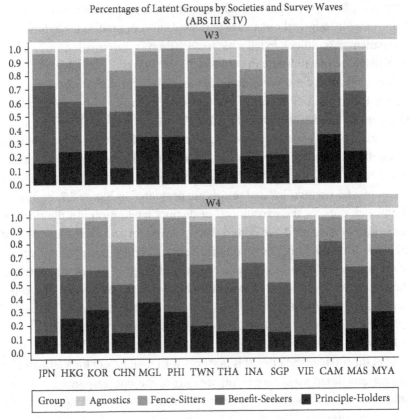

Figure 3.6 Compositions of LCA Latent Groups in ABS III and IV

(e.g., Thaksin's populist mobilization, street protests, and the subsequent military coup), it is quite understandable that some Benefit-Seekers (who were always ready to trade off key democratic principles for instrumental gains) might have been shocked by the socioeconomic and political chaos due to the lack of stable institutions and procedures in sustaining Thailand's democracy. These original Benefit-Seekers might start to show more appreciation of the values of key democratic principles and lower their willingness to engage in such trade-offs, thus transforming into Fence-Sitters. The significant changes in Vietnam have primarily been driven by the varying non-response rate: in ABS III, the non-response rate for the PUD instruments in Vietnam was more than 50%; while, in ABS IV, the corresponding non-response rate plummeted to around 5%. With more citizens being willing to or capable of giving meaningful answers to the PUD instruments, it should not be surprising to see the significant changes in Vietnam as illustrated in Figure 3.6. Unfortunately, without access to related survey paradata for appropriate assessment, it is difficult to tell what has driven such a dramatic change in the non-response rate in Vietnam between the two waves of ABS surveys.[15]

Similar to what we have done for assessing the longitudinal correlation between the IRT scores of popular understandings of democracies in the thirteen East Asian societies, we have also examined the longitudinal correlations between the compositions of the latent groups of people with distinct democratic conceptions in these societies (i.e., weighted percentages of the latent groups identified by the four-class LCA model) from the two waves of ABS surveys. Related results are presented in Figure 3.7. Again, we used black dots for the percentages of distinct latent group in the thirteen societies. We also used the dotted diagonal line for the ideal scenario that all black dots should fall on, had there been no change in the compositions of these societies' respective popular understandings of democracy between the two waves of surveys. Empirically, the closer the black dots fall to the dotted line, the greater longitudinal stability in popular understandings of democracy (as operationalized by the PUD instruments' latent groups).

Figure 3.7a presents how the percentages of Principle-Holders varies overtime in the thirteen societies. It is quite obvious that, except for Vietnam (for the reasons noted earlier regarding its fluctuating non-response rates), the other twelve black dots fall very close to the dotted line, indicating sufficiently high longitudinal stability. A Pearson's correlation coefficient of 0.88 (with a 95% confidence interval between 0.61 and 0.97) confirms the existence of a strong positive correlation between the two waves of ABS surveys regarding the presence of Principle-Holders among the East Asians over time. As we move to Figure 3.7b, we see a quite similar but less consistent pattern regarding the presence of Benefit-Seekers. In addition to Vietnam, Thailand seems to have witnessed some significant change (for reasons discussed earlier). A Pearson's correlation coefficient of 0.59 (with a 95% confidence interval between 0.02 and 0.87) suggests some moderate positive correlation between the two waves of ABS surveys in this regard. Similarly, Figures 3c and 3d illustrate the presence of Fence-Sitters and Agnostics, respectively, in the thirteen East Asian societies between the two waves of ABS surveys. Correlation analyses suggest a Pearson's correlation coefficient of 0.75 (with a 95% confidence interval between 0.31 and 0.93) for the presence of Fence-Sitters and 0.74 (with a 95% confidence interval between 0.29 and 0.92) for

VARYING UNDERSTANDINGS OF DEMOCRACY 65

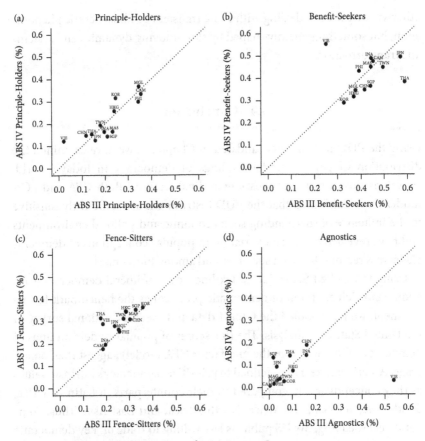

Figure 3.7 Longitudinal Features of LCA Latent Groups

the presence of Agnostics.[16] Both indicate a somewhat strong positive correlation over time, which, in turn, suggests high longitudinal stability.

Overall, our findings based on the CFA and LCA models have established the sufficiently high longitudinal stability in popular understandings of democracy, at least at the aggregate level. Although our evidence is primarily from the East Asian context, given our earlier discussions and findings on the validity and reliability of the PUD instruments in uncovering comparable latent constructs/groups in East Asia, South Asia, Latin America, North Africa, sub-Saharan Africa, and the United States, we have sufficient reason to believe in the longitudinal stability of this critical political attitude despite distinct surrounding socioeconomic and political contexts. Put

3.4 Conclusion

Using the PUD instruments validated in Chapter 2, we have examined the distribution of popular understandings of democracy in today's world, as well as this critical attitude's longitudinal features. Both CFA and LCA models have confirmed that the PUD instruments are sufficiently sensitive to the influence of surrounding socioeconomic and political environments and have revealed significant variation in popular conceptions of democracies across regions, between societies, and among individuals.

Using the United States (i.e., a textbook case of liberal democracy with a long and rich tradition of democratic practice) as the benchmark for assessment, we have pooled the GBS II data and the 2017 national survey of the United States for analysis. The IRT scores of popular understandings of democracy (extracted from the one-factor CFA model) suggest that, on average, Americans are more inclined to prioritize democracy's intrinsic values as they conceptualize it, compared to their counterparts in Latin America, South Asia, sub-Saharan Africa, North Africa, and East Asia. Thus, comparatively speaking, the US public is less willing to trade off key democratic principles for instrumental gains. Meanwhile, people living in East Asia and North Africa, on average, are more inclined to emphasize democracy's instrumental values and therefore more willing to engage in such trade-offs when necessary.

Further analysis suggests substantial variation within each of the regions. For instance, citizens of Latin American countries like Ecuador, Nicaragua, Guatemala, and Paraguay, on average, are more inclined to embrace the substantive understanding of democracy, despite the fact that most of their Latin American neighbors are more attracted to the procedural understanding. Similarly, citizens of Mongolia, Cambodia, India, and Philippines are more inclined to prioritize the intrinsic values of democracy, despite the prevailing emphasis on its instrumental values in other Asian societies. There is more heterogeneity among the citizens of African countries in terms of how they conceptualize democracy. One the one hand, those living in societies like Morocco, Swaziland, Mali, and Niger think more like their East Asian counterparts in mainland China and Singapore, emphasizing the instrumental values of democracy. On the other hand, those living in societies like Tanzania and Cameroon think more like their Latin American counterparts in Mexico or Dominican Republic, prioritizing the intrinsic values of democracy. Meanwhile, those living in societies like Kenya, Burundi, and Mozambique hold somewhat balanced and mixed views of democracy, without systematically prioritizing its instrumental or intrinsic values.

Our LCA models cross-validate these findings on the significant variation in popular conceptions of democracy between regions and between societies. In addition to confirming the relative standing established by the IRT scores for the seventy-two societies, the LCA models further reveal nuanced compositions of citizens with distinct conceptions of democracy in each of the seventy-two societies. More specifically, the LCA models differentiate between Principle-Holders, Benefit-Seekers, Fence-Sitters, and Agnostics as four latent groups of people showing distinct willingness to engage in the trade-offs between key democratic principles and instrumental gains. The United States and Latin America outperform other regions by boasting the largest percentage of Principle-Holders (who prioritize the intrinsic values of democracy). Meanwhile, both Latin America and Asia are quite homogenous in their respective popular conceptions of democracy. In the former, most societies have a larger percentage of Principle-Holders; while in the latter, most societies have a larger percentage of Benefit-Seekers (who emphasize the instrumental values of democracy). The heterogeneity among African societies in this regard is noteworthy, with some of them behaving like Asian societies and others behaving like Latin American countries. It is also important to note that, in all seventy-two societies, the presence of Fence-Sitters (whose willingness to trade off key democratic principles might be conditional upon the nature of instrumental gains under examination) is substantial. Even in the United States, around 33% of citizens are Fence-Sitters: they do not clearly prioritize democracy's instrumental or intrinsic values and are willing to sacrifice key democratic principles when the expected return of instrumental gains is sufficiently attractive.

To ensure that the variation documented in popular conceptions of democracy around the world (as captured by the PUD instruments) is not something transient or idiosyncratic, given the cross-sectional nature of the GBS data under examination, we have further explored the longitudinal features of this critical attitude using the ABS two-wave rolling-cross-sectional surveys from thirteen East Asian societies. Basically, we have information on popular conceptions of democracy (captured by the same PUD instruments) collected at two time points separated by three to four years in the thirteen societies, using comparable national representative samples. Although not ideal, these longitudinal data allow us to assess, indirectly at least, how popular understandings of democracy might have evolved over time, which, in turn, indicates potential roles played by slow-moving dynamics and systematic transformations in driving this critical political attitude.

Both CFA and LCA models have uncovered a high level of longitudinal stability in how East Asians, on average, conceptualize democracy. With a few exceptions like Vietnam, mainland China, and Thailand, popular understandings of democracy in the other East Asian societies demonstrate high consistency between the two waves of surveys. Although we do not have enough information (e.g., related survey paradata) to scrutinize the significant change in the non-response rates to the PUD instruments in Vietnam, the documented changes in democratic conceptions in mainland China and Thailand are quite consistent with the two societies' macro socioeconomic and political changes between the two waves of ABS surveys. Overall, we have sufficient reasons to believe in the longitudinal stability of this critical attitude, that is, popular understandings of democracy are unlikely to be transient and hyper-sensitive to idiosyncratic factors, but more likely to be mainly shaped by slow-moving dynamics and systematic transformations. Therefore, our subsequent analysis of the origins and attitudinal and behavioral consequences of varying popular conceptions of democracy should be highly informative for understanding the politics in contemporary authoritarian regimes and democracies, as well as for interpreting these societies' evolving political dynamics.

VARYING UNDERSTANDINGS OF DEMOCRACY 69

Appendix

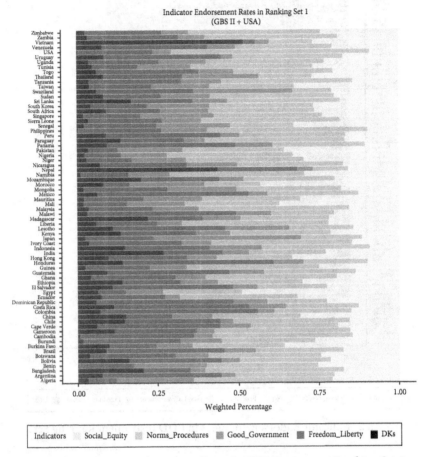

Figure A3.1 Indicator Endorsement Rates in PUD Instrument Ranking Set 1

70 UNDERSTANDINGS OF DEMOCRACY

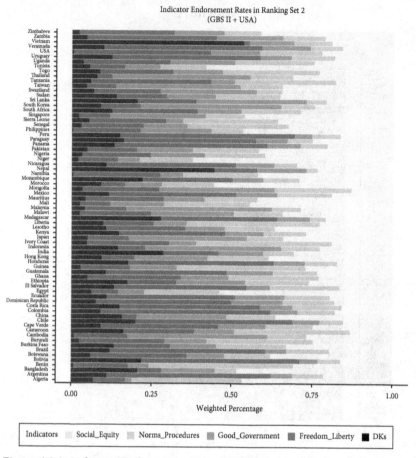

Figure A3.2 Indicator Endorsement Rates in PUD Instrument Ranking Set 2

VARYING UNDERSTANDINGS OF DEMOCRACY 71

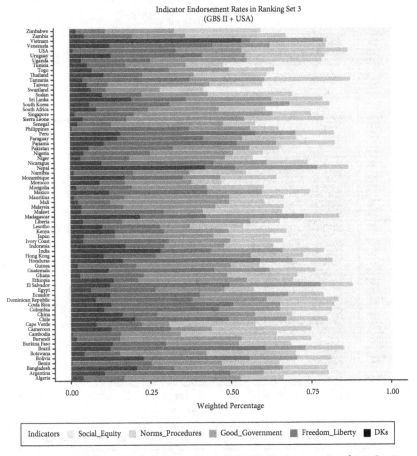

Figure A3.3 Indicator Endorsement Rates in PUD Instrument Ranking Set 3

72 UNDERSTANDINGS OF DEMOCRACY

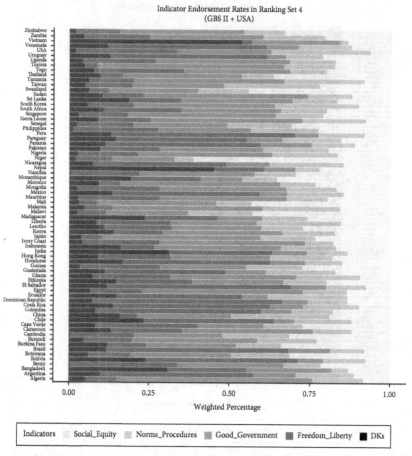

Figure A3.4 Indicator Endorsement Rates in PUD Instrument Ranking Set 4

4
Origins of Varying Understandings of Democracy

As shown in previous chapters, popular understandings of democracy vary significantly across regions, between societies, and even within societies. After establishing the patterns of varying conceptions of democracy in the contemporary world, it is a natural extension to examine the origins of such variations. More specifically, what might have driven people's varying propensities to prioritize democracy's instrumental or intrinsic values when they conceptualize democracy, especially when the potential trade-offs between the two are highlighted (as captured by the PUD instruments)? In this chapter, we scrutinize both individual- and societal-level factors that might contribute to the varying understandings of democracy found in the GBS II data. Basically, we attempt to profile which groups of people are more likely to trade off key democratic principles for instrumental gains, as well as the influence of economic, political, and cultural contextual factors on the willingness to engage in such trade-offs.

Most existing related research focuses on either a single case (Lu and Shi 2015; Lu et al. 2014; Crow 2010) or a number of cases in a single region (Canache 2012; Bratton and Mattes 2001; Ferrin and Kriesi 2016; Kriesi and Morlino 2016). Given our main interest in understanding how economic, political, and cultural environments shape popular democratic conceptions, it is crucial to maximize the contextual variation in the data. This is a key advantage offered by the GBS, which covers a large number of developing countries across the world. However, for such comparative survey projects, it is quite a challenge to incorporate and enforce the administration of an extensive module collecting pertinent individual features using identical or comparable instruments.[1] We have decided to include as many societies as possible, even at the cost of sacrificing some of the explanatory power at the individual level. As a consequence, to make full use of the much broader geographical coverage of GBS II to achieve maximum variation in economic, political, and cultural environments, we are not able to account for an extensive list of individual-level factors that have been examined in related scholarship.

We also want to be upfront regarding the nature of our subsequent analyses and discussions. Given the observational and cross-sectional nature of the GBS II data, it is very difficult to empirically demonstrate the causal effects of our explanatory variables on how people differ when they conceptualize democracy. Our empirical findings, therefore, are primarily about correlations. Nevertheless, we do have sufficient theoretical reasons to justify incorporation of the explanatory variables as legitimate and possible causes of varying understandings of democracy. For instance, at the individual level, democratic, cognitive, and socioeconomic characteristics are more likely to shape how people conceptualize democracy, rather than the other way around. Similarly, at the societal level, socioeconomic and political features (as objective indicators of surrounding contexts) are more likely to cast their influence over how people vary in their democratic conceptions, rather than being shaped by such understandings.[2]

Technically, for statistical inference we mainly use mixed-effect models, also recognized as hierarchical or multilevel models in the literature (Gelman and Hill 2007; Stegmueller 2013; Luke 2004; Raudenbush and Bryk 2002; Steenbergen and Jones 2002), for the following reasons. First, mixed-effect models enable us to integrate the survey data collected from a large number of individuals living in different societies with these societies' respective socioeconomic, political, and cultural features for effective and efficient analyses. Second, mixed-effect models can easily estimate varying relationships across societies via appropriate model specifications, thus accommodating our interest in examining the contextualized dynamics that shape popular understandings of democracy. Overall, to effectively accommodate the nested structure of our data (i.e., respondents embedded in different socioeconomic and political contexts) and efficiently estimate the impact of both individual- and societal-level factors, mixed-effect models are the most appropriate statistical tool for our empirical analysis.

4.1 Non-response to the PUD instruments

As discussed in Chapter 3, non-response to the PUD instruments is observed in all GBS II societies, and there is also noticeable variation in this regard.[3] If

ORIGINS OF VARYING UNDERSTANDINGS OF DEMOCRACY 75

we operationalize popular understandings of democracy as a continuous latent feature (as measured by the IRT scores of the PUD instruments), people offering non-response to all four ranking sets of the PUD instruments are recorded as missing values in corresponding IRT scores. If we operationalize democratic conceptions as a discrete latent construct (as measured by the LCA groups of the PUD instruments), people offering non-responses to three or more ranking sets are classified as Agnostics in the LCA latent groups.

Theoretically, we can apply a classic psychological-process model to understand how people respond to the PUD instruments (Tourangeau et al. 2000). Typically, after receiving stimuli from an interviewer, a respondent needs to understand what has been asked for, search for related information in memory, go through various calculations and evaluations, map the results of calculations and evaluations back to the answer categories provided by the interviewer, and, finally, report the choice of answer categories to the interviewer. Accordingly, an item non-response may be the result of various issues, including cognitive deficiency, lack of related information, social desirability concerns, political awareness, difficulties in choosing from the provided answer categories, or other idiosyncratic factors. Knowing the possible underlying, driving forces of non-response to the PUD instruments can help us more effectively interpret the meaningful responses recorded in the GBS II data.

Cognitive deficiency and lack of related information have been repeatedly identified as a key driver of survey non-response (Yan 2008; Zhu 1996; Jessee 2017; Reilly and Zigerell 2012; Luskin and Bullock 2011; Berinsky and Tucker 2006; Carnaghan 1996). When people cannot effectively understand what they have been asked for, "I don't know" should be expected and recorded as a legitimate response. Even if people do understand what they have been asked for, they may still not be able to provide a meaningful response if they do not have related information. That is one reason why some scholars have criticized the use of the standard "satisfaction with democracy" instrument to examine global popular support for democracy, since not everyone has pertinent experience to make an effective assessment (Anderson 2002; Canache et al. 2001; Ananda and Bol Forthcoming; Kiewiet de Jonge 2016; Panel 2019). Meanwhile, as discussed earlier, ranking is cognitively more challenging than rating, since the former requires simultaneous assessment of and comparison between multiple indicators. Thus, for the PUD instruments, cognitive deficiency might be a salient driving force for non-responses. Furthermore, as shown in Table 2.1, in order to make meaningful choices for the PUD instruments, people are expected to be familiar with terms like "democracy," "state aid," "public money," "corruption," "elections," "legislature," etc. It is reasonable to argue that the exposure to and engagement with such terms vary greatly between and within societies. Therefore, a lack of related information might also play some role in driving non-responses.

In the meantime, due to political or social desirability concerns, people might be induced to self-censor (Shen and Truex Forthcoming; Hayes et al. 2010; Hayes et al. 2005) or even engage in preference falsification (Kuran 1995; Atkeson et al. 2014; Tourangeau and Yan 2007; Lei and Lu 2017) during surveys. The influence of such concerns might be of particular salience in comparative surveys like the GBS II (covering societies with varying political and cultural contexts). The PUD instruments do not ask people to assess their regime or government directly (which can be politically sensitive under some conditions), but simply probe their views on which aspects of democracy should be more essential. Furthermore, as discussed earlier, few politicians publicly denounce democracy per se. Even authoritarian leaders actively use democratic discourse when talking about their regimes. Thus, given the nature of the PUD instruments and the fact that democracy is widely embraced as "something good," the role of political or social desirability concerns in driving non-responses should be limited.

To examine the hypothesis of cognitive deficiency, we relied on self-reported educational attainment as the key proxy: *people with better education are more likely to offer meaningful responses to the PUD instruments, thus showing a lower non-response propensity (**Hypothesis C4.1_1**)*. Educational attainment was incorporated as an ordinal variable with five categories, indicating varying levels of education from the lowest of illiteracy to the highest of postgraduate study.

To examine the hypothesis of lack of information, we relied on self-reported interest in politics as a key proxy: *people reporting a higher level of political interest are more likely to offer meaningful responses to the PUD instruments, thus showing a lower non-response propensity (**Hypothesis C4.1_2**)*. Political interest was incorporated as an ordinal variable measured with a four-point Likert scale, with a larger value indicating a higher level of interest in politics.[4] Besides the varying level of personal initiative required to acquire related information (as captured by political interest), we also included societal political features that might moderate the impact of personal initiative: *the influence of political interest on non-response is less strong in societies with better practice of democratic politics* **(Hypothesis C4.1_3)**. The reasoning for this is quite straightforward: in societies with better practice of democratic politics, even people with low interest in politics might have sufficient exposure to various forms of democratic practice and discourse, given the permeation of such information through media platforms and their daily lives. The political contextual feature was measured by a reversed Freedom House seven-point rating scale, with a larger value indicating better practice democratic politics.

To examine the hypothesis of political or social desirability bias, we relied on societal political regime features as a key proxy: *people living in societies with better protection of civil liberties and political rights are more likely to offer meaningful responses to the PUD instruments, thus showing lower non-response propensity* **(Hypothesis C4.1_4)**. Again, we used the reversed Freedom House seven-point rating scale for measurement, with a larger value indicating better protection of civil liberties and political rights.

Following best practice in related literature, six age groups (i.e., differentiating between the following age cohorts, 16–24, 25–34, 35–44, 45–54, 55–64, and 65+) and one gender indicator (i.e., 1 for males and 0 for females) were included as key democratic features for control. Furthermore, per capita GDP (transformed via a natural logarithm function), as a key socioeconomic contextual feature, was also included as a control.[5]

The outcome variable (i.e., non-response to the PUD instruments) can be measured in different ways. We can calculate a summary index of non-responses to the four ranking sets of the PUD instruments, thus getting an interval variable ranging from 0 to 4. We can code all missing values in the IRT scores of the PUD instrument as non-responses, thus getting a dichotomous variable. We also can code all Agnostics in the LCA groups of the PUD instruments as non-responses, again getting a dichotomous variable. All these measures are theoretically legitimate, but they differ in the distinct modeling strategies involved. The summary index offers richer information on how people differ in their propensity to give non-responses to the PUD instruments. However, using raw scores based on the survey data might introduce unwanted measurement errors into our analyses, given the influence of idiosyncratic factors on non-responses. Both IRT scores and LCA groups have taken appropriate statistical procedures to address the influence of such idiosyncratic factors, thus reducing unwanted measurement errors. However, different statistical procedures might uncover distinct patterns of non-responses in the data. For instance, only those giving non-responses to all four ranking sets of the PUD instruments are recorded as missing values in the IRT scores; while those offering non-responses to three or more ranking sets are classified as Agnostics in the LCA groups. Thus, non-responses identified using the IRT scores should be a subset of non-responses identified using the LCA groups.[6] To check the robustness of our findings, we ran the mixed-effect models using all three measures of non-responses with the same set of explanatory variables.[7] It is very encouraging that the findings are highly consistent across the model specifications. For an easier interpretation, we focused on regression results of the summary index (estimated via mixed-effect linear models) and presented the findings in Figure 4.1.

Technically, we ran a mixed-effect linear model with a random intercept, which accommodates possible variation in the average non-response rates across societies that cannot be fully captured by the specified individual and societal-level features. In Figure 4.1, as well as all subsequent figures, black

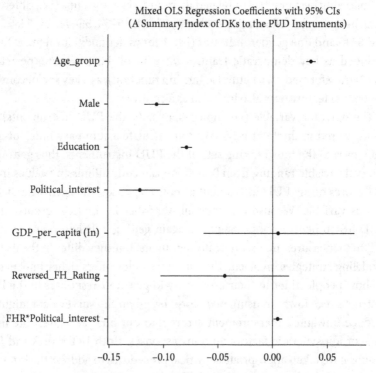

Figure 4.1 Mixed-Effect Linear Model on Non-Responses to the PUD Instruments

dots stand for regression coefficients for each of the included explanatory variables and horizontal segments stand for the 95% confidence intervals associated with the regression coefficients. The vertical line of zero stands for the conventional null hypothesis that the regression coefficients are statistically not different from zero (i.e., the lack of meaningful influence). If any of the horizontal segments intersects with the vertical line, the corresponding regression coefficient is not statistically different from zero at the 0.05 level. Put otherwise, the associated variable has little statistically meaningful impact on the outcome variable under examination.

As illustrated in Figure 4.1, better education, ceteris paribus, is associated with a lower propensity of offering non-response to the PUD instruments. In other words, when confronted with the trade-offs between key democratic principles and instrumental gains, better-educated people are more likely to make a choice, rather than saying "I don't know." This is consistent with Hypothesis C4.1_1: cognitive deficiency plays some role in driving non-response to the PUD instruments.

Although the regression coefficient associated with political interest is negative and statistically significant, we cannot make any meaningful interpretation solely based on that coefficient, given the incorporation of the interactive item between political interest and regime features (i.e., measured by the reversed Freedom House rating). Following best practice in interpreting interaction effects, we plotted the marginal effect of political interest given each Freedom House rating in Figure 4.2.

As shown in Figure 4.2, regardless of the regime features under examination, the impact of political interest on the propensity of giving non-responses to the PUD instruments is consistently negative. In other words, people who are more interested in politics are much less likely to avoid making a choice when confronted with the trade-offs between key democratic principles and instrumental gains. This finding is consistent with Hypothesis C4.1_2, that is, the lack of related information plays some role in driving non-responses to the PUD instruments.

Furthermore, as shown in Figure 4.2, the negative impact of political interest is much stronger in autocracies than in democracies, and this difference is statistically significant at the 0.05 level. Basically, the impact of this information inequality (shaped by individual initiatives) is reduced in democracies, where most people have sufficient exposure to democratic practice and related discourse through media channels and in their daily lives. This finding is consistent with Hypothesis C4.1_3, that is, political

80 UNDERSTANDINGS OF DEMOCRACY

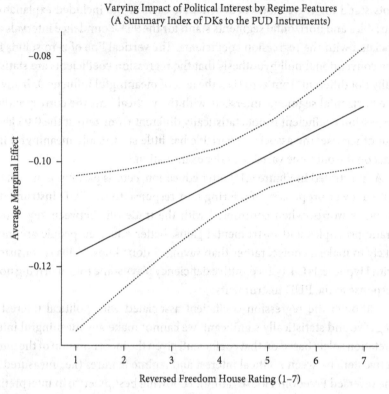

Figure 4.2 Average Marginal Effect of Political Interest under Different Political Contexts

context moderates how the lack of related information drives non-response to the PUD instrument.

The regression coefficient associated with reversed Freedom House rating is negative, which indicates, on average, a lower non-response propensity in democracies than in autocracies, especially among the people with very low interest in politics. However, the corresponding 95% confidence interval is so large that it covers the vertical line, suggesting statistical insignificance. Further simulations reveal that, despite the statistically significant interaction between reversed Freedom House rating and political interest, the impact of reversed Freedom House rating is negative but statistically insignificant at all levels of political interest. In other words, our empirical evidence does not strongly support Hypothesis C4.1_4, and we have not found strong evidence for the influence of political or social desirability bias on non-responses to the PUD instruments.

The performance of some control variables also merits discussion. On average, as shown in Figure 4.1, younger males are more likely to make a choice when probed for their views on the trade-offs between key democratic principles and instrumental gains. Although we do not have enough information to uncover associated underlying mechanisms, this pattern is highly consistent with the existing literature's conclusions on the critical role of cognitive sophistication and capability of information acquisition in shaping political attitudes. Overall, it is fair to argue that meaningful responses to the PUD instruments (as recorded in the GBS II data) are neither random nor uncontemplated reflections. In other words, when confronted with the contrast between democracy's intrinsic versus instrumental values, people do try to make informed choices. Thus, the meaningful responses to the PUD instruments provide valuable information for us to explore why people might be willing to trade off key democratic principles for instrumental gains.

4.2 Multilevel dynamics that drive varying understandings of democracy

Having demonstrated the dominant influence of cognitive deficiency and lack of pertinent information on non-responses to the PUD instruments, we have more confidence in examining people's meaningful responses to the PUD instrument as informed choices between democracy's intrinsic and instrumental values. As demonstrated in Chapter 3, in addition to the substantive cross-regional and between society variations, there is also significant variation within each of the seventy-two societies under examination (i.e., seventy-one GBS II societies plus the United States). Our analysis of the data further reveals that close to 84% of the variation in popular understandings of democracy (measured by either the continuous IRT scores or discrete LCA groups) should be attributed to individual-level dynamics; and the rest of the variation should be attributed to societal level dynamics.[8] Basically, to effectively account for why people vary in their willingness to trade off key democratic principles for instrumental gains, we need to incorporate multi-level dynamics for integrated analyses.

Impact of individual features: Above all, popular conceptions of democracy are attitudes held by individuals. Therefore, individual cognitive and psychological dynamics are expected to play a major role in shaping such attitudes. Existing scholarship on popular understandings of democracy and other related political attitudes has highlighted the significance of how people engage in political communication, as well as their socioeconomic status, in shaping their conceptions of democracy.

As Norris and Inglehart (2009) have argued, cosmopolitan communications have some significant and lasting impact on critical political values in today's world. How people engage in cosmopolitan communications is greatly shaped by their access to socioeconomic resources, cognitive capacity, and self-initiative. Better access to socioeconomic resources, greater cognitive capacity, and more self-initiative generally enable more effective engagement. As a consequence, people with such access are more likely to embrace self-expression or emancipative values, which, in turn, is likely to boost their support for institutional arrangements that promote and protect such values (Inglehart 2018; Inglehart and Welzel 2005; Welzel 2013). Following this line of research, it is reasonable to argue that, *ceteris paribus*, such people also are more inclined to cherish democracy's intrinsic values and are therefore less willing to trade off key democratic principles for instrumental gains.

Meanwhile, some recent research suggests that socioeconomic status may create cognitive bias regarding popular commitment to liberal democracy. Basically, people who can secure socioeconomic benefits and, accordingly, improve their status within an existing political system are more likely to hold favorable views toward the status quo (Ceka and Magalhães 2020). Therefore, in illiberal societies, richer people are less likely to conceptualize democracy following the liberal tradition. Conversely, in liberal societies, richer people are more likely to endorse liberal democracy as the authentic version of democracy. In other words, economic benefits attached to the existing political system might generate cognitive bias favoring the political status quo when people conceptualize democracy. This argument runs against the cosmopolitan communications thesis, especially regarding the possible influence of socioeconomic resources on popular understandings of democracy.

To examine the influence of cognitive capacity, we relied on self-reported educational attainment as a key proxy: *better-educated people are more likely to prioritize the intrinsic values of democracy and are thus less willing to trade off key democratic principles for instrumental gains* (**Hypothesis C4.2_1**). The same five-category ordinal indicator of educational attainment used earlier was incorporated for analysis.

To examine the influence of self-initiative, we relied on self-reported political interest as a key proxy: *people reporting a higher interest in politics are more likely to emphasize democracy's intrinsic values and are thus less willing to trade off key democratic principles for instrumental gains (**Hypothesis C4.2_2**)*. The same four-point Likert scale of political interest used earlier was used for analysis.

It is reasonable to argue that the influence of cognitive capacity and self-initiative on how people conceptualize democracy might be conditional upon the socioeconomic context. Basically, in societies with better information infrastructure, higher penetration of information technology, and a higher standard of living enabling more international travel, the difference in how people engage in cosmopolitan communications as a consequence of their varying cognitive capacity and self-initiative might shrink. Furthermore, in richer societies, the relative attractiveness of instrumental gains (as compared to key democratic principles) may also be dramatically weakened. Thus, to examine the moderating effect of socioeconomic context, we relied on a society's per capita GDP (transformed via a natural logarithm function) as a key proxy: *the influence of educational attainment and political interest on people's willingness to trade off key democratic principles for instrumental gains is stronger in societies with a lower per capita GDP (**Hypothesis C4.2_3**)*. The interactions between per capita GDP, on the one hand, and educational attainment and political interest, on the other, were included for analysis.

To examine the influence of socioeconomic resources, we relied on self-evaluations of family economic situation at the time of the survey as a key proxy. However, given the aforementioned distinct theoretical conjectures, different hypotheses were derived. On the one hand, the influence of socioeconomic resources on how people conceptualize democracy might be independent from the political context: *people who enjoy more socioeconomic resources are more likely to prioritize democracy's intrinsic values and are thus less willing to trade off key democratic principles for instrumental gains (**Hypothesis C4.2_4_1**)*. On the other hand, the influence of socioeconomic resources might be conditional upon the nature of the existing political regime: *in autocracies, people enjoying more socioeconomic resources are more willing to trade off key democratic principles for instrumental gains; while, in liberal democracies, they are less willing to engage in such trade-offs (**Hypothesis C4.2_4_2**)*. Self-evaluations of family economic situation at the time of the survey were measured by a five-category ordinal indicator, ranging from the lowest end of "Very bad" to the highest end of "Very good." The same reversed Freedom House seven-point rating scale was used to measure the nature of political regimes. These two variables and their interactive item were incorporated in the analysis.

Besides these three key individual features of interest, we followed the best practice in the literature of political attitudes and behavior and included age and gender as controls (Verba et al. 1978; Leighley and Vedlitz 1999; Shi 1999; Gimpel et al. 2004; Grasso 2014; Jennings 1998; Burns et al. 2001). The same six-category indicator of age groups and the binary indicator of female/male were incorporated in the analysis.[9]

Impact of economic contexts: The relationship between societies' economic conditions and political features has been extensively examined by students of political science and economics since the 1950s (Lipset 1959; Przeworski et al. 2000; Barro 1999; Acemoglu and Robinson 2006). Although scholars cannot agree upon the specific underlying causal mechanisms (Boix and Stokes 2003; Feng and Zak 1999), some positive correlation between economic development and democracy has been repeatedly demonstrated and confirmed through numerous exercises. One growing literature that contributes to our understanding of the relationship between societies' economic conditions and political features emphasizes the mediating role played by political values and norms (Inglehart 1990, 1997a; Inglehart and Welzel 2005, 2010; Welzel and Alvarez 2014; Welzel 2013; Inglehart 2018, 1997b). This literature has significant implications for our examination of how popular understandings of democracy might be shaped by economic contexts.

More specifically, according to the revised modernization theory (also identified by its key contributor Ronald Inglehart as evolutionary modernization theory), thanks to the sustained and continuous economic growth in industrial societies, post-materialist (Inglehart 1997b, 1990, 1997a) or emancipative values (Inglehart and Welzel 2005; Welzel 2013) are likely to be cultivated among the people. Such values encourage people to be politically more expressive and active, and their demands are upgraded from subsistence and basic material needs, with increasing emphasis on political freedom, liberty, rights, and individual dignity (Inglehart 2018; Inglehart and Welzel 2010). As people become politically more expressive, active, and demanding in terms of their rights and liberties, the pressure for adjustments in the political regime to accommodate such requests and demands through institutional changes (e.g., liberalization and democratization) grows accordingly. A natural extension and application of the aforementioned arguments to our examination of popular conceptions of democracy is that, as people enjoy more benefits delivered by sustained and continuous economic development, their understandings of democracy may shift as well. They are likely to prioritize the instrumental values of democracy less and its intrinsic values more. Therefore, their willingness to trade off key democratic principles for instrumental gains is likely to be substantially weakened. Overall, we hypothesized that: *on average, people living in a society with better economic performance are more likely to prioritize democracy's intrinsic values and are thus less willing to trade off key democratic principles for instrumental gains* **(Hypothesis C4.2_5).**

To effectively examine the impact of economic contexts, we relied on three indicators. The first indicator is per capita GDP (transformed via a natural logarithm function) of the seventy-one societies at the time of the GBS II survey. This is probably the most widely used indicator in the literature for a society's general trajectory of economic development. In the GBS II, there are poor societies with per capita GDP of less than $500 such as Burundi, Malawi, Liberia, Niger, and Madagascar. There also are rich societies with per capita GDP of more than $15,000 such as Chile, Uruguay, Taiwan, South Korea, Hong Kong, Singapore, and Japan. Such substantial and significant variation makes the GBS II sample ideal for exploring the influence of societies' economic context on how their citizens conceptualize democracy.

The other two indicators are concerned with a society's short-term economic context: (1) whether it was in economic recession at the time of the GBS II survey; and (2) whether it had recovered from the 2008–2009 global financial crisis by the time of the GBS II survey. When feelings of existential security are challenged (for instance, by an economic recession or the 2008–2009 global financial crisis), as Inglehart (2018) has forcefully argued, a regression from post-materialist or emancipative values to survival values is likely to be triggered. Thus, economic recessions (i.e., negative growth) may pose a unique and significant challenge for regime legitimacy and significantly affect how people assess the trade-offs between key democratic principles and instrumental gains. The coding of economic recession is quite straightforward, with positive economic growth at the time of the GBS II survey coded as 1 and the rest coded as 0. In the GBS II sample, only two societies were in economic recession at the time of the survey: Mali and Japan.

Furthermore, due to the economic shock of the 2008–2009 global financial crisis, people in many societies have been forced to live with less vibrant economies as well as lower levels of economic growth. Although their living standards may still improve, frustration and anxiety due to unmet economic expectations (driven by their earlier experience of much faster economic growth) might grow and spread.[10] The growing frustration and anxiety might reshape how citizens assess the relative significance of democracy's instrumental and intrinsic values. We compared the growth rates of GBS II societies at the time of the survey with their respective growth rates in 2007. Societies were coded 1 if their survey-year growth rate was more than or equal to their growth rate in 2007; and the rest are coded as 0. In the GBS II sample, fifty societies had not fully recovered from the damage done by the 2008–2009 global financial crisis by the time of the survey.

Impact of political and cultural contexts: In addition to its economic context, a society's political and cultural environment is expected to have critical implications for its public opinion as well. Living in a democratic regime (as compared to living in an authoritarian regime) provides different experiences for people to assess and understand democracy based on their personal engagement (Mattes and Bratton 2007; Bratton et al. 2005; Bratton and Mattes 2001; Preuss 2006; Cho 2014). Theoretically, as people accumulate more life experiences regarding the protections of their political liberties and rights, as well as their dignity as human beings, by democratic institutions and procedures, they are expected to be more inclined to prioritize democracy's intrinsic values when confronted with the trade-offs between democracy's intrinsic and instrumental values. Conversely, authoritarian regimes have both an interest in and the necessary resources to indoctrinate their citizens with notions of democracy that strip off the key institutions and procedures of liberal democracy and lead their citizens astray in how they conceptualize democracy (Kirsch and Welzel 2019; Kruse et al. 2019). Therefore, when confronted with the trade-offs between democracy's intrinsic and instrumental values, people indoctrinated by authoritarian regimes might be more inclined to eschew the former for the latter. Overall, we hypothesize that: *on average, people living in a society with richer experience of liberal democratic politics are more inclined to prioritize democracy's intrinsic values and thus less willing to trade off key democratic principles for instrumental gains (Hypothesis C4.2_6)*.

Furthermore, existing research has established the distinctions between various authoritarian regimes, including but not limited to the salience and level of institutionalization of political practice. Compared to other types of authoritarian regimes, single-party regimes demonstrate the highest level of institutionalization, while personal dictatorships generally have a minimum level of or negligible institutionalization (Svolik 2012; Gandhi 2008; Geddes 1999; Magaloni 2008). Theoretically, we might expect that people living in a society with a history of personal dictatorships are more likely to have memories of (via either their personal experience or second-hand information from various sources) the chaotic and even catastrophic situations driven by the high instability and uncertainty under dictatorial rule. Therefore, these people might be more inclined to appreciate the significance and value of institutions and procedures for politics, and thus more likely prioritize democracy's intrinsic values. Thus, we hypothesized that: *on average, people living in a society with a history of personal dictatorships are more likely to emphasize democracy's intrinsic values and thus less willing to trade off key democratic principles for instrumental gains* (**Hypothesis C4.2_7**).

Moreover, as some recent research has shown, a society's cultural traditions also matter for its citizens' political values and norms (e.g., Lu and Shi 2015; Shi and Lu 2010; Lorenzo 2013; Bell 2015; Bell and Li 2013; Fukuyama 1995b). Despite some conflicting conclusions about whether so-called "Asian values" or "Confucian traditions" significantly shape people's political attitudes and behavior (Shi 2008; Welzel 2011; Shin 2012, 2013; Fukuyama 1995a), existing evidence suggests that some authoritarian leaders have been quite skillful and effective in using culturally embedded political discourse to indoctrinate their citizens with non-liberal views of democracy (Lu and Shi 2015; Lu et al. 2014; Lu 2013). Relevant research further suggests that the Confucian emphasis on and promotion of paternalistic meritocracy as the ideal form of governance may work as a key competitor against liberal democracy in shaping how people conceptualize democracy (Chan 2007, 2013, 2014; Bell 2015; Bell and Fan 2012; Bell and Li 2013). Thus, we hypothesized that: *on average, people living in a Confucian society are more inclined to emphasize democracy's instrumental values and thus more willing to trade off key democratic principles for instrumental gains* (**Hypothesis C4.2_8**).

To effectively examine the impact of political and cultural contexts, we relied on a number of indicators. The first indicator is the Freedom House seven-point rating, which has been widely used in the literature on democracy and democratization.[11] We included the reversed Freedom House rating (ranging from the lowest indicating a full autocracy to the highest indicating a full democracy) of the seventy-one societies at the time of their respective surveys. In the GBS II sample, according to the Freedom House rating, there are full autocracies like Sudan, China, Vietnam, and Zimbabwe; and there also are full democracies like Cape Verde, Ghana, Chile, Uruguay, Japan, and South Korea. The second indicator measures a society's historical record of democratic practice. We included this indicator to account for the long-term dynamics of democratic practice (e.g., democratic capital), which has been demonstrated to be useful for understanding contemporary political dynamics (Persson and Tabellini 2009; Fuchs-Schündeln and Schündeln 2015). We created an indicator documenting a society's historically accumulated capital of political rights and civil liberties since 1972. Following the verified empirical approach (Fuchs-Schündeln and Schündeln 2015; Persson and Tabellini 2009), we used a discount factor of 0.98 to calculate each society's accumulated capital of political rights and civil liberties between 1972 and the year of its GBS II survey.[12] In the GBS II sample, accumulated democratic capital ranges from the lowest of 0 (e.g., China and Vietnam) to the highest of around 27 (e.g., Japan, Botswana, and Costa Rica). In addition, using a new data set on the history of regime transitions (Geddes et al. 2014, 2018), we created two binary indicators for the history of single-party regimes and personal dictatorships respectively for each of the GBS II societies. And, following best practice in related scholarship, we also created a binary indicator for the seven Confucian societies covered in the GBS II sample, namely Japan, Hong Kong, mainland China, South Korea, Taiwan, Singapore, and Vietnam.

As demonstrated earlier, non-response to the PUD instrument has been primarily driven by cognitive deficiency and lack of related information. For this section, our research question is: among the people who can associate abstract concepts of democracy with concrete features, what individual and societal features might be associated with their varying willingness to trade off key democratic principles for instrumental gains? Therefore, we focused on respondents who provided meaningful responses to the PUD instruments in the GBS II sample.

The outcome variable can again be operationalized as either a latent continuous construct (i.e., IRT scores of the PUD instruments) or latent groups (i.e., LCA groups of the PUD instruments). To examine the robustness of our findings, we ran the mixed-effect models using both IRT scores and LCA groups with the same set of explanatory variables.[13] It is very encouraging that the findings are highly consistent across the models. For an easier interpretation, we focused on the regression results of the IRT scores (estimated via mixed-effect linear models) and presented the findings in Figure 4.3. As previously, black dots and horizontal segments stand for

ORIGINS OF VARYING UNDERSTANDINGS OF DEMOCRACY   89

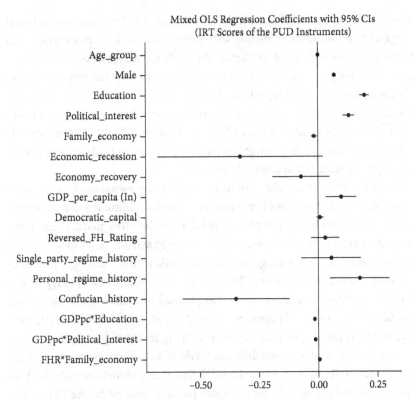

Figure 4.3 Mixed-Effect Linear Model of Popular Understandings of Democracy

regression coefficients and related 95% confidence intervals respectively. The vertical line of zero stands for the conventional null hypothesis that the regression coefficients are statistically not different from zero. It is worth noting that, given our coding of the PUD instruments, a larger value of the IRT scores suggest more appreciation of democracy's intrinsic values and thus lower willingness to trade off key democratic principles for instrumental gains.

As shown in Figure 4.3, the regression coefficients associated with educational attainment and political interest are positive, with the lower boundary of corresponding 95% confidence intervals to the right side of the vertical line of zero. Meanwhile, their interactions with per capita GDP are associated with negative regression coefficients, with the upper boundary of corresponding 95% confidence intervals to the left side of the vertical line. Further information reported Table A4.2 (i.e., the results of M2 without interactions) suggests that, on average, people with better education or more interest in politics are more inclined to cherish the intrinsic values of democracy and thus less willing to trade off key democratic principles for instrumental gains. This is consistent with Hypotheses C4.2_1 and C4.2_2. Basically, cognitive sophistication and high self-initiative enable more effective engagement with cosmopolitan communications, which, in turn, may highlight the intrinsic values of democracy and lower people's willingness to trade off key democratic principles for instrumental gains.

However, the statistically significant negative regression coefficients associated with the interactions between educational attainment and political interest, on the one hand, and per capita GDP, on the other hand, suggest that the influence of cognitive sophistication and high self-initiative in weakening people's willingness to engage in such trade-offs is much stronger in poorer societies than in richer ones. This finding is consistent with Hypothesis C4.2_3. To help understand these complicated moderating effects further, we ran a series of simulations and plotted the marginal effect of education and political interest in societies with varying levels of per capita GDP in Figure 4.4. The x-axis shows different levels of socioeconomic development in an ascending order of per capita GDP. The y-axis shows the estimated average marginal impact of education and political interest on the IRT scores. More specifically, Figure 4.4 presents the estimated impact of education (Figure 4.4a) and political interest (Figure 4.4b) on how people differ when they conceptualize democracy when a society's per capita GDP increases from around 400 USD (e.g., societies like Liberia and Niger) to about 36,000 USD (e.g., societies like Hong Kong and Singapore), while holding other individual and societal level features constant.

As shown in Figure 4.4a, better-educated citizens in societies such as Liberia or Niger are significantly more inclined to prioritize democracy's intrinsic values and thus less willing to trade off key democratic principles for instrumental gains. Their better-educated counterparts living in societies like Hong Kong or Singapore are also significantly less willing to engage in such trade-offs. Nevertheless, the impact of education is much weaker in these better-off societies. More specifically, as we move from poor societies like Liberia or Niger to rich societies like Hong Kong or Singapore, the substantive impact of education on popular willingness to trade off key democratic principles for instrumental gains is reduced by a factor of three.

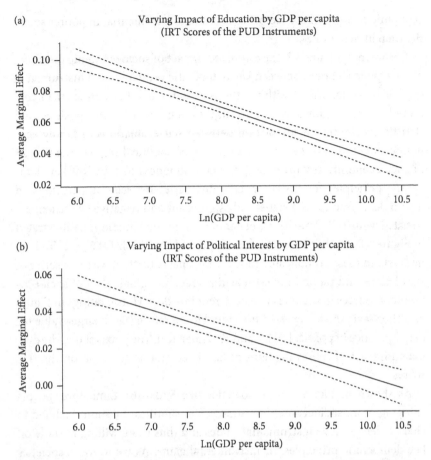

Figure 4.4 Average Marginal Effects of Cognitive Capacity and Self-Initiative

Similarly, as illustrated in Figure 4.4a, when confronted with such trade-offs, citizens of poor societies like Liberia or Niger reporting more interest in politics are significantly more likely to prioritize democracy's intrinsic values. Similar citizens in rich societies like Hong Kong or Singapore, on the contrary, are no longer substantially different from their fellow citizens with lower interest in politics in terms of their appreciation of democracy's intrinsic values.[14] In other words, in rich societies like Hong Kong or Singapore, political interest is no longer a significant factor that shapes how people conceptualize democracy. Clearly, how education and political interest affect popular understandings of democracy is highly conditional upon a society's economic context. These factors are much more influential in poorer societies than in richer ones.

As shown in Figure 4.3, the estimated impact of socioeconomic resources on how people choose between key democratic principles and instrumental gains is more consistent with the thesis of status-quo bias, rather than cosmopolitan communications. Basically, as suggested by the positive and statistically significant interaction between self-evaluations of family economic situation and the features of a society's political regime, the impact of socioeconomic resources on popular willingness to trade off key democratic principles for instrumental gains varies between autocracies and liberal democracies. The statistically significant and negative coefficient associated with self-evaluations of family economic situation, as illustrated in Figure 4.3, further attests to the validity of Hypothesis C4.2_4_2. To help understand these complicated moderating effects further, we ran a series of simulations and plotted the estimated average marginal effect of socioeconomic resources in societies with different Freedom House ratings in Figure 4.5. The x-axis shows reversed Freedom House rating (i.e., a larger value for better practice of political rights and civil liberties). The y-axis shows the estimated impact of self-evaluations of family economic situation on the IRT scores.

As shown in Figure 4.5, in societies like Sudan or Zimbabwe, people enjoying more socioeconomic resources are significantly more inclined to cherish democracy's instrumental values and thus more willing to trade off key democratic principles for instrumental gains. As we move to societies with better practice of democratic politics (as assessed by Freedom House ratings), the negative impact is gradually weakened. As we further move to liberal democracies like Chile or Uruguay, the relationship is reversed; that is, people enjoying more socioeconomic resources are significantly more inclined to cherish democracy's intrinsic values and thus less willing to engage in such trade-offs. It seems that the cognitive status-quo bias associated with socioeconomic resources has effectively counterweighted the empowerment effect (i.e., via engaging in cosmopolitan communications) in shaping how people conceptualize democracy.

At the societal level, our evidence for the impact of economic, political, and cultural contexts varies. As displayed in Figure 4.3, although the coefficients associated with economic recession and recovery from the 2008–2009 global financial crisis are negative, there is large uncertainty associated with the estimations. Further analysis reported in Table A4.2 (i.e., results of

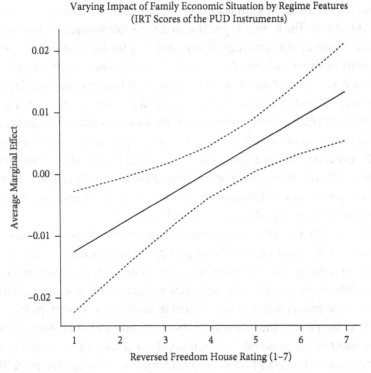

Figure 4.5 Average Marginal Effect of Socioeconomic Resources

M2 without interactions) indicates that, on average, the estimated impact of per capita GDP is positive but also associated with large uncertainty. Overall, our evidence is not strong enough to support Hypothesis C4.2_5.

As theoretically expected, the regression coefficients of democratic capital and reversed Freedom House rating, as illustrated in Figure 4.3, are positive. Further analysis reported in Table A4.2 (i.e., the results of M2 without interactions) confirms this finding. Basically, in societies with richer experience and better practice of democratic politics, on average, people are more likely to cherish democracy's intrinsic values and thus less willing to trade off key democratic principles for instrumental gains. Nevertheless, the uncertainties associated with such estimations are too large to enable any statistically justifiable conclusion. Thus, our evidence is not strong enough to support Hypothesis C4.2_6.

It is worth noting that the regression coefficients associated with the binary indicators of a political history of personal dictatorships and Confucian legacies are statistically significant across all model specifications (as reported in Table A4.2). The former is positive, and the latter is negative. Basically, in societies with a political history of personal dictatorships, on average, people are more likely to prioritize democracy's intrinsic values when they conceptualize democracy. Meanwhile, in societies with lasting Confucian legacies, on average, people are more willing to trade off key democratic principles for instrumental gains. As discussed earlier, the former could be mainly affected by the memories of the chaotic and even catastrophic situations driven by the high instability and uncertainty under dictatorial rule; while the latter might be primarily driven by glorification of paternalistic meritocracy as the ideal form of governance in Confucian political traditions. Overall, our evidence is consistent with Hypotheses C4.2_7 and C4.2_8.

The control variables' performance also reveals some interesting dynamics. As shown in Figure 4.3, age groups are not associated with the IRT scores in a statistically meaningful way. It seems that, after accounting for their differences in cognitive sophistication (i.e., with educational attainment as the proxy) and access to related information (i.e., with political interest as the proxy), the difference between young and old cohorts in their assessment of the trade-offs between key democratic principles and instrumental gains is limited. Meanwhile, on average, males are not just more likely to offer meaningful responses to the PUD instruments (as reported in Figure 4.1), they are also more inclined to prioritize democracy's intrinsic values when they conceptualize democracy. Although our data limitations do not allow further investigations of related underlying mechanisms, the evidence does suggest that, *ceteris paribus*, males are less willing to trade off key democratic principles for instrumental gains.

4.3 Conclusion

In this chapter, we used a series of mixed-effect models to examine the origins of varying popular conceptions of democracy. The observational and cross-sectional nature of our data does not allow for rigorous causal inference. However, we have sufficient theoretical reasons to argue for and defend the correlates at both individual and societal levels as potential drivers that shape how people vary in their understandings of democracy. Due to data limitations, we only accounted for certain key demographic, cognitive, psychological, and socioeconomic features at the individual level, as we focused on the impact of the economic, political, and cultural contexts. Our findings are generally consistent with the conclusions of existing research, but also reveal some nuanced dynamics that have been overlooked in the literature.

First of all, cognitive deficiency and lack of related information are the two main drivers of non-responses to the PUD instruments. There is little evidence for the possible role of political or social desirability bias in shaping non-response to the PUD instruments. Overall, it should be fair to conclude that meaningful responses to the PUD instruments (as recorded in the GBS II data) are neither random nor uncontemplated reflections. In other words, when confronted with the contrast between democracy's intrinsic versus instrumental values, people do try to make informed choices. Thus, the meaningful responses to the PUD instruments provide valuable information to explore why people might be willing to trade off key democratic principles for instrumental gains.

Second, on average, when confronted with the choice between key democratic principles and instrumental gains, males with a higher level of education and more interest in politics are significantly less inclined to trade off the former for the latter, given their deeper appreciation of democracy's intrinsic values. This pattern is consistent with the cosmopolitan communications thesis, which emphasizes the significance of cognitive capacity and self-initiative in enabling more effective engagement with cosmopolitan communications. Such engagement leads to more exposure to and embracement of self-expression or emancipative values, which, in turn, are likely to boost popular support for institutional arrangements that promote and protect such values. Accordingly, people are more inclined to prioritize its intrinsic values when they conceptualize democracy. And their willingness to trade off key democratic principles for instrumental gains is then much lower. Furthermore, our evidence also suggests some significant role for socioeconomic contexts (i.e., proxied by per capita GDP) in moderating the influence of education and political interest: overall, such influence is much stronger in poorer societies than in richer ones. This could be primarily related to how a rich society's better informational infrastructure, higher penetration of information technologies, and higher living standards might have helped level engagement with cosmopolitan communications for citizens with varying cognitive capacity and self-initiative.

Third, the cosmopolitan communications thesis suggests that individuals' access to more socioeconomic resources should facilitate their engagement with cosmopolitan communications, thus generally increasing their appreciation of democracy's intrinsic values. Nevertheless, the cognitive status-quo bias thesis argues that such people's willingness to trade off key democratic principles for instrumental gains should be conditional upon the particular political context, due to their attachment to the existing political regime. Our findings are more consistent with the latter, showing a statistically significant interaction between self-reported family economic situation and a society's Freedom House rating in shaping popular democratic conceptions. More specifically, in illiberal societies, richer people are less likely to conceptualize democracy following the liberal tradition by prioritizing its intrinsic values. In addition, their willingness to trade off key democratic principles for instrumental gain is significantly higher. Conversely, in liberal societies, richer people are more likely to endorse liberal democracy as the authentic version of democracy by prioritizing its intrinsic values. Therefore, their willingness to engage in such trade-offs is much lower.

Fourth, societies' varying economic contexts mold their respective popular understandings of democracy in a nuanced way. Although our evidence on the influence of short-term economic dynamics like recession or crisis is not conclusive, it does suggest how such short-term economic challenges might amplify the significance of the regime's performance in delivering good governance for its citizens. This further highlights the salience and necessity of democracy's instrumental values, which, in turn, might tilt popular assessment of the trade-offs between key democratic principles and instrumental gains in the latter's favor. Meanwhile, a society's general socioeconomic development (as measured by per capita GDP) dramatically moderates the influence of education and political interest on popular democratic conceptions. In short, a society's better economic performance and enhanced socioeconomic development not only make its people overall more appreciative of democracy's intrinsic values and less willing to trade off key democratic principles for instrumental gains, but also make its population more homogenous in their understandings by reducing the disparities that might have been driven by their varying cognitive capacity and self-initiative.

Fifth, societies' distinct political contexts and cultural traditions also matter in terms of how their citizens conceptualize democracy. Although our evidence on the influence of societies' accumulated democratic capital is not conclusive, it does indicate that people's richer experience with liberal democratic practice enables them to learn of and appreciate the significance of democratic institutions, procedures, values, and norms in ensuring their political rights and liberties as well as their dignity as human beings. Thus, they are more likely to prioritize democracy's intrinsic values and less willing to trade off key democratic principles for instrumental gains. Better democratic practice also greatly moderates how the cognitive status-quo bias shapes popular understandings of democracy: richer people in autocracies and liberal democracies are likely to make contradictory choices when confronted with the trade-offs between key democratic principles and instrumental gains: democracy's intrinsic values are more appreciated by wealthier people in liberal democracies. Furthermore, our evidence suggests that memories (individual or collective) of the chaos and calamities associated with political instability and uncertainty under personal dictatorships have made people more appreciative of the significance of institutions and procedures in politics; therefore, under the shadow of personal dictatorships, people are more likely to emphasize democracy's intrinsic values. In addition, when the trade-offs between key democratic principles and instrumental gains are highlighted, Confucian political traditions in a society significantly tilt its popular preference toward the latter. This finding seems to be associated with the paternalistic meritocracy discourse in Confucian societies, which has been sustained and promoted through cultural traditions and political socialization.

In a sum, our findings have effectively established the salience of economic, political, and cultural contexts for understanding how people conceptualize democracy. Factors driven by short-term events (like economic growth or recession), mid-term evolutions (like democratic practice assessed by the Freedom House rating and economic development measured by per capita GDP), and long-term dynamics (like the history of personal dictatorships and Confucian political traditions) all play some role in shaping popular understandings of democracy. Put otherwise, incorporating contextual features into existing research for a more comprehensive and dynamic explanation of why people understand democracy in different ways is both fruitful and necessary. Our empirical findings not only confirm the value of various modernization theories for understanding micro dynamics involved in democratic transition and consolidation (Brunkert et al. 2019; Inglehart and Welzel 2010; Welzel 2013; Zavadskaya and Welzel 2015) but also echo recent calls from students of comparative politics on the importance of systematically incorporating and theorizing historical legacies (both political and cultural) for understanding contemporary politics (Beissinger and Kotkin 2014; Pop-Eleches and Tucker 2017; Simpser et al. 2018).

It is also important to remind our readers that most of the variation (around 84%) in popular understandings of democracy should be attributed to individual-level dynamics. Due to data limitations, we could not extensively and comprehensively explore such dynamics by including a long list of individual-level factors. Nevertheless, despite our shorter list of individual demographic, cognitive, psychological, and socioeconomic factors, we did find robust evidence on the roles played by education, political interest, gender-related socialization, and socioeconomic resources in shaping how people conceptualize democracy. More interestingly, we identified some nuanced but significant cross-level interactive effects on how economic and political environments moderate the influence of such individual-level dynamics. Clearly, political cognitive and psychological dynamics unfold in specific contexts and are molded by these contextual features. For further analysis, it is important to integrate the literature on political psychology and public opinion with the literature on political institutions and structural forces. We will take this approach in subsequent analyses of how popular conceptions of democracy shape political behavior and other critical political attitudes under distinct socioeconomic, political, and cultural contexts.

Appendix

Table A4.1 Mixed-Effect Models for Non-Response to the PUD Instruments

	M1 (Summary index of DKs) Mixed OLS	M2 (Summary index of DKs) Mixed OLS	M3 (Summary index of DKs) Mixed OLS	M4 (Missings in IRT Scores) Mixed Logit	M5 (Agnostics in LCA Groups) Mixed Logit
Fixed effects					
Age_group	**0.034 (0.002)**	0.035 (0.22)		**0.114 (0.011)**	**0.098 (0.008)**
Polynomial (Age, 2)_1			**18.080 (1.007)**		
Polynomial (Age, 2)_2			**8.881 (0.946)**		
Male	**−0.107 (0.006)**	**−0.107 (0.006)**	**−0.109 (0.006)**	**−0.441 (0.033)**	**−0.350 (0.024)**
Education	**−0.080 (0.002)**	**−0.079 (0.002)**	**−0.078 (0.002)**	**−0.401 (0.017)**	**−0.306 (0.011)**
Political_interest	**−0.122 (0.009)**	**−0.101 (0.003)**	**−0.121 (0.009)**	**−0.372 (0.054)**	**−0.347 (0.040)**
GDP_per_capita (ln)	0.005 (0.035)	0.005 (0.035)	0.004 (0.035)	0.202 (0.134)	0.144 (0.120)
Reversed_FH_rating	−0.044 (0.030)	−0.032 (0.030)	−0.044 (0.030)	−0.150 (0.116)	−0.082 (0.097)
RFH*Political_interest	**0.005 (0.002)**		**0.005 (0.002)**	−0.014 (0.012)	−0.007 (0.009)
Intercept	**0.915 (0.261)**	**0.863 (0.260)**	**1.029 (0.261)**	**−2.891 (0.995)**	−2.069 (0.910)
Random effects (variance)					
Intercept	0.118	0.117	0.118	1.652	1.187
Residual	0.873	0.873	0.872		
# of societies	71	71	71	71	71
# of observations	101,855	101,855	101,855	101,855	101,855

Source: Global Barometer Surveys II (N = 104,248).

Notes:
Robust standard errors in parentheses.
Statistically significant coefficients are bolded (at the 0.05 level).

Table A4.2 Mixed-Effect Models for Popular Understandings of Democracy

	M1 (IRT scores)	M2 (IRT scores)	M3 (IRT scores)	M4 (LCA Principle-Holders vs. Benefit-Seekers)	M5 (LCA Fence-Sitters vs. Benefit-Seekers)
	Mixed OLS	Mixed OLS	Mixed OLS	Mixed Logit	Mixed Logit
Fixed effects					
Age_group	0.000 (0.001)	0.001 (0.001)		0.010 (0.007)	0.010 (0.006)
Polynomial (Age, 2)_1			−0.231 (0.678)		
Polynomial (Age, 2)_2			−1.959 (0.641)		
Male	0.066 (0.004)	0.068 (0.004)	0.067 (0.004)	0.220 (0.019)	0.207 (0.018)
Education	0.195 (0.011)	0.067 (0.002)	0.198 (0.011)	0.706 (0.052)	0.529 (0.048)
Political_interest	0.127 (0.012)	0.031 (0.002)	0.126 (0.012)	0.434 (0.059)	0.256 (0.054)
Family_economy	−0.017 (0.006)	0.002 (0.002)	−0.017 (0.006)	−0.121 (0.031)	−0.050 (0.027)
Economic_recession	−0.329 (0.178)	−0.365 (0.180)	−0.327 (0.178)	−1.393 (0.617)	−0.669 (0.402)
Economic_recovery	−0.072 (0.006)	−0.072 (0.062)	−0.072 (0.061)	−0.137 (0.211)	−0.192 (0.138)
GDP_per_capita (ln)	0.095 (0.032)	0.033 (0.032)	0.096 (0.032)	0.319 (0.114)	0.106 (0.073)
Democratic_capital	0.007 (0.007)	0.007 (0.007)	0.007 (0.007)	0.042 (0.025)	0.011 (0.016)
Reversed_FH_rating	0.028 (0.030)	0.038 (0.030)	0.028 (0.030)	0.003 (0.105)	−0.020 (0.069)
Single_party_regime_history	0.054 (0.064)	0.053 (0.064)	0.054 (0.064)	0.192 (0.221)	0.277 (0.144)
Personal_regime_history	0.174 (0.064)	0.171 (0.064)	0.174 (0.064)	0.494 (0.221)	0.422 (0.144)
Confucian_history	−0.348 (0.116)	−0.381 (0.117)	−0.347 (0.116)	−1.312 (0.402)	−0.201 (0.261)

GDPpc*Education	−0.016 (0.001)	−0.016 (0.001)	−0.054 (0.006)	−0.042 (0.006)
GDPpc*Political_interest	−0.012 (0.002)	−0.012 (0.002)	−0.044 (0.007)	−0.018 (0.007)
RFH*Family_economy	0.004 (0.001)	0.004 (0.001)	0.029 (0.006)	0.024 (0.006)
Intercept	−1.319 (0.265)	−0.866 (0.264)	−1.325 (0.266)	−4.669 (0.044)	−2.498 (0.603)
Random effects (variance)				
Intercept	0.050	0.051	0.050	0.598	0.253
Residual	0.364	0.365	0.364		
# of societies	71	71	71	71	71
# of observations	95,880	95,880	95,880	63,890	64,622

Source: Global Barometer Surveys II ($N = 104,248$).

Notes:

Robust standard errors in parentheses.

Statistically significant coefficients are bolded (at the 0.05 level).

5
Democratic Assessment Colored by Understandings of Democracy

In Chapters 3 and 4, we established the salience of varying understandings of democracy within and between societies in today's world, as well as the underlying socioeconomic, political, and cognitive dynamics that might have contributed to such different conceptions. Now, we need to address the million-dollar question for any social science research: Why should we care? Put otherwise, what extra analytical leverage can we gain by examining popular understandings of democracy?

Our general response to this question is quite straightforward: people holding different understandings of democracy are inclined to focus on distinct aspects of political practices and performance when they assess political regimes (their democratic nature, in particular). Furthermore, given the respective priorities assigned to procedural arrangements versus substantive outputs as defining features of democracy, people's varying willingness to trade off key democratic principles for instrumental gains might also be associated with different ways of political participation. Overall, we argue that popular understandings of democracy should have significant implications for critical political attitudes and behaviors. In this chapter, we focused on the influence of varying democratic conceptions on how people assess the practice of democracy in both foreign countries and their home society. As with Chapter 4, we relied on the GBS II data and mixed-effect models for empirical analysis.

To kick-off subsequent discussions, the result of a simple correlation analysis is presented in Figure 5.1. The y-axis presents the weighted popular average of perceived levels of democracy in the seventy-one societies covered by the GBS II, based on a ten-point scale ranging from the lowest end of "1: Completely undemocratic" to the highest end of "10: Completely democratic." The x-axis presents the corresponding Freedom House ratings of the seventy-one societies at the year of their respective GBS II survey, based on a seven-point scale ranging from the lowest end of "1: least free" to the highest

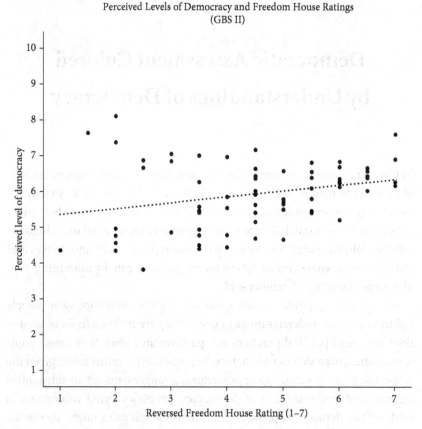

Figure 5.1 Ordinary People's versus Experts' Evaluations of Democratic Practice

end of "7: most free."[1] Unlike the information collected by the GBS II, the Freedom House ratings are based on country experts' evaluations of the situation of political freedom and civil rights in each society, following the same criteria and framework specified by Freedom House (which define democracy closely following the liberal tradition). Thus, the Freedom House ratings are immune from the impact of varying understandings of democracy and can be used as a meaningful benchmark for assessing the salience and influence of different democratic conceptions. If ordinary people share the same conceptions of democracy as the Freedom House country experts, we should expect a strong and positive correlation between popular assessment of the levels of democracy (as captured in the GBS II) and country experts' evaluations of democracy (as reported by Freedom House).

As illustrated in Figure 5.1, we found a positive correlation between the two measures; however, the correlation was not as strong as expected.[2] Furthermore, as illustrated in Figure 5.1, even in societies rated as equally democratic or undemocratic by Freedom House, corresponding popular evaluations of the level of democracy vary significantly. For instance, among the seven GBS II societies rated by Freedom House at 2/7 (i.e., very low level of political freedom and lack of meaningful protection of civil rights), namely, Vietnam, Mali, Zimbabwe, Cameron, Ethiopia, and Swaziland, citizens' assessment of their home society's respective level of democracy fluctuates wildly between 4.35/10 in Swaziland and 8.10/10 in Vietnam. In other words, despite similar levels of political oppression and constraints on political freedom and rights, citizens of Swaziland are far more critical than their counterparts in Vietnam when they assess the democratic nature of their political regime. Similarly, among the eight GBS II societies rated by Freedom House at 6/7 (i.e., high level of political freedom and sufficient protection of civil rights), namely, Mongolia, Benin, Namibia, Senegal, South Africa, Argentina, Brazil, and Panama, citizens' evaluations of their home society's respective level of democracy also vary between 5.20/10 in Mongolia and 6.83/10 in Argentina. It seems that, despite these countries' similar level of institutionalization in ensuring political rights and liberties (at least from the country experts' point of view), their citizens' assessment is at best lukewarm. Political and socioeconomic environments clearly play some role here. Nevertheless, they definitely cannot tell the whole story. To more effectively account for such variation, we believe it is necessary to take varying democratic conceptions (which shape the benchmark for assessment) into consideration.

5.1 Assessing democratic practices in the United States and mainland China

Before examining the influence of varying understandings of democracy on how people view their own political regimes, we ran this variable through a critical test to scrutinize its usefulness for empirical analysis. More specifically, we examined how distinct democratic conceptions could have shaped popular views about democratic practices in the United States (in sixty-six GBS II societies) and mainland China (in the same GBS II societies excluding mainland China).[3] The logic behind this critical test is threefold.

First, it is reasonable to expect a much higher level of objectivity in how people assess democratic practice in a foreign country than in the corresponding evaluations of their home society, thanks to the much lower influence of emotions and prejudices shaped by country-specific political practices and dynamics. This higher level of objectivity, in turn, enables more meaningful and effective comparisons between societies. This may not be a salient issue for studies that explore within-society variation, which, by design, hold almost all country-unique features constant. However, for comparative analysis covering a large number of societies (as we conducted here), the influence of country-unique features might be highly salient and significant.[4] Therefore, methodologically, popular assessment of democratic practices in specified foreign societies provides the "most-likely case" (Eckstein 1975; Gerring 2012, 2007) for examining the influence of popular conceptions of democracy. Put otherwise, if varying understandings of democracy do shape how people assess the democratic nature of political practice, such influence is most likely to be detected in their evaluations of foreign societies' democratic practices, thanks to the higher level of objectivity in evaluations of foreign societies. Conversely, if we cannot find unambiguous and significant evidence for this, our empirical journey should end here.

Second, asking people to assess democratic practices in the United States and mainland China also provides the most likely scenario for examining the usefulness of the PUD instruments as proxies for popular willingness to trade off key democratic principles for instrumental gains. As discussed earlier, the PUD instruments feature a contrast between democracy's intrinsic and instrumental values and gauge the extent to which people are willing to trade off the former for the latter when they conceptualize democracy. In today's world, the United States and China represent two distinct models of governance, with prominent and defining features that are hard to miss for most people around the world. Furthermore, both countries have been quite active in promoting (at least, campaigning for defending and justifying) their own governance models worldwide via distinct discourses. For most people, the US model represents the classical practice of liberal democracy, characterized by the institutionalization of division of power, checks and balances, and protection of freedom and rights. Meanwhile, the Chinese model, characterized by a one-party regime with satisfying performance in securing political order and stability as well as continuous economic growth, has also proven to be attractive, especially among the politicians and citizens of developing societies. Such a crystal-clear contrast between the United States and China in terms of their democratic practices, as well as the high profile and salience of both countries for contemporary political discourses on governance and democracy, provides the most likely candidate to detect the role (if there is any) that distinct democratic conceptions (as measured by the PUD instruments) may play in coloring popular assessment of democratic practice.

Finally, a lower level of social desirability bias is expected in self-reported assessment of democratic practices in foreign countries, as compared to that in self-reported evaluations of respondents' home society. Social desirability bias (or more generally, preference falsification) has haunted survey research since the very beginning of the industry. It is driven by a number of factors, including but not limited to political fear, political correctness, and peer pressure (Comşa and Postelnicu 2013; Tourangeau and Yan 2007; Kuran 1995). In different political contexts, social desirability bias might drive popular responses to the same survey instruments in distinct ways. For instance, in authoritarian societies, respondents might be inclined to report more positive views of their political regimes given the lurking threat of political oppression. Meanwhile, citizens of democracies might be socialized into the mindset of being more critical of their regimes, especially when asked to offer their opinions in public. As a result, these critical democratic citizens might be inclined to report more negative views of their political regimes. When the social desirability bias is highly salient, the validity of conclusions based on survey data may be severely compromised. Comparatively speaking, social desirability bias should be much less salient when foreign countries are under examination, which, in turn, provides a much friendlier and less challenging environment for drawing solid conclusions.

Comparatively speaking, the United States outperforms China in more effectively establishing and running democratic institutions and procedures, as well as delivering better substantive governance outcomes (if we take GDP per capita as the key indicator). Therefore, regardless of whether people emphasize democracy's intrinsic values or prioritize its instrumental values, their overall assessment of the United States' democratic practice, on average, should be more positive than their assessment of China's. To examine this conjecture, we relied on self-reported evaluations of the levels of democracy in the United States and mainland China as a key proxy: *on average, popular* *perception of the level of democracy in the United States should be higher than for mainland China (**Hypothesis C5.1_1**)*. A ten-point scale of perceived levels of democracy (ranging from the lowest end of "1: Completely undemocratic" to the highest end of "10: Completely democratic") in the United States and mainland China was incorporated for analysis.

We also expect that popular evaluations of democratic practices in China and the United States may vary depending on distinct conceptions of democracy, since these varying understandings of democracy may lead people to prioritize distinct aspects of democratic practice in their assessments. Given the beacon status of the United States for liberal democracy, it is reasonable to expect that people who are less willing to trade off key democratic principles for instrumental gains (i.e., prioritizing democracy's intrinsic values) might hold even more positive assessments of the United States' democratic practice and even more negative views of China's democratic practice. Meanwhile, China's stunning performance in sustaining economic growth despite the 2008–2009 global financial crisis, as well as exacerbating inequality and polarization and rising populism after the financial crisis in the United States, might have triggered some unique dynamics in related evaluations, especially among those who are more willing to trade off key democratic principles for instrumental gains (i.e., emphasizing democracy's instrumental values). These people might hold much less negative evaluations of China's democratic practice and much less positive assessments of US democratic practice. To examine this conjecture, we relied on the PUD instruments' IRT scores and LCA groups as key proxies: *people with higher IRT scores are likely to assess the United States' democratic practice more positively and view China's democratic practice more negatively (**Hypothesis C5.1_2_1**)*. In addition, *people classified as Principle-Holders (as compared to their counterparts of Benefit-Seekers) are likely to assess the United States' democratic practice more positively and view China's democratic practice more negatively (**Hypothesis C5.1_2_2**)*.

Figure 5.2 presents the weighted average of popular evaluations of democratic practices in the United States and mainland China from sixty-five GBS II societies. Two patterns are quite outstanding. First, given the ten-point scale, the average assessment of US democracy is consistently above the midpoint and ranges between 5.92 (Malaysia) and 8.95 (Algeria). Meanwhile, average evaluations of China's democratic practice show much more variation, ranging between 2.70 (Japan) and 7.59 (Ethiopia). Second, in almost all GBS II societies, respondents, on average, hold a more positive view of the

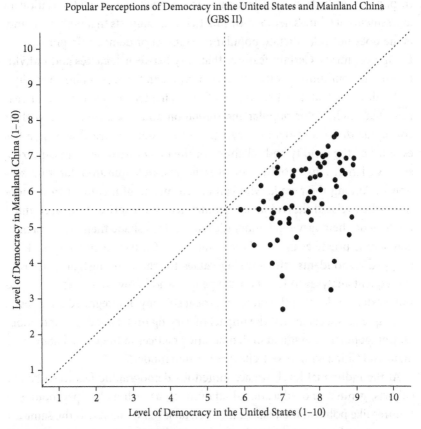

Figure 5.2 Perceived Levels of Democracy in the United States and Mainland China

democratic practice in the United States than in China, except for those in Vietnam (who assessed US democracy at 6.93/10 and rated China's democratic practice at 7.01/10). This more positive assessment of US democratic practice is even found among Chinese respondents, who, on average, rated US democratic practice at 6.90/10 and Chinese democratic practice at 6.67/10.

These findings not only confirm our earlier expectation on the higher level of objectivity in popular assessments of democratic practices in foreign societies, but also provide supporting evidence for Hypothesis C5.1_1. Put otherwise, the GBS II respondents were not blind to the political reality in the United States and China and did incorporate the two countries' political practices into their evaluations. Nevertheless, the noticeable variation in popular evaluations of US democracy, as well as the wild variation in assessments of China's democratic practice, also suggests that political reality alone does not fully dictate popular assessment of democratic practices in foreign countries. Certain features that vary between societies and individuals might condition how individuals interpret and process political reality.

As discussed at the beginning of this chapter, a key individual feature that might color popular interpretation and assessment is how their conceptualizations of democracy vary. So far, our empirical evidence has established the validity and reliability of the PUD instruments in capturing such variations. Essentially, our specific research question for this section is: Among the people who can attach meaningful content to democracy, when related individual and contextual characteristics are accounted for, how do their varying democratic conceptions shape their assessment of democratic practices in the United States and China? As in Chapter 4, we dropped respondents with missing values for the PUD instruments from subsequent analyses to focus on the people who know about democracy to some extent. Adopting the same empirical strategy of integrated analyses as in Chapter 4, we examined the impact of varying understandings of democracy on popular assessment of democratic practices in the United States and mainland China with mixed-effect regression models.

At the individual level, we accounted for demographic features like age cohorts, gender, and educational attainment, as well as key psychological features like political interest. At the societal level, we included the same set of indicators for pertinent socioeconomic, political, and cultural contextual features at the time of the survey. For socioeconomic contextual features, we included indicators of general economic development (per capita GDP transformed via a logarithm function), economic recession, and recovery from the 2008 financial crisis. For political and cultural contextual characteristics, we included reversed Freedom House ratings, historically accumulated capital of political rights and civil liberties since 1972, history of single-party regimes and personal dictatorships, and Confucian cultural traditions as indicators. Theoretically, the socioeconomic, political, and cultural contexts of respondents' home societies are not expected to moderate the individual dynamics that drive their assessment of foreign countries' democratic practices (i.e., the United States and China); thus, we did not specify cross-level interactions in the mixed-effect models.

To check for robustness, we ran the same mixed-effect models with popular understandings of democracy operationalized as either a continuous

DEMOCRATIC ASSESSMENT 111

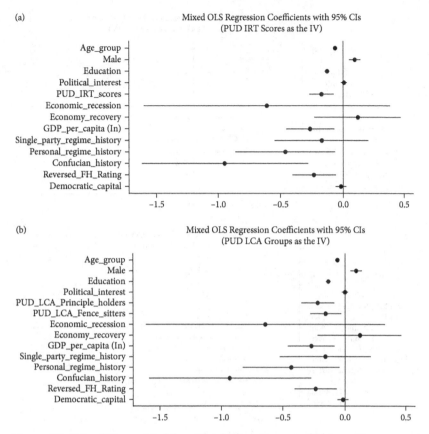

Figure 5.3 Mixed Linear Model on Popular Assessment of Chinese Democracy

latent construct (i.e., the IRT scores) or nominal latent groups (i.e., the LCA groups).[5] Figure 5.3 presents the regression coefficients and associated 95% confidence intervals for popular evaluations of China's democratic practice. Figure 5.4 presents the corresponding regression results for popular assessment of the United States' democratic practice. We adopted the same set of legends used earlier for illustration: black dots stand for regression coefficients and horizontal segments stand for associated 95% confidence intervals. The vertical line stands for the conventional null hypothesis that the influence under examination is statistically not different from zero.[6]

Figure 5.3 shows the influence of individual and societal-level factors on how the citizens of sixty-five GBS II societies (excluding China and five South Asian countries) assess China's democratic practice. The only difference between Figure 5.3a and Figure 5.3b is how popular understandings

112 UNDERSTANDINGS OF DEMOCRACY

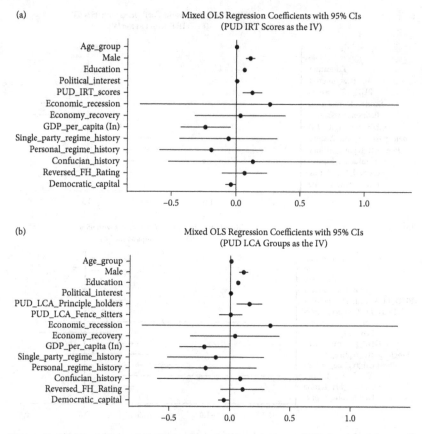

Figure 5.4 Mixed Linear Model on Popular Assessment of US Democracy

of democracy are operationalized, which is captured by continuous latent IRT scores in the former and by nominal latent LCA groups in the latter. Nevertheless, regardless of the specific operationalization of democratic conceptions, we secured highly consistent findings. As illustrated in Figure 5.3a, the regression coefficient for the IRT scores is negative and significantly different from zero. Since a larger IRT score indicates a lower willingness to trade off key democratic principles for instrumental gains, this negative coefficient suggests that, *ceteris paribus*, respondents who appreciate the intrinsic values of democracy in protecting political liberty and rights more are inclined to assess China's democratic practice more negatively. Similarly, as shown in Figure 5.3b, compared to Benefit-Seekers (the baseline group who are generally willing to trade off key democratic principles for instrumental gains), Principle-Holders and Fence-Sitters (both of which are less willing to engage in such trade-offs) are inclined to evaluate China's democratic practice more negatively.

Basically, despite both China's stunning performance in promoting economic growth and securing political order and stability and the CCP regime's charm offensive aimed at presenting itself as a genuine democracy, people who have a deeper appreciation of democracy's intrinsic values and prioritize its institutions, procedures, and related norms and values are much less likely to be led astray in their assessments of the CCP regime's democratic practice. Compared with these people's belief in democracy as a way of life that secures individuals' inalienable rights and freedoms through established institutions and procedures, China's lack of competitive and regular elections for national leaders, absence of competitive party politics, and the inadequacy of its institutionalized protection of political freedom and rights represent deficiencies in its democratic practice. Meanwhile, respondents who put more emphasis on democracy's instrumental values are much more likely to be impressed by the CCP regime's performance and competence in delivering quality governance. The Chinese government has not only survived the 2008–2009 financial crisis but also outperformed most Western democracies in spreading the benefits of economic growth among the largest section of its population. Furthermore, despite grave problems of environmental pollution and corruption, the Chinese government has launched effective campaigns to reduce its greenhouse gas emissions, secure more blue-sky-days, and fight corruption. The Chinese government's competence and efficiency in sustaining growth, spreading the benefits of development, curbing corruption, and responding to popular demands all highlight the country's achievements in democratic practice for respondents who view democracy as a way of governance that satisfies popular needs through effective public policies. Clearly, varying understandings of democracy have oriented people toward different aspects of Chinese society as they assess its democratic practice.

We found similar dynamics in popular evaluations of US democratic practice. Figure 5.4 shows the influence of individual and societal-level factors on how people view US democracy in sixty-six GBS II societies (including China). Despite different ways of operationalizing popular understandings of democracy for Figure 5.4a (continuous latent IRT scores) and Figure 5.4b (nominal latent LCA groups), the findings again are highly consistent. In particular, the impact of the PUD instruments shows an almost mirror image between Figure 5.3 and Figure 5.4. More specifically, as shown in

Figure 5.4a, the positive coefficient of the IRT scores suggests that, *ceteris paribus*, respondents who appreciate the intrinsic values of democracy in ensuring people's dignity and protecting their liberties and rights through established institutions and procedures are more inclined to assess the United States' democratic practice more positively. Similarly, as illustrated in Figure 5.4b, compared to Benefit-Seekers, Principle-Holders are likely to evaluate its democratic practice more positively. Meanwhile, Fence-Sitters are not significantly different from Benefit-Seekers in this regard.

Put otherwise, as many US politicians have boasted, as the beacon of liberal democracy, the United States indeed has impressed many people around the world with its practice of democracy, especially those who prioritize democratic institutions and procedures as defining features of democracy and are less willing to trade off key democratic principles for instrumental gains. More specifically, democratic practice in the United States, characterized by its division of power, checks and balances, and the deep-rooted liberal tradition that has been vigilantly guarding individual liberties and rights against possible transgression from the government, has effectively won the hearts and minds of these people and boosted their evaluations of US democracy. However, for those who put more emphasis on the instrumental values of democracy in satisfying popular demands through quality governance, the rising partisan gridlock in the United States, as well as its growing inequality, worsening racial confrontation, and exacerbated political polarization, might make their assessment of US democracy much less rosy. Again, different conceptions of democracy have oriented people toward distinct aspects of US society as they assess its democratic practice. The evidence is highly consistent with Hypotheses C5.1_2_1 and C5.1_2_2.

Despite the similarities in how democratic conceptions shape popular assessment of democratic practices in the United States and China, there are some noticeable differences between the dynamics that might have driven how people view the two countries' democratic practices. As shown in Figure 5.3, on average, people with a higher level of education are more critical of China's democratic practice. Meanwhile, as shown in Figure 5.4, the same group of better-educated people hold a more favorable view of the way US democracy works. It seems a higher level of political sophistication and better access to information (both possibly because of more education) might have made people more sensitive to the political deficiencies of the Chinese one-party regime and enable them to appreciate more the political merits of US-style checks and balances and division of power.

Some societal features play significant roles in shaping their citizens' views of democratic practices in the United States and China. More specifically, citizens of richer societies (i.e., higher per capita GDP) are generally more critical of both countries' democratic practices. These societies' better socioeconomic performance might have raised the bar for evaluating foreign countries among their citizens. This makes perfect sense, given that most people are naturally inclined to use their own experiences of democratic practice in their home society as a meaningful baseline for assessing foreign countries' practices. Meanwhile, citizens of more democratic societies (i.e., better Freedom Houser rating) are also generally more critical of China's democratic practice. It is likely that their home society's better protection of political liberty and rights might have amplified citizens' awareness of the deficiencies in China's democratic practice. Furthermore, societies with a history of personalist regimes or a significant legacy of Confucian traditions are also more critical of China's democratic practice. Although we do not have enough data to examine the underlying dynamics in detail, we can draw some reasonable conjectures. People living in countries with a history of personalist regimes might still share memories of their earlier sufferings under such regimes. Although the CCP regime is characterized by one-party rule rather than a personalist dictator, the similarities in political power concentration, media censorship, and heavy-handed control over some aspects of society may resonate with these memories, thus worsening their assessment of China's democratic practice. Meanwhile, the negative influence of the legacy of Confucian traditions on popular views of China's democratic practice is likely unrelated to the cultural contexts of Confucian societies and more likely to have been driven by geopolitical concerns triggered by China's rise. All Confucian societies are located in East Asia and witnessed at close hand China's expanding influence and growing strength over the past decades. Given their geopolitical concerns, it is understandable that these societies hold varying levels of uneasiness and even fear about how China's rise might reconfigure the geopolitics in East Asia, as well as the implications for their security and economic prosperity. Such uneasiness and fear might affect how their citizens assess China's democratic practice. Of course, we need more appropriate data to test the validity of these conjectures.

It should be fair to argue that, given the evidence presented so far, varying understandings of democracy play a critical role in shaping people's assessment of democratic practices in foreign countries. In other words, examining how people conceptualize democracy in different ways provides extra analytical leverage for our understanding of popular views of democracy. Here, the PUD instruments have been shown to be analytically useful. Nevertheless, as discussed earlier, popular evaluations of democratic practices in the United States and China are most-likely cases for testing the influence of varying democratic conceptions on political attitudes. Therefore, the supportive evidence presented so far is neither sufficient nor persuasive enough for us to draw generalizable conclusions on the empirical and theoretical values of incorporating popular understandings of democracy (as captured by the PUD instruments) into our examination of how people assess democratic practices. For this, we need additional empirical evidence from distinct and more challenging scenarios.

5.2 Assessing democratic practice at home

Having demonstrated the benefits of incorporating popular conceptions of democracy (as captured by the PUD instruments) into our analysis of how people assess democratic practices in foreign countries (the United States and China), we have more confidence in using this key variable to further our understanding of other popular views of democracy. More specifically, we are particularly interested in examining how varying understandings of democracy shape citizens' assessment of their own political regime's democratic nature.

For this exercise, we relied on two instruments in the GBS II survey. The first instrument asked for respondents' satisfaction with how democracy works in their home society, using a four-point Likert scale ranging from "1: Not at all satisfied" to "4: Very satisfied." The second instrument adopted the same ten-point scale used earlier for assessing democratic practices in the United States and China to capture respondents' perceptions of their home society's democratic practice, ranging from "1: Completely undemocratic" to "10: Completely democratic." Empirically, there is a moderate positive correlation between the two measures: the Pearson's correlation coefficient between the two instruments is 0.44, with a p-value of 0.000. This moderately strong and significant correlation suggests some meaningful overlap between the two measures, but also some critical distinction between them.[7] If we can secure similar supportive evidence regarding the influence of varying democratic conceptions on the two different but related measures of how people view democratic practices in their home societies, we should have

DEMOCRATIC ASSESSMENT 117

more confidence in concluding that popular understandings of democracy indeed shape assessment of democratic practices.

To give our readers some intuitive understanding of how people around the world assess their home society's democratic practice, we plotted the weighted population averages of the two measures from the seventy-one GBS II societies on a world map. To simplify our presentation and readers' interpretation, we recoded the four-point Likert scale of popular satisfaction with democratic practices into a binary measure to highlight the contrast between satisfaction and dissatisfaction. Then we calculated the weighted percentages of respondents reporting satisfaction with their home society's democratic practice at the time of the GBS II survey and presented the percentages in Figure 5.5a. For the perceived levels of democratic practice, we used the original ten-point scale, calculated the weighted population means for the

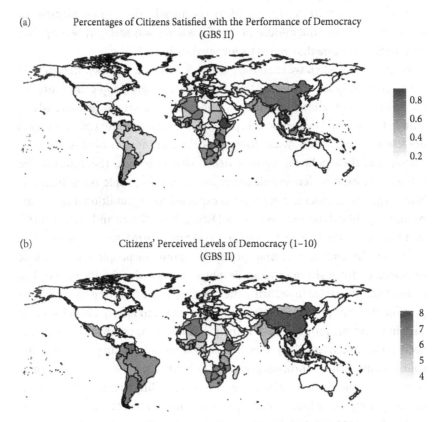

Figure 5.5 Assessment of Democratic Practice in Today's World

seventy-one GBS II societies, and plotted them on the same world map in Figure 5.5b.

Above all, the significant variation between the GBS II societies' respective popular views of their democratic practices is hard to miss. As shown in Figure 5.5a, the percentage of citizens who are satisfied with their home society's democratic practice varies between 19.9% (Honduras) and 91.6% (Singapore). In countries like Honduras, Madagascar, Mexico, Togo, Paraguay, Peru, Brazil, and Colombia, less than 30% of citizens are satisfied with the way democracy works. Meanwhile, more than 70% of their counterparts in societies like Taiwan, Senegal, Botswana, Mauritius, Malaysia, Ghana, mainland China, Tanzania, Thailand, Cambodia, Uruguay, Vietnam, Ethiopia, and Singapore are satisfied with the way democracy works. Similarly, as displayed in Figure 5.5b, the national averages for evaluations of respective levels of democracy in the seventy-one societies also vary greatly, ranging from the lowest of around 3.81 (Egypt) to the highest of about 8.10 (Vietnam). More specifically, the average assessment is less than 5.5 (i.e., the middle-point of the ten-point scale) in twenty-four countries[8] and more than 6.5 in twenty-two societies.[9]

Furthermore, when we examine Figures 5.5 and 3.2 together, the contrast is too great to ignore. It seems that in societies where people are more inclined to conceptualize democracy by prioritizing its intrinsic values and less willing to trade off key democratic principles for instrumental gains, citizens are less satisfied with how democracy works and more critical in their assessment of their political regimes' democratic practices. Theoretically, the influence of varying democratic conceptions on how people assess their political regimes' democratic practices is expected to be conditional upon surrounding political contexts (Ferrin and Kriesi 2016; Kirsch and Welzel 2019). In autocracies, the lack of meaningful institutionalized protection of basic political rights and liberties may greatly disappoint the people who prioritize democracy's intrinsic values and deeply appreciate the significance of key democratic principles in securing their dignity and protecting them against possible abuse of power. Even in autocracies that can effectively deliver and sustain economic growth, these Principle-Holders (as compared to Benefit-Seekers) are much less likely to be led astray by authoritarian politicians' discourse manipulation, propaganda, and indoctrination. As a consequence, compared to their fellow citizens who are more willing to trade off key democratic principles for instrumental gains and more subject to the influence of such political maneuvers, these people are expected to be more critical when they assess their political regimes' democratic practices. Conversely, in liberal democracies, well-established democratic institutions and procedures might have fulfilled the expectations of those who cherish democracy's intrinsic values. Even when their societies witness short-term economic difficulties, given their low willingness to trade off key democratic principles for instrumental gains, these people are expected to be less critical when they assess their political regimes' democratic practices. To examine this conjecture, we focused on the cross-level interaction between popular understandings of democracy (proxied by the PUD instruments) and societies' political features (proxied by reversed Freedom House ratings): *the influence of people's willingness to trade off key democratic principles for instrumental gains on how they assess their home society's democratic practice is conditional upon the features of the surrounding political environment* (**Hypothesis C5.2_1**).

For effective analysis, we included the same set of controls used in the previous section to account for respondents' demographic and psychological features, as well as societies' socioeconomic and political characteristics. Furthermore, unlike popular assessment of democratic practices in foreign countries, how citizens assess their home society's democratic practice is highly likely to be affected by the quality of governance in the society (e.g., Kumlin and Esaiasson 2011; Dahlberg and Holmberg 2014; Markowski 2016; Park 2002). There are two related survey questions in GBS II: one asked for respondents' evaluations of their national economic situation at the time of the survey; the other asked for evaluations of their family's economic situation at the time of the survey. The former corresponds to so-called sociotropic economic evaluations, while the latter corresponds to so-called pocketbook economic evaluations (e.g., Anderson 2007; Ansolabehere et al. 2012). We relied on the two instruments to examine the governance hypothesis: *people holding better perceptions of their family or national economic situation are inclined to assess their home society's democratic practice more favorably* (**Hypothesis C5.2_2**). Both instruments were incorporated for analysis as ordinal variables, using the same five-point Likert scale ranging from "1: Very bad" to "5: Very good."

Again, we ran mixed-effect models to examine how varying understandings of democracy may shift citizens' assessments of their home society's democratic practice. To ensure the robustness of our findings, we ran the same mixed-effect models with the PUD instruments operationalized in different ways (i.e., continuous IRT scores versus nominal LCA groups). To facilitate subsequent interpretations, we focused on the mixed-effect models

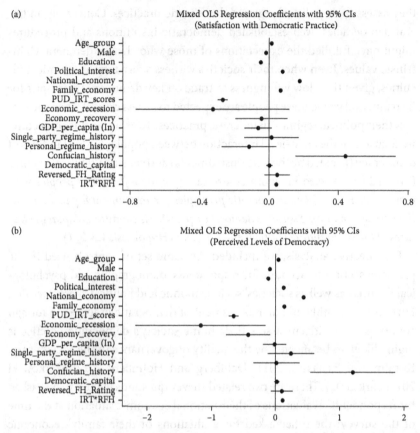

Figure 5.6 Mixed-Effect Linear Model on Assessment of Home Society's Democratic Practice

with popular understandings of democracy measured by the IRT scores. Similar findings were established when the LCA groups were used. Using the same set of legends, Figure 5.6 presents the regression coefficients and related 95% confidence intervals from the two mixed-effect models for popular satisfaction with democratic practice (Figure 5.6a) and perceived levels of democratic practice (Figure 5.6b) respectively in the seventy-one GBS II societies.[10]

For us, the key and consistent findings are: (1) the regression coefficient for the IRT scores of the PUD instruments is negative and statistically significant; and (2) the interaction between individuals' understandings of democracy and their home society's regime features (i.e., assessed by the reversed

Freedom House ratings, with a larger value for a higher level of democracy) is positive and statistically significant. Additional analysis suggests that, on average, citizens who are less willing to trade off key democratic principles for instrumental gains are inclined to be less satisfied with and more critical of their home society's democratic practice.[11] Furthermore, as indicated by the positive and significant coefficient of the interaction term, this impact is much stronger in autocracies and weaker in societies with improved protection of political rights and civil liberties. We also ran a series of simulations based on the mixed-effect regression results and plotted the estimated average marginal impact of varying democratic conceptions on popular satisfaction with and perceived levels of democratic practices in the GBS II societies rated by Freedom House from the lowest level of "Least free" to the highest level of "Most free" in Figure 5.7. The solid lines stand for the simulated regression coefficients (i.e., average marginal effect) associated with the IRT scores of the PUD instruments. The dotted lines stand for the corresponding 95% confidence intervals. When its 95% confidence interval covers the horizontal dotted line (which stands for zero or the lack of any impact), the impact of varying understandings of democracy is statistically not different from zero.

As illustrated in Figure 5.7a, in countries like Japan, South Korea, Ghana, Senegal, Argentina, and Brazil (rated by Freedom House as democracies with minor issues),[12] *ceteris paribus*, citizens who embrace different understandings of democracy are not essentially different from each other in their reported satisfaction with how democracy works in their home country. However, in countries like Sudan, China, Vietnam, Mali, Zimbabwe, Swaziland, and Ethiopia (rated by Freedom House as autocracies),[13] on average, citizens who prioritize democracy's intrinsic values are significantly less satisfied with their home country's democratic practice as compared to their fellow citizens who emphasize democracy's instrumental values. In hybrid regimes like Malaysia, Singapore, Nigeria, Nepal, Pakistan, Honduras, and Venezuela,[14] citizens' varying willingness to trade off key democratic principles for instrumental gains still significantly shapes popular satisfaction with their home country's democratic practice. Less willingness to engage in such trade-offs is associated with lower democratic satisfaction. However, the magnitude of such impact is weakened and reduced to about 50% of that in autocracies. Furthermore, in full democracies like Cape Verde, Chile, Costa Rica, and Uruguay,[15] the impact is no longer negative but positive. Basically, in full democracies, citizens' deeper appreciation of

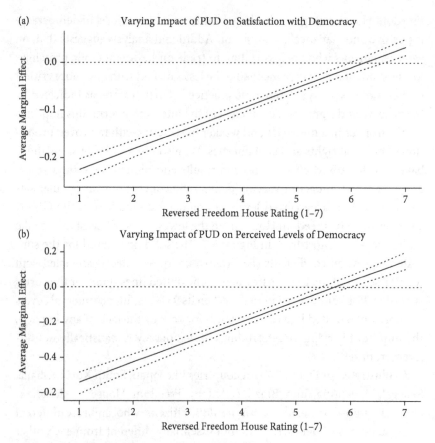

Figure 5.7 Average Marginal Effects of Democratic Conceptions under Different Political Contexts

democracy's intrinsic values is associated with higher satisfaction with their home country's democratic practice. Clearly, people who conceptualize democracy in different ways are inclined to assess their home society's democratic practice using distinct benchmarks. And this disparity in democratic satisfaction between people with varying willingness to trade off key democratic principles for instrumental gains is also highly responsive to their immediate political contexts.

An almost identical pattern is illustrated in Figure 5.7b using a different proxy for assessment of democratic practice. As shown in Figure 5.7b, in democracies with some issues like Mongolia, Indonesia, India, South Africa, Namibia, Peru, and Panama,[16] the impact of democratic conceptions on assessment of democratic practice is negligible. Meanwhile, in societies rated by Freedom House as less democratic and more autocratic, the impact becomes increasingly negative and statistically significant. Put otherwise, in autocracies and hybrid regimes, people who prioritize the intrinsic values of democracy, *ceteris paribus*, are inclined to report much lower assessment of their own society's democratic practice. And such impact almost doubles in societies like Sudan, China, and Vietnam when compared to countries like Malaysia, Burkina Faso, Nigeria, Honduras, and Nepal. Again, it is interesting to find that, in full democracies like Cape Verde, Chile, Costa Rica, and Uruguay, as well as democracies with minor issues like Japan, South Korea, and Ghana, the impact is no longer negative but positive and statistically significant. Basically, in these democracies, citizens who are less willing to trade off key democratic principles for instrumental gains are inclined to report better evaluations of their home society's democratic practice. Given the limited number of such cases in our data, we do not want to over-interpret this finding; nevertheless, the patterns and dynamics of change in the influence of popular understandings of democracy on how people assess their own society's democratic practice are highly consistent with Hypothesis C5.2_1.

Most control variables perform as expected (as displayed in Figure 5.6). At the individual level, on average, people who perceive improvement in their national or personal economic situation are likely to report more satisfaction with or a higher rating of their own society's democratic practice. Clearly, quality governance matters in popular assessment of democracy, regardless of how people understand democracy. This finding is consistent with Hypothesis C5.2_2, as well as the conclusions drawn by some recent research on democratic recession or deconsolidation, which is generally attributed to democracies' lackluster performance in delivering good governance (Mounk 2018; Diamond and Plattner 2015; Plattner 2017). Meanwhile, younger males with a higher level of education, *ceteris paribus*, are more critical when they assess their own society's democratic practice (i.e., reporting less satisfaction and a lower rating). It seems that the new socialization dynamics among the youth (further exacerbated by the increasing challenges in fulfilling their socioeconomic and political ambitions) (Foa and Mounk 2016; Markowski 2016; Foa and Mounk 2017)[17] and the enhanced political sophistication due to a higher level of education might also make citizens more critical in related assessments.

At the societal level, another consistent finding, aside from the interaction between popular understandings of democracy and regimes' democratic features, is the legacy of Confucian history and cultural traditions. On average, citizens living in Confucian societies are inclined to report more satisfaction with and a higher rating of their home society's democratic practice. It is worth noting that this relationship holds even after accounting for the socioeconomic and political features of societies, as well as individuals' demographic and psychological characteristics and their varying understandings of democracy. It seems that certain normative (e.g., hierarchical orientations toward authority) and cognitive features (e.g., inclination to avoid conflict and eschew negative sentiments) driven by long-term socialization under the shadow of Confucian traditions might play some role here. This finding is consistent with the conclusions drawn by the scholarship on political culture and psychology in East Asia (e.g., Shi 2015; Shin 2013; Choi and Nisbett 1998; Miller 2001).

5.3 Conclusion

Having established the existence of varying democratic conceptions and explored possible related dynamics at both individual and societal levels in earlier chapters, we examined the attitudinal consequences of this critical mass opinion in this chapter. More specifically, we focused on how popular understandings of democracy shape people's assessment of democratic practices in both foreign countries and their home society. Theoretically, people's varying willingness to trade off key democratic principles for instrumental gains may orient them toward different aspects of democratic practice in their assessments. For those who deeply appreciate democracy's intrinsic values, the quality of core democratic institutional settings and procedural arrangements, as well as related norms and values, in ensuring political rights, liberties, and dignity are central to their assessment of democratic practice. For those who prioritize democracy's instrumental values, the quality of delivered governance, including but not limited to improved social equity and living standards, are essential. As a consequence, confronted with the same regime's democratic practice (either foreign or home), people with varying democratic conceptions are likely to draw distinct conclusions in their assessments.

Given the salience of the United States and China in today's global politics and economy, their respective models of ruling and governance are of significance for contemporary political discourses on democracy and governance. In addition to its indisputable status as the world's number one economy, the United States has been widely recognized as a beacon of liberal democracy and a pioneer in technological innovations. Meanwhile, besides its outstanding performance in engineering continuous economic growth, China has been widely recognized for its high resilience and competence in sustaining its one-party regime against various domestic and international pressures for political change and for ensuring political order and stability in the face of dramatic socioeconomic transformations. Furthermore, both countries have claimed themselves as genuine democracies and have made industrious efforts in launching global campaigns to justify, defend, and even promote their preferred ways of engaging in democratic politics.

Thus, we first tested how varying understandings of democracy could have shaped GBS II respondents' assessments of democratic practices in the United States and China. In almost all GBS II societies (including China), on average, people offer a higher rating of democratic practice in the United States than in China, which further validates the GBS II data's effectiveness in capturing popular views of democracy. Meanwhile, there is a noticeable variation in respondents' evaluations, with much more variation in how people assess China's democratic practice. Mixed-effect regressions confirm that, regardless of how popular understandings of democracy are operationalized (i.e., as continuous IRT scores or nominal LCA groups), *ceteris paribus*, people who prioritize democracy's intrinsic values by emphasizing its institutions and procedures in protecting basic rights and liberties are more critical of China's democratic practice and hold more favorable attitudes toward US democracy. Those who are more willing to trade off key democratic principles for instrumental gains, on average, are less impressed by the performance of US democracy and show more appreciation of democratic practice with Chinese characteristics. Given the aforementioned contrast between the United States and China in terms of their respective ways of ruling and governance, it should be reasonable to argue that the established impact of varying understandings of democracy on how people assess democratic practices in the United States and China has clearly demonstrated the salience of varying benchmarks that people adopt to assess democratic practice due to their distinct conceptions of democracy (as captured by the PUD instruments).

We further examined how such varying conceptions of democracy could have affected popular views of democratic practice in their home society. To ensure the robustness of our findings, we adopted two proxies (with distinct measurement strategies and scales): citizens' self-reported satisfaction with and perceived levels of democratic practice in their home society. There is a moderate but significant positive correlation between the two proxies, which provides an assuring setting for our robustness check. Similar mixed-effect regressions reveal that, again, people's different understandings of democracy significantly shape how they assess their home society's democratic practice. On average, people who prioritize democracy's intrinsic values (compared to their fellow citizens who are more willing to trade off key democratic principles for instrumental gains) are less satisfied with their regime's democratic practice. A nuanced but critical finding is that this impact is highly conditional upon surrounding political contexts. More specifically, after accounting for other relevant features, the impact in full autocracies is twice as strong as in hybrid regimes. In democracies with minor issues, the impact further diminishes and is no longer statistically significant. In full democracies, the impact is reversed. In other words, in full democracies, the more people appreciate democracy's intrinsic values (i.e., the lower the willingness to trade off key democratic principles for instrumental gains), the more favorably they view their home society's democratic practice. Put otherwise, people are highly responsive to the features of their immediate political environment when they assess their home society's democratic practice.

Our analysis also establishes that, regardless of how people differ in their conceptions of democracy, younger males with a higher level of education are generally more critical of their home society's democratic practice. Moreover, even a full democracy also needs to deliver (i.e., provide good governance through better economic and political performance) to win over its citizen's hearts and minds and foster its popular support. Furthermore, political regimes in Confucian societies might have benefited from the lasting influence of Confucian cultural traditions and enjoyed some premium in its popular democratic assessment.

Our findings have critical implications for existing research on regime transition and democratic consolidation. In authoritarian regimes, citizens who prioritize democracy's intrinsic values and appreciate key democratic principles more than instrumental gains are much less likely to be led astray or even blinded by the regime's discourse manipulation, media indoctrination, and propaganda. These citizens can effectively see through the nondemocratic nature of such regimes, even in the context of their impressive performance in delivering satisfying governance (of course, at the cost of violating basic human rights and liberties). When these citizens account for a significant portion of the masses, they form a considerable force that eases and contributes to democratic transitions. Similarly, to avoid recession or deconsolidation in established democracies, the unwavering support from citizens who are not willing to trade off key democratic principles for instrumental gains is critical and indispensable. Given their deep-rooted appreciation of democracy's intrinsic values, these citizens are unlikely to withdraw their support for democracy, despite the vicissitudes, challenges, and even hardships in governance. Thus, democracies wherein the majority of citizens prioritize democracy's intrinsic values are expected to be much more resilient and robust against authoritarian populism. On the contrary, when people who are more willing to trade off key democratic principles for instrumental gains account for a significant portion of the masses, authoritarian regimes (if they can deliver) may appear more resilient while democracies (if they cannot deliver) are more likely to be in trouble.

Public opinion is critical for examining politics in any society. In this chapter, we have established the significance of varying understandings of democracy in shaping the benchmarks people use to assess both foreign countries' and their home society's democratic practices. To further demonstrate the importance of popular democratic conceptions for understanding political change, more concrete evidence on attitude-behavior connections is needed. More specifically, we need to demonstrate that the variation in how people conceptualize democracy also has critical implications for whether and how they engage in politics, that is, their political participation. Chapter 6 addresses these issues in detail.

Appendix

Table A5.1 Mixed-Effect Linear Models on Assessment of Democratic Practices in the United States and China

	M1 (PRC + IRT) Mixed OLS	M2 (PRC + LCA) Mixed OLS	M3 (USA + IRT) Mixed OLS	M4 (USA + LCA) Mixed OLS
Fixed effects				
Age_group	−0.064 (0.008)	−0.060 (0.008)	0.004 (0.006)	0.007 (0.006)
Male	0.098 (0.024)	0.092 (0.024)	0.110 (0.018)	0.109 (0.018)
Education	−0.128 (0.009)	−0.132 (0.009)	0.064 (0.007)	0.065 (0.007)
Political_interest	0.008 (0.012)	0.001 (0.013)	0.006 (0.009)	0.005 (0.010)
PUD_IRT_scores	−0.171 (0.049)		0.125 (0.038)	
PUD_LCA_Principle_holders		−0.218 (0.069)		0.158 (0.054)
PUD_LCA_Fence_sitters		−0.153 (0.063)		0.004 (0.048)
Economic_recession	−0.607 (0.506)	−0.640 (0.496)	0.262 (0.512)	0.334 (0.537)
Economic_recovery	0.123 (0.179)	0.123 (0.175)	0.034 (0.179)	0.042 (0.187)
GDP_per_capita (ln)	−0.262 (0.098)	−0.272 (0.097)	−0.235 (0.099)	−0.210 (0.104)
Single_party_regime_history	−0.169 (0.193)	−0.155 (0.189)	−0.058 (0.193)	−0.116 (0.203)
Personal_regime_history	−0.462 (0.203)	−0.432 (0.199)	−0.189 (0.204)	−0.199 (0.214)
Confucian_history	−0.947 (0.342)	−0.930 (0.335)	0.131 (0.332)	0.087 (0.348)
Reversed_FH_rating	−0.232 (0.089)	−0.236 (0.087)	0.067 (0.089)	0.106 (0.093)
Democratic_capital	−0.018 (0.022)	−0.016 (0.021)	−0.039 (0.022)	−0.049 (0.023)
Intercept	10.222 (0.844)	10.408 (0.827)	9.632 (0.847)	9.393 (0.888)

Random effects (variance)			
Intercept	0.387	0.409	0.459	0.593
PUD_IRT_scores	0.125		0.080	
PUD_LCA_Principle_holders		0.235		0.148
PUD_LCA_Fence_sitters		0.192		0.116
Residual	7.178	7.140	5.020	4.945
# of societies	65	65	66	66
# of observations	48800	47928	58931	57098

Source: Global Barometer Surveys II ($N = 104{,}248$).

Notes:

Robust standard errors in parentheses.

Statistically significant coefficients are bolded (at the 0.05 level).

Table A5.2 Mixed-Effect Linear Models on Satisfaction with Democratic Practice of Home Society

	M1 Mixed OLS	M2 Mixed OLS	M3 Mixed OLS
Fixed effects			
Age_group	**0.015 (0.002)**	**0.015 (0.002)**	**0.017 (0.002)**
Male	**−0.018 (0.006)**	**−0.019 (0.006)**	**−0.022 (0.006)**
Education	**−0.048 (0.002)**	**−0.048 (0.002)**	**−0.049 (0.002)**
Political_interest	**0.080 (0.003)**	**0.080 (0.003)**	**0.076 (0.003)**
National_economy	**0.178 (0.003)**	**0.179 (0.003)**	**0.178 (0.003)**
Family_economy	**0.068 (0.003)**	**0.068 (0.003)**	**0.065 (0.003)**
PUD_IRT_scores	**−0.268 (0.014)**	**−0.071 (0.005)**	
PUD_LCA_Principle_holders			**−0.386 (0.024)**
PUD_LCA_Fence_sitters			**−0.174 (0.021)**
Economic_recession	−0.325 (0.226)	−0.325 (0.227)	−0.320 (0.228)
Economic_recovery	−0.044 (0.077)	−0.047 (0.078)	−0.043 (0.078)
GDP_per_capita (ln)	−0.062 (0.041)	−0.059 (0.041)	−0.058 (0.041)
Single_party_regime_history	0.015 (0.081)	0.008 (0.081)	0.013 (0.081)
Personal_regime_history	−0.115 (0.081)	−0.115 (0.081)	−0.122 (0.082)
Confucian_history	**0.441 (0.147)**	**0.434 (0.147)**	**0.433 (0.148)**
Democratic_capital	0.003 (0.009)	0.003 (0.009)	0.003 (0.009)
Reversed_FH_rating	0.048 (0.038)	0.046 (0.038)	0.015 (0.038)
IRT*RFH	**0.043 (0.003)**		
LCA_PH*RFH			**0.063 (0.005)**
LCA_FS*RFH			**0.039 (0.005)**
Intercept	**1.992 (0.333)**	**1.993 (0.335)**	**2.161 (0.336)**
Random effects (variance)			
Intercept	0.081	0.082	0.082
Residual	0.676	0.678	0.674
# of societies	71	71	71
# of observations	91046	91046	87347

Source: Global Barometer Surveys II (N = 104,248).

Notes:
Robust standard errors in parentheses.
Statistically significant coefficients are bolded (at the 0.05 level).

Table A5.3 Mixed-Effect Linear Models on Perceived Levels of Democracy in Home Society

	M1 Mixed OLS	M2 Mixed OLS	M3 Mixed OLS
Fixed effects			
Age_group	**0.045 (0.006)**	**0.045 (0.006)**	**0.044 (0.006)**
Male	**−0.089 (0.016)**	**−0.094 (0.016)**	**−0.098 (0.016)**
Education	**−0.115 (0.007)**	**−0.116 (0.007)**	**−0.117 (0.007)**
Political_interest	**0.126 (0.008)**	**0.126 (0.008)**	**0.122 (0.008)**
National_economy	**0.437 (0.009)**	**0.439 (0.009)**	**0.440 (0.009)**
Family_economy	**0.138 (0.009)**	**0.138 (0.009)**	**0.135 (0.009)**
PUD_IRT_scores	**−0.658 (0.041)**	**−0.131 (0.013)**	
PUD_LCA_Principle_holders			**−0.853 (0.067)**
PUD_LCA_Fence_sitters			**−0.250 (0.060)**
Economic_recession	**−1.168 (0.515)**	**−1.170 (0.518)**	**−1.176 (0.520)**
Economic_recovery	**−0.428 (0.177)**	**−0.438 (0.178)**	**−0.440 (0.178)**
GDP_per_capita (ln)	−0.012 (0.093)	−0.004 (0.093)	−0.007 (0.094)
Single_party_regime_history	0.245 (0.184)	0.230 (0.186)	0.246 (0.186)
Personal_regime_history	0.017 (0.185)	0.018 (0.186)	0.016 (0.186)
Confucian_history	**1.204 (0.335)**	**1.186 (0.337)**	**1.211 (0.337)**
Democratic_capital	0.026 (0.021)	0.025 (0.021)	0.026 (0.021)
Reversed_FH_rating	0.103 (0.086)	0.097 (0.087)	0.036 (0.087)
IRT*RFH	**0.116 (0.008)**		
LCA_PH*RFH			**0.151 (0.014)**
LCA_FS*RFH			**0.044 (0.013)**
Intercept	**3.344 (0.760)**	**3.344 (0.765)**	**3.703 (0.767)**
Random effects (variance)			
Intercept	0.419	0.425	0.427
Residual	5.439	5.450	5.388
# of societies	71	71	71
# of observations	89391	89931	85942

Source: Global Barometer Surveys II ($N = 104{,}248$).
Notes:
Robust standard errors in parentheses.
Statistically significant coefficients are bolded (at the 0.05 level).

6
Political Participation and Varying Understandings of Democracy

In Chapter 5, we demonstrated the influence of popular understandings of democracy on how people assess democratic practices in foreign countries and their home societies. Overall, due to their varying conceptions of democracy (i.e., different willingness to trade off key democratic principles for instrumental gains), people are inclined to adopt distinct benchmarks for assessing democratic practice. We are inclined to interpret this as critical evidence for the significance and necessity of incorporating popular understandings of democracy in comparative research on democratic transition and consolidation, or crisis and deconsolidation. Nevertheless, since both outcome variables and the key explanatory variable in Chapter 5 are self-reported attitudinal measures, we can only, at best, show some robust correlations. Despite our efforts to account for possible confounders in the mixed-effect models and theoretical justification for the causal nature of the correlations, there might still be some concerns regarding the influence of some omitted variables (which might simultaneously drive all self-reported attitude measures, thus making the correlations spurious). To address such concerns and reservations, in this chapter we examine the relationships between popular understandings of democracy and various political participatory activities, again using the GBS II data.

Theoretically, the distinction between attitudes (e.g., varying democratic conceptions) and behaviors (e.g., political participatory activities) is much more recognizable than the distinction between different attitudes. Therefore, our analyses and interpretations are much less likely to be challenged by omitted variables. Furthermore, the relationships between attitudes and behaviors have always been a central but thorny issue in the contemporary literature on public opinion and political behavior. Although it is widely acknowledged that attitudes only matter in real-life politics when they can effectively shape how people participate in politics (which is indispensable for meaningful political changes), demonstrating the behavioral impact of political attitudes has been difficult. Thus, if we can establish robust relationships between popular understandings of democracy and various political participatory activities, as well as possible moderating effects of surrounding socioeconomic and political environments, we should be on a much better footing to argue for the significance and necessity of incorporating popular understandings of democracy into the agenda of related research.

6.1 Varying understandings of democracy and electoral participation

Historically, since its first appearance in ancient Greek political thought, electoral politics has been at the heart of democracy (Dahl 1956, 1989; Ober 1989). Thus, it is not surprising that when ordinary people talk about democracy, elections are likely to be the very first thing that comes to their mind (Shin and Kim 2018). Furthermore, when scholars engage in democracy-related research, regardless of how they conceptualize democracy, the practice of electoral politics has always been central to their operationalization and measurement. In other words, scholars have widely acknowledged the indispensability of regular, competitive, and fair elections for any democracy (Schmitter and Karl 1991; Przeworski et al. 2000; Przeworski 2016). Experts working for international organizations (e.g., the World Bank) and Nongovernmental organizations (NGOs) (e.g., Freedom House) may also choose different indicators to assess the quality of democratic practices around the world, but they all include the integrity of electoral politics as a key indicator. Meanwhile, elections have also been adopted by a large number of authoritarian regimes for various purposes (Gandhi and Lust-Okar 2009); and competitive authoritarianism is a growing phenomenon documented by students of comparative politics (Levitsky and Way 2010; Schedler 2013; Bunce and Wolchik 2010). Thus, if we were only allowed to pick one domain of political participation to examine the influence of popular understandings of democracy, electoral participation would be the unquestionable choice.

In democracies, elections are expected to provide vital and institutionalized mechanisms for people to voice their concerns and preferences, shape public policies, select political leaders, and, more importantly, hold political leaders accountable (Przeworski et al. 1999). Above all, in democracies, elections are an indispensable component of the core political institutions and procedures. Although many authoritarian regimes also have embraced elections and engaged in regular electoral politics, in most cases, such elections have been designed or manipulated to provide authoritarian leaders with advantages in mobilizing popular support, collecting critical information from the people, identifying potential challengers for preemptive attacks or cooptation, and showcasing their power and capability in sustaining effective control (Morse 2012; Schedler 2013). Thus, in these authoritarian regimes, elections primarily serve as tools furthering the interests of authoritarian leaders rather than serving the people's needs. Given such clear contrasts between the practices of electoral politics under different regimes, how do citizens with varying understandings of democracy engage in electoral participation?

As the existing literature on electoral participation has demonstrated, in most cases, participation in electoral politics (including voting, attending rallies, and assisting campaign activities) cannot be satisfactorily explained by instrumental calculations alone (Aldrich 1993; Miller and Shanks 1996; Leighley and Nagler 2014). In many cases, electoral participation serves critical expressive values (Drinkwater and Jennings 2007; Brennan and Hamlin 1998). Put otherwise, given the negligible probability of any particular individual's secret ballot being decisive in shaping an election's outcome, any benefits associated with winning the election per se are unlikely to be the key driver of electoral participation. Therefore, for an effective understanding of electoral participation, we need to examine the expressive considerations of voters. For us, the key argument is that electoral participation stands for essentially different things to people who conceptualize democracy in distinct ways.

As previously discussed, for those prioritizing democracy's intrinsic values in protecting liberties and basic rights via appropriate institutions and procedures, electoral politics is the backbone and a defining institutional component of democracy. Conversely, for those emphasizing democracy's instrumental values in delivering good governance, electoral politics is just one of many channels through which the needs of citizens are fulfilled. At the same time, for the latter group, electoral participation may not even be the most effective channel for serving their material needs. Therefore, people's varying willingness to trade off key democratic principles for instrumental gains could be a key driver of their expressive considerations in electoral participation. Furthermore, the expressive values associated with electoral participation should be much higher among those who emphasize the key principles of democracy, primarily as a way of demonstrating adherence to democracy's intrinsic values. To examine this conjecture, we relied on the PUD instruments: *on average, people who are less willing to trade off key democratic principles for instrumental gains are more likely to engage in electoral participation* (**Hypothesis C6.1_1**).

However, given the varying practices of and distinct functions served by electoral politics in different regimes, surrounding political contexts are also expected to significantly moderate the relationship between varying democratic conceptions and electoral participation. More specifically, the relationship is expected to be much more substantial and significant in authoritarian societies than in democracies. The reasoning is quite straightforward: the most salient difference between democracies and authoritarian societies lies in how the origins and practices of political power are constrained and regulated by well-established institutions and procedures to strengthen political accountability, minimize potential abuse of power, and ensure the protection of basic rights and liberties. Authoritarian leaders attempt to manipulate electoral politics for their political goals and preferred agendas rather than offering their citizens meaningful choices and participation. Nevertheless, elections in authoritarian societies still provide a rare opportunity for citizens to participate in high-profile focal-point events (Schelling 1960) and to collectively (not necessarily via intentional coordination or mobilization) demonstrate their unhappiness and concerns with the regimes' institutional deficiencies, or even to challenge the political boundaries set by the authoritarian leaders. Under some conditions, such challenges may result in meaningful political changes and may even lead to transitions to democracy (Beaulieu and Hyde 2009; Kelley 2011, 2012), such as the Color Revolutions in Central and Eastern Europe. Thus, in authoritarian societies, citizens prioritizing democracy's intrinsic values are much more likely to take advantage of such high-profile focal-point events (i.e., elections) to demonstrate their adherence to democracy as a way of life when compared to their fellow citizens who emphasize democracy's instrumental values more. Meanwhile, in established democracies, because regular and competitive elections are such a deeply ingrained practice, many people may take electoral participation for granted (or even have established a habitual response) (Aldrich et al. 2011). In addition, procedure-wise, there is limited room for further improvement in electoral politics in democracies.[1] Therefore, given the contrast between the nature and practices of electoral politics under different regime types, the expressive values associated with electoral participation might be much higher in authoritarian societies than in democracies due to the risks, stakes, and passions involved. To test this conjecture, we focused on the interaction between popular understandings of democracy (proxied by the PUD instruments) and societies' political features (proxied by reversed Freedom House ratings): *the influence of people's willingness to trade off key democratic principles for instrumental gains on their participation in electoral politics is conditional upon the features of the surrounding political environment* **(Hypothesis C6.1_2)**.

For our dependent variable (i.e., electoral participation), we relied on the summary index of three survey instruments to (1) maximize the inclusion of societies with varying socioeconomic and political contexts[2] and (2) minimize the influence of measurement errors. The first instrument asked whether respondents voted in the last election. The second instrument asked whether they worked for a certain candidate or party in the last election. The third instrument asked whether they tried to persuade others to vote for a certain candidate or party in the last election.[3] The average of individual responses to the three instruments was adopted as our measure of individuals' electoral participation, which ranges between zero and one. Again, we relied on mixed-effect models for empirical analysis. As in Chapter 5, we dropped respondents with missing values for the PUD instruments from subsequent analyses to focus on the people who know about democracy to some extent.[4]

At the individual level, we accounted for demographic features like age cohorts, gender, and educational attainment, key psychological features like political interest, as well as sociotropic and pocketbook economic evaluations. At the societal level, we included the same set of indicators for pertinent socioeconomic, political, and cultural contextual features at the time of the survey. For socioeconomic contextual features, we included indicators of general economic development (per capita GDP transformed via a logarithm function), economic recession, and recovery from the 2008 financial crisis. For political and cultural contextual characteristics, we included indicators like reversed Freedom House ratings, historically accumulated capital of political rights and civil liberties since 1972, history of single-party regimes and personal dictatorships, and Confucian cultural traditions. For reasons discussed later, we also specified a cross-level interaction between educational attainment and reversed Freedom House rating in the mixed-effect models.

For robustness checks, we ran the same mixed-effect models with popular understandings of democracy operationalized as either a continuous latent construct (i.e., the IRT scores) or nominal latent groups (i.e., the LCA groups). To ease subsequent interpretations, we focused on the mixed-effect models with popular understandings of democracy measured by the IRT scores. Similar findings were established when the LCA groups were used. Figure 6.1 presents the regression coefficients and associated 95% confidence intervals for electoral participation. We adopted the same set of legends used

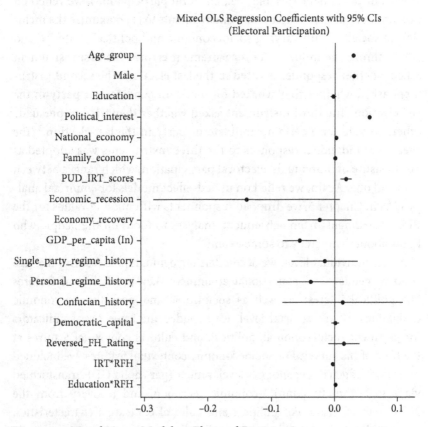

Figure 6.1 Mixed Linear Model on Electoral Participation

in other figures for illustration: black dots stand for regression coefficients, and horizontal segments stand for associated 95% confidence intervals. The vertical line stands for the conventional null hypothesis that the influence under examination is statistically not different from zero.[5]

The general pattern, presented in Figure 6.1, is quite consistent with the conclusions of the existing literature: older males with more interest in politics are significantly more like to participate in electoral politics.[6] Furthermore, on average, citizens of richer societies (i.e., as captured by a higher level of per capita GDP) are significantly less likely to participate in electoral politics, which is also consistent with the well-known low turnout rates in contemporary industrial democracies. What interests us most is how popular democratic conceptions shape electoral participation. Additional analyses reveal that, on average, a larger IRT score of the PUD instruments is associated with a significantly higher propensity to engage in electoral participation.[7] Basically, the lower the willingness to trade off key democratic principles for instrumental gains (i.e., prioritizing democracy's intrinsic values in related conceptions), the more active the engagement in electoral participation (i.e., casting ballots and joining electoral campaigns). This is consistent with Hypothesis C6.1_1.

A more interesting and revealing finding is that the interaction between popular understandings of democracy and a society's reversed Freedom House rating (i.e., a higher rating for a higher level of democracy) is also statistically significant but with a negative regression coefficient. Put otherwise, although, on average, citizens prioritizing democracy's intrinsic values are more likely to participate in electoral politics than their fellow citizens emphasizing democracy's instrumental values, such a difference is much more salient in authoritarian societies and much less so in democracies. At the same time, we also found an interesting and significant positive interaction between citizens' educational attainment and their society's reversed Freedom House rating in shaping their propensity to participate in electoral politics. To enable more straightforward and transparent interpretations of these critical but nuanced findings, we ran a series of simulations on the estimated average marginal impact of democratic conceptions, as well as that of educational attainment, on electoral participation in societies ranked by Freedom House in different ways (ranging from the lowest level of a full autocracy to the highest level of a full democracy). Figure 6.2 summarizes the results of our simulations. Again, the solid lines stand for the main effects and the dotted lines stand for corresponding 95% confidence intervals.

140 UNDERSTANDINGS OF DEMOCRACY

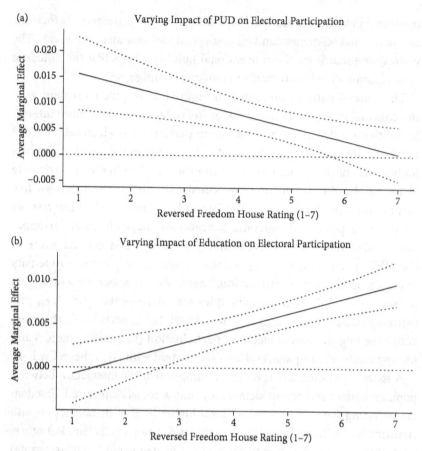

Figure 6.2 Average Marginal Effects of Democratic Conceptions and Education on Electoral Participation

Figure 6.2a shows the varying impact of popular understandings of democracy (measured by the IRT scores of the PUD instruments) on electoral participation in autocracies, hybrid regimes, and democracies. It is quite clear that, in GBS II societies like Sudan, China, Vietnam, Mali, and Zimbabwe (rated by Freedom House at 6 or higher), citizens who are unwilling to trade off key democratic principles for instrumental gains are significantly more likely to participate in electoral politics than their fellow citizens who are much more likely to engage in such trade-offs. Meanwhile, in societies like Malaysia, Burkina Faso, Nigeria, Honduras, and Nepal (rated by Freedom House at 4), citizens prioritizing the intrinsic values of democracy are still significantly more active in electoral participation than their counterparts emphasizing democracy's instrumental values. Nevertheless, the associated impact is substantially weakened by about 50%. Furthermore, in societies like Argentina, Brazil, Japan, South Korea, Ghana, Chile, and Uruguay (rated by Freedom House at 2 or lower), the difference between citizens endorsing distinct democratic conceptions in terms of their participation in electoral politics is no longer statistically significant after taking other factors into consideration. This is highly consistent with Hypothesis C6.1_2.

Figure 6.2b presents similar simulation results on the changing impact of citizens' educational attainment on electoral participation in regimes with varying levels of democratic politics, showing a mirror-image of Figure 6.2a. More specifically, in authoritarian societies, better-educated citizens are less inclined to participate in electoral politics, although the difference is not statistically significant. The impact of education on electoral participation becomes statistically significant, more salient, and positive in hybrid regimes. Such positive impact keeps growing and achieves its maximum in liberal democracies. This dynamic is highly consistent with the existing literature's findings: in autocracies, elections are manipulated by authoritarian leaders for their preferred political goals and agenda. Such rigged elections cannot provide meaningful channels and mechanisms for citizens to shape public policies or hold politicians accountable. Therefore, given their higher level of political sophistication, better-educated citizens are more likely to see through the nature of such rigged elections and less likely to participate in electoral politics in autocracies. In some cases, better-educated citizens in autocracies may even intentionally avoid such elections to demonstrate their resentment against authoritarian leaders' political manipulation and propaganda (Karklins 1986; Shi 1997, 1999; Croke et al. 2016). In democracies, electoral politics provides a key channel for people to shape public policies by choosing their preferred candidates and a meaningful mechanism to hold their politicians accountable by evaluating politicians' performance with their secret ballots. Embedded in such a political context, better-educated people are not only more capable of processing pertinent political information and assessing policy platforms (thanks to their higher level of political sophistication) but also more capable of shaping public policies in their favor (given their better access to resources). Thus, they are more willing and much more likely to participate in electoral politics (Verba et al. 1978; Erikson 2015; Sondheimer and Green 2010; Leighley and Nagler 2014; Tenn 2007). In democracies, better-educated citizens' more active participation in electoral politics also enables them to shape public policies more effectively by having their preferences and concerns much better embodied in such policies (Verba and Orren 1985; Gilens 2005, 2012).

This crystal-clear contrast illustrated in Figure 6.2 regarding the varying impact of democratic conceptions versus education resonates with our earlier discussions on the dynamics of expressive considerations in electoral participation. As a widely acknowledged proxy for political sophistication, education's performance in our models (as summarized in Figures 6.1 and 6.2) is highly consistent with instrumental calculations for participation in electoral politics (Verba et al. 1978; Erikson 2015; Sondheimer and Green 2010; Leighley and Nagler 2014; Tenn 2007). Having accounted for the dynamics of instrumental calculations in our models, we have more confidence in arguing that the varying impact of popular understandings of democracy (proxied by the PUD instruments) might have effectively captured the dynamics of expressive considerations for participation in electoral politics. More specifically, for those who deeply appreciate democracy's intrinsic values, taking advantage of elections as high-profile focal-point events to demonstrate their adherence to key democratic principles in an authoritarian setting (e.g., casting ballots against the incumbents or for write-in candidates, campaigning against incumbents, etc.) offers much more in terms of expressive values than engaging in similar participatory activities in a democracy, given the challenges, risks, stakes, and passions involved.

These findings further demonstrate the GBS II data's validity in measuring participation in electoral politics, as well as its sensitivity to the varying dynamics of electoral politics under different political regimes. It should be fair to argue that our findings regarding the role of popular willingness to trade off key democratic principles for instrumental gains in shaping electoral participation are unlikely to be completely driven by measurement errors or some idiosyncratic factors. Therefore, such findings enable us to establish the substantive impact of popular democratic conceptions on electoral participation, which varies in interesting ways depending on the features of the surrounding political environment. Nevertheless, political participation is more than just voting and attending rallies. For students of political participation, electoral participation is just a small domain of the whole universe of participatory activities and may not even be the domain of most interest and significance, especially in non-democratic settings. For a more systematic examination of how popular understandings of democracy may affect political participation, we scrutinize other participatory activities in subsequent sections.

6.2 Varying understandings of democracy and conventional participation

Although electoral politics plays a key role in political participation, especially for democratic politics, people are only able to cast their ballots, join rallies, or campaign for their preferred politicians every few years (depending on the electoral cycles of their societies). Between elections, people also engage in numerous participatory activities to promote their interests and address their concerns (Verba et al. 1971). According to the pioneering work of Barnes and Kasse (1979), political participation can be broadly categorized as conventional and unconventional participatory activities. The former refers to all modes of participation embedded in established legal institutional frameworks, including voting, contacting politicians, or attending hearings. The latter refers to all modes of participation not embedded in established legal institutional frameworks such as petitioning, demonstrating, striking, or boycotting. Our earlier discussions focused exclusively on electoral participation, given its central role in democratic politics and its high salience for how people conceptualize democracy. In this section, we focus on other modes of conventional participation, primarily contacting various political and government representatives or agencies.

There are several reasons why we decided to focus on contacting as the proxy for conventional political participation. First, aside from electoral participation, this is the most widely used channel of conventional political participation in both democracies and non-democracies (Verba et al. 1971; Shi 1997; Hough 1976; Tsai and Xu 2018). Thus, focusing on political contacting enables us to engage in a richer comparative and contextual analysis of similar participatory activities initiated under varying political contexts. Second, unlike electoral participation, which is attached to high-profile focal-point events (e.g., national or local elections) that usually involve a large number of citizens, citizens mostly engage in political contacting individually for their own concerns and issues. While expressive considerations are highly salient for electoral participation, the instrumental concerns of political contacting are highly salient among and widely appreciated by ordinary citizens. Therefore, focusing on political contacting offers a distinct scenario for testing the impact of popular conceptions of democracy on political participation. Third, empirically, political contacting is the most widely asked question on political participation in the GBS II survey. Thus, focusing on political contacting helps us maximize the power of statistical inference by including the largest number of GBS II societies in the analysis.

Unlike in our earlier discussions on the relationship between popular conceptions of democracy and electoral participation, we cannot unequivocally specify how varying understandings of democracy may shape people's political contacting, given the strong instrumental incentives involved. In democracies, contacting legislative representatives or government bureaucrats is built into representative institutions and is generally perceived as a legitimate and effective (at least to some extent) means of political participation. Meanwhile, in contrast to the previous conventional wisdom on the lack of meaningful institutionalization of political representativeness and responsiveness in authoritarian societies, recent research suggests a different picture of political participation in non-democracies. Citizens in authoritarian societies may still take advantage of their informal networks (Tsai and Xu 2018; Shi 1997) and even some institutional opportunities to effectively voice their concerns and address their needs via political contacting. (Distelhorst and Hou 2017; Chen et al. 2016; Truex 2016; Manion 2016; Pepinsky 2013). Thus, given the inherent incentives to contact political and government agents or agencies to address specific personal needs and concerns, as well as the accessibility of effective channels for such participation in both democracies and authoritarian regimes, we may not expect substantial differences between people embracing distinct understandings of democracy (by prioritizing its intrinsic or instrumental values) in this regard. To test this conjecture, we relied on the PUD instruments: *on average, there is no significant difference between people with varying willingness to trade off key democratic principles for instrumental gains regarding their engagement in political contacting (Hypothesis C6.2_1).*

Despite the dominance of instrumental concerns in driving conventional participatory activities like political contacting, it may still be reasonable to expect that the expressive considerations associated with such activities may offer extra rewards for engaging in institutionalized participation. Theoretically, this should be of particular salience for people who prioritize democracy's intrinsic values embodied in its core institutions, procedures, principles, and norms. Consistent with this reasoning, recent studies have found that democratic ideals and values have a noticeable impact on institutionalized participation (e.g., political contacting) in European democracies, and the level of institutionalized participation is significantly higher among Europeans who place particular emphasis on classic political rights when they conceptualize democracy (Oser and Hooghe 2018; Bakule Forthcoming).[8] Following this line of reasoning, it might be further argued that such extra rewards based on expressive considerations might be more substantial in authoritarian societies, given that participatory activities like political contacting may offer opportunities to challenge the political boundaries set by authoritarian leaders and might even push for further political opening and reform. To examine this conjecture, we relied on the interaction between popular understandings of democracy (proxied by the PUD instruments) and societies' political features (proxied by reversed Freedom House ratings): *people who are less willing to trade off key democratic principles for instrumental gains are more likely to engage in political contacting; however, the influence of such willingness is conditional upon the features of the surrounding political environment* **(Hypothesis C6.2_2)**.

To measure political contacting, we adopted three instruments administered in all seventy-one GBS II societies. All respondents were asked whether they "have never, once, or more than once done the following because of personal, family, or neighborhood problems, or problems with government officials and policies in the past three years": (1) contacting elected officials or legislative representatives at any level, (2) contacting government officials at a higher level, or (3) contacting officials of political parties or other political organizations.[9] The average of individual responses to the three instruments was adopted as our measure of political contacting, which ranges between zero and one. In addition to our key explanatory variable (i.e., popular understandings of democracy measured by the PUD instruments), we included the same set of controls for both individual and societal features that were used for the earlier analysis on electoral participation. To enable meaningful and effective comparisons of the dynamics between different modes of political participation, we also included the same cross-level interaction between individuals' educational attainment and a society's reversed Freedom House rating.

For robustness checks, we ran the same mixed-effect models with popular understandings of democracy operationalized as either a continuous latent construct (i.e., the IRT scores) or nominal latent groups (i.e., the LCA groups). To ease subsequent interpretations, we focused on the mixed-effect models with popular understandings of democracy measured by the IRT scores. Similar findings were established when the LCA groups were used. Figure 6.3 summarizes the mixed-effect regression results, using the same legends for regression coefficients and associated 95% confidence intervals.[10] Quite similar to the findings reported in Figure 6.1 on the correlates of electoral participation, older males with a higher level of political interest are significantly more likely to contact political and government agents or agencies for their needs and concerns. Unlike the socioeconomic and political dynamics shaping electoral participation (as illustrated in Figure 6.1), a society's general level of development (proxied by per capita GDP) plays little role in shaping how its citizens

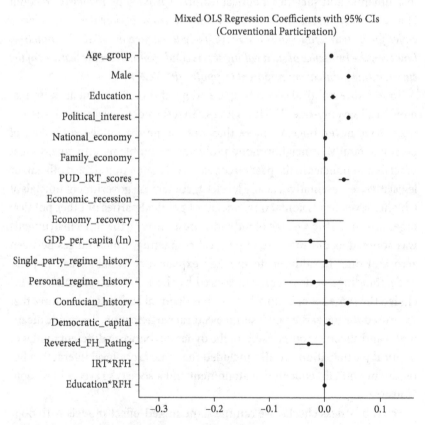

Figure 6.3 Mixed Linear Model on Political Contacting

engage in political contacting. However, citizens in societies witnessing economic recession are, on average, much less inclined to engage in political contacting.[11] At the same time, citizens living in societies with a richer tradition of democratic politics (measured by more accumulated capital of political rights and civil liberties since 1972) are, on average, significantly more active in contacting their political and government agents or agencies to fulfill their needs and address their concerns. It seems that the higher initiatives required by political contacting are more likely to be activated and sustained by the richer tradition of democratic politics. Although there is little data here for further investigation, related political socialization might have played some key role in this regard.

More interestingly, the extra rewards of expressive values associated with political contacting seem to have generated a significantly higher propensity among the people prioritizing democracy's intrinsic values for political contacting, as indicated by the positive and significant regression coefficient of the IRT scores of the PUD instruments. Additional analyses reveal that, on average, a larger IRT score is associated with a significantly higher propensity of engaging in political contacting.[12] Basically, the lower the willingness to trade off key democratic principles for instrumental gains (i.e., prioritizing democracy's intrinsic values in related conceptions) the more active the engagement in political contacting (i.e., contacting representatives, elected officials, government agents, etc.). It seems that, besides shared instrumental concerns, citizens who deeply appreciate key democratic principles, institutions, and norms are more likely to enjoy the rewards of expressive values associated with political contacting (as compared to their fellow citizens who are more willing to trade off key democratic principles for instrumental gains), thus demonstrating a higher propensity to contact political and government agents or agencies. This is inconsistent with Hypothesis C6.2_1 but compatible with Hypothesis C6.2_2.

Furthermore, consistent with our theoretical expectation, such extra rewards from expressive values seem to be far more substantial in authoritarian societies, as suggested by the statistically significant and negative interaction between the IRT scores and a society's reversed Freedom House rating. Meanwhile, the interaction between citizens' educational attainment and a society's reversed Freedom House rating is not statistically significant. Basically, better-educated citizens are generally equally more inclined to contact their political and government agents or agencies to advocate for their needs and concerns regardless of the surrounding political context.[13] This finding is different from the growing positive impact of educational attainment on electoral participation as we move from full autocracies to full democracies (as reported in Figure 6.1). Again, we ran a series of simulations on how a society's political context (assessed by Freedom House ratings) moderates the respective influence of popular understandings of democracy and educational attainment on political contacting for more straightforward and transparent interpretations of the interactions.

Figure 6.4a shows the shifting influence of varying democratic conceptions on citizens' propensity to engage in political contacting in different regimes.

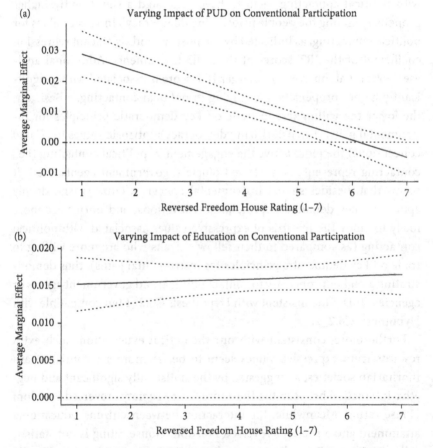

Figure 6.4 Average Marginal Effects of Democratic Conceptions and Education on Political Contacting

POLITICAL PARTICIPATION 149

Very similar to the findings on electoral participation presented in Figure 6.3a, people who are less willing to trade off key democratic principles for instrumental gains are significantly more inclined to contact their political and government agents or agencies to advocate for their needs and concerns in societies that Freedom House has rated as unfree. In hybrid regimes, while these citizens still significantly outperform their counterparts emphasizing democracy's instrumental values by engaging in political contacting more actively, the advantage is substantially weakened by more than 60%. In free societies (as rated by Freedom House), the difference shrinks further and is no longer statistically significant. This finding is consistent with Hypothesis C6.2_2.

The question remains: is the finding in Figure 6.4a mainly driven by the extra rewards of expressive values associated with political contacting rather than by any additional instrumental concerns, as we argued earlier? The findings presented in Figure 6.4b provide additional clues and evidence in this regard. As our previous discussion emphasized, educational attainment has been widely acknowledged as a critical and valid proxy for political sophistication, awareness, skills, and related resources. Thus, incorporating education as a key control variable can effectively account for pertinent instrumental calculations in political contacting. As shown in Figure 6.4b, the positive and significant impact of educational attainment on citizens' inclination to engage in political contacting is highly consistent between societies with varying political regimes. Put otherwise, better-educated people are equally more likely to contact their political and government agents or agencies to advocate for their needs and concerns, regardless of whether they live in democracies or autocracies. It is reasonable to argue that this consistent positive influence of education is primarily shaped by underlying instrumental concerns that drive political contacting (Schlozman et al. 2010; Burns et al. 2001; Verba et al. 1995). Given our model specification, the impact of democratic conceptions on political contacting (i.e., reported in Figure 6.4a) was estimated after accounting for citizens' educational attainment and other related features (e.g., age, gender, and political interest). Therefore, we have high confidence in arguing that the varying impact of democratic conceptions on political contacting is primarily driven by the extra rewards of expressive values associated with engaging in these participatory activities. In addition, as the expressive values are more salient, significant, and rewarding in non-democracies, people prioritizing democracy's intrinsic values (and therefore less willing to trade off key democratic principles for instrumental gains and also more sensitive to such expressive values) are likely to outperform their fellow citizens who emphasize democracy's instrumental values by contacting political and government agents or agencies more actively in authoritarian settings.

Will we observe similar dynamics when examining more resource and initiative-demanding participatory activities, like marching in a demonstration or protest, or more radical ways of participation associated with political violence? What role will popular understandings of democracy play in such participatory activities outside of established legal institutional frameworks?

6.3 Varying understandings of democracy and unconventional participation

Electoral participation and political contacting are meaningful and critical participatory activities in both democracies and authoritarian regimes. While the former serves both expressive and instrumental values, the latter has more instrumental significance for ordinary citizens. In most cases, people engage in electoral participation and political contacting by themselves and primarily to address their individual (expressive or instrumental) needs and concerns. Meanwhile, people may also join a large number of their fellow citizens in petitions, demonstrations, protests, or even radical actions to advocate for collective needs and goods. The "Me Too" movement against sexual harassment and assault, the NIMBY (i.e., Not-In-My-Back-Yard) movement against unwanted local development projects, and the anti-government protests, uprisings, and armed rebellions that contributed to the Color Revolutions in Central and Eastern Europe and the Arab Spring in the Middle East all are recent, well-known examples of such participatory activities. Although the frequencies of such collective, large-scale, and even radical participatory activities are relatively low (as compared to electoral participation and political contacting), people's involvement in such unconventional political participation plays a critical role in our understanding of major political changes in general and regime transitions (including democratic transition, consolidation, or deconsolidation) in particular.

Compared to electoral participation and political contacting, unconventional political participation is much more demanding in terms of resource mobilization and overcoming the thorny issue of collective action (Olson 1971; Hardin 1995; Lichbach 1995). It has been widely acknowledged that, given the collective nature of such participatory activities, people may strategically choose not to get involved to minimize their risks and costs, while still enjoying the collective benefits (e.g., improved living conditions, more equal and fair treatment of minorities, or a freer society) once other people's collective efforts and sacrifices pay off. It is no wonder that existing research on social movements, political violence, and revolutions pays more attention to structural, institutional, and communal features than to individual dynamics (McAdam et al. 2001; Tilly 2008; McAdam et al. 1996; Goodwin 2001). Here, we are not trying to examine and offer better explanations for contentious politics per se; instead, we are interested in understanding the role that varying democratic conceptions might play in shaping individuals' propensity to engage in such unconventional participatory activities.

Similar to previous discussions on electoral participation and political contacting, the expressive values associated with unconventional political participation are central to understanding the influence of democratic conceptions. On average, people prioritizing democracy's intrinsic values are expected to be more sensitive and attracted to the expressive values associated with joining petitions, demonstration, protests, or rebellions, as long as such unconventional and even radical participatory activities are consistent with their adherence to democracy's key principles, institutions, and norms. It is noteworthy that such participatory activities are recognized as unconventional exactly because of their challenges to and possible conflicts with a society's established legal institutional frameworks (Barnes and Kasse 1979). Thus, the extent to which the associated expressive values are consistent with popular adherence to democracy's key principles, institutions, and norms is conditional upon the nature of the surrounding political context.

Much like elections in authoritarian societies, petitions, demonstrations, and protests also serve as focal-point events with high salience that may allow people to collectively challenge the boundaries set by authoritarian leaders in a more direct and forceful way. Different from electoral participation, unconventional political participation in authoritarian regimes features large-scale mobilization and coordination, which may enable people to experience more psychological satisfaction by standing with fellow citizens to fight for shared goals, such as a better life in a freer society. Embedded in such an authoritarian context, people who deeply appreciate democracy as a way of life and prioritize its intrinsic values are expected to significantly outperform their counterparts who emphasize democracy's instrumental values by engaging in unconventional political participation more actively. As the political context becomes less authoritarian and more democratic, the difference in citizens' propensity to engage in unconventional participatory activities (as driven by their distinct willingness to trade off key democratic principles for instrumental gains) is expected to shrink accordingly.

It is also likely that, in a fully free society, people who prioritize democracy's intrinsic values might be much less likely to join petitions, demonstrations, protests, or rebellions, exactly because of their deep appreciation of the significance and value of democratic institutions and procedures. For these citizens, it may be preferable to address issues and solve problems through established institutional channels and procedures, rather than resorting to street politics. Conversely, their counterparts who are more willing to trade off key democratic principles for instrumental gains might have much fewer concerns about circumventing or challenging established democratic institutions and procedures and will therefore be more likely to engage in unconventional political participation. In a nutshell, a significant interaction between popular understandings of democracy (proxied by the PUD instruments) and regime features (proxied by reversed Freedom House ratings) in shaping how people engage in unconventional participatory activities is expected: *in autocracies, people who are less willing to trade off key democratic principles for instrumental gains are more likely to engage in political contacting; in democracies, the influence of such willingness is weakened or might even be reversed (**Hypothesis C6.3_1**).*

There are two instruments in the GBS II survey tapping unconventional political participation. Respondents were asked whether they "have never, once, or more than once done any of the following things during the past three years": (1) attending a demonstration or protest march; and (2) using force or violence for a political cause.[14] Again, the average of individual responses to the two instruments was adopted as our measure of unconventional political participation, which ranges between zero and one. Besides our key explanatory variable (i.e., popular understandings of democracy measured by the PUD instruments), we again included the same set of controls for both individual and societal features incorporated in our earlier analysis on electoral participation and political contacting. For meaningful and effective comparisons of the dynamics between different modes of political participation, the same cross-level interaction between a society's reversed Freedom House rating and respondents' educational attainment was specified in the mixed-effect regressions. Again, for robustness checks, we ran the same mixed-effect models with popular understandings of democracy operationalized as either a continuous latent construct (i.e., the IRT scores) or nominal latent groups (i.e., the LCA groups). To ease subsequent interpretations, we focused on the mixed-effect models with popular understandings of democracy measured by the IRT scores.

Figure 6.5 summarizes the mixed-effect regression results using the same legends for regression coefficients and associated 95% confidence intervals.[15] Different from the findings reported in Figures 6.1 and 6.3, younger males (rather than older ones) showing more interest in politics are significantly more likely to join a demonstration, march in a protest, or engage in political violence. It seems that getting old may equip people with more resources

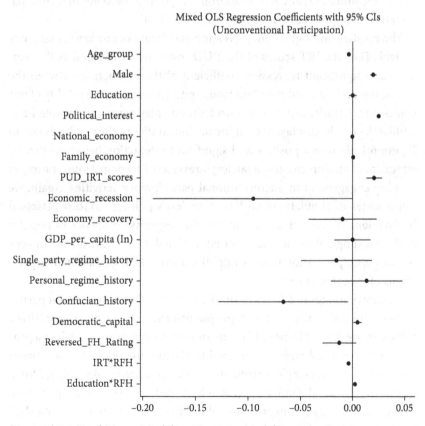

Figure 6.5 Mixed Linear Model on Unconventional Participation

(including material, relational, and cognitive resources) for more effective electoral participation and political contacting; however, aging may also deprive people of the necessary passion for engaging in more radical activities. Consequently, compared to their older cohorts, the youth with sufficient interest in politics are more attracted to unconventional participatory activities. A society's richer democratic tradition (measured by more accumulated capital of political rights and civil liberties since 1972) also significantly enhances its citizens' average propensity to engage in unconventional participation. This might be related to democracies' higher tolerance of such unconventional and even radical participatory activities, as well as the influence of political socialization. Meanwhile, citizens of Confucian societies, on average, are much less inclined to engage in unconventional political participation. This finding is consistent with existing scholarship's conclusion on the salience of the norm of conflict avoidance in Confucian political culture (Shi 2015; Shin 2012) and its implications for political behavior in Confucian societies (Ulbig and Funk 1999; Kung and Ma 2014).

The positive and significant regression coefficient of our key explanatory variable (i.e., the IRT scores of the PUD instruments), as well as the negative and significant regression coefficient of the interaction between the IRT scores and reversed Freedom House ratings, suggests the validity of our conjecture. Clearly, expressive considerations play some crucial role here. Unlike the results displayed in Figure 6.3 but similar to the results shown in Figure 6.1, there is a positive and significant interaction between citizens' educational attainment and a society's reversed Freedom House rating in shaping engagement in unconventional participatory activities. Again, we ran a series of simulations on how a society's political context (assessed by Freedom House ratings) moderates the respective influence of popular understandings of democracy and educational attainment on unconventional participation for more straightforward and transparent interpretations of the interactions.

As shown in Figure 6.6a, very similar to our findings on electoral participation and political contacting, people prioritizing democracy's intrinsic values are significantly more likely to join a demonstration, march in a protest, or use political violence for a political cause than their fellow citizens emphasizing democracy's instrumental values in countries like Sudan, China, Vietnam, Mali, and Zimbabwe (rated by Freedom House at 6 or higher). The same disparity in unconventional political participation is established in other authoritarian or hybrid regimes (rated by Freedom House between

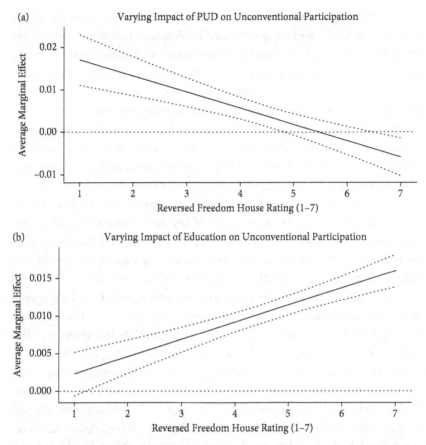

Figure 6.6 Average Marginal Effects of Democratic Conceptions and Education on Unconventional Participation

4 and 5); nevertheless, the corresponding gap shrinks. For instance, in countries like Malaysia, Burkina Faso, Nigeria, Honduras, and Nepal, the impact of popular understandings of democracy on unconventional political participation is weakened by about 65%. Furthermore, this disparity disappears in societies witnessing better democratic practices (rated by Freedom House between 2 and 3) like the Philippines, Bolivia, Mexico, Indonesia, Sierra Leone, India, Mongolia, Namibia, Argentina, and Brazil. In these societies, there is no longer any meaningful difference between people holding varying willingness to trade off democratic principles for instrumental gains regarding their engagement in unconventional political participation.

Finally, in free societies like Japan, South Korea, Taiwan, Ghana, Mauritius, Cape Verde, Chile, and Uruguay (rated by Freedom House at 1.5 or 1), the impact of varying democratic conceptions becomes negative and statistically significant. Citizens prioritizing democracy's intrinsic values are actually much less likely to join a demonstration, march in a protest, or use violence for a political cause. Their fellow citizens emphasizing democracy's instrumental values are significantly more likely to engage in such unconventional participatory activities. It seems that, in established democracies, citizens' adherence to core democratic principles, institutions, and procedures may discourage them from engaging in participatory activities that circumvent or even challenge established institutions and procedures. Meanwhile, citizens with greater willingness to trade off key democratic principles for instrumental gains may be less constrained by such concerns and may even be empowered to engage in such unconventional participatory activities. Recent examples of street politics and political violence that have challenged core institutions (i.e., blocking legislatures) and norms (i.e., hate speech and white supremacy) in established democracies such as the United States, United Kingdom, France, and Taiwan all substantiate the validity of this finding. And this is highly consistent with Hypothesis C6.3_1.

Figure 6.6b presents the changing impact of educational attainment on unconventional political participation in societies with distinct regime features. This is almost a mirror image of Figure 6.6a. Furthermore, the pattern in Figure 6.6b is very similar to that in Figure 6.2b (i.e., the average marginal impact of education on electoral participation) but highly different from that in Figure 6.4b (i.e., the average marginal impact of education on political contacting). As discussed earlier, we are inclined to argue the impact of educational attainment on unconventional political participation is primarily driven by people's instrumental calculations of the associated costs and benefits. Better-educated people clearly have access to more resources that enable effective unconventional political participation. However, their enhanced political sophistication also makes them more informed of the potential risks and costs associated with such participatory activities. Therefore, in authoritarian regimes like Sudan, the lurking threat of political oppression and the authoritarian leaders' determination to use violence against dissidents or potential challengers might deter most people from joining a demonstration or marching in a protest. As shown in Figure 6.6b, under such a political environment, better-educated people are no different from their less-educated fellow citizens in staying away from street politics. Not surprisingly, in this scenario, the impact of educational attainment is not statistically different from zero.

As a society gradually moves away from the tightened control of authoritarian leaders by providing more room and opportunities for people to voice their concerns and preferences, better-educated people's access to more resources may enable them to effectively overcome or compensate for the costs and risks of engaging in unconventional participatory activities. Thanks to the reduced political risks and costs associated with such participatory activities, better-educated people's enhanced political sophistication may also help them better understand and appreciate the potential benefits associated with such participatory activities. Therefore, given the less constraining political context, better-educated people might more actively engage in unconventional political participation. Finally, in free societies, the risk and costs of unconventional political participation are significantly reduced or almost eliminated in many cases (especially for activities like signing petitions, joining demonstrations, or marching in protests). Under this free political environment and thanks to their higher political sophistication and access to more resources, *ceteris paribus*, better-educated people are significantly more likely to join a demonstration, march in a protest, or (in very rare cases) use violence for a political cause to voice their concerns and demand change. As illustrated in Figure 6.6b, when we move from an authoritarian country like Zimbabwe (rated by Freedom House at 6) to a liberal democracy like Chile (rated by Freedom House at 1), the impact of educational attainment on people's propensity to join a demonstration, march in a protest, or use violence for a political cause is boosted by about three times.

Overall, the contrast between educational attainment's increasing impact on people's engagement in unconventional political participation in freer societies (shown in Figure 6.6b) and the decreasing and even reversed influence of democratic conceptions on unconventional participatory activities in freer societies (displayed in Figure 6.6a) confirms the validity of our earlier differentiation between the instrumental and expressive values associated with various modes of political participation. Therefore, it is reasonable to argue that incorporating educational attainment in our models has effectively captured the dynamics of instrumental calculations in unconventional participation, while including popular willingness to trade off key democratic principles for instrumental gains enables us to establish and focus on the dynamics of expressive considerations.

6.4 Conclusion

In Chapter 5, we demonstrated how varying understandings of democracy have shaped people's assessment of democratic practices in their home societies and foreign countries. Given their distinct baselines for evaluations, people who conceptualize democracy in different ways offer varying assessments of democratic practices in the United States, China, and their home societies. Although such attitude-to-attitude connections are of great value for comparative research on public opinion, there might still be questions about the value-added of democratic conceptions as a key explanatory variable for understanding contemporary politics (given the proximity between two attitudes and the challenge of omitted variables). In this chapter, we focused on the implications of democratic conceptions for political behavior, that is, the attitude-to-behavior connections with longer causal distance and space between our key explanatory variable and outcome variables. Following best practices in political behavior research, we examined both conventional and unconventional political participation. Furthermore, given the salience and indispensability of electoral politics for democracies, as well as the adoption of manipulated or rigged elections in many autocracies and hybrid regimes, we also examined electoral participation separately from political contacting (although both are conceptualized as critical components of conventional political participation).

Overall, we have found that, compared to their fellow citizens who emphasize the instrumental values of democracy in delivering good governance, people who prioritize democracy's intrinsic values in ensuring individual dignity and basic rights and liberties through appropriate institutions and procedures are significantly more likely to engage in a range of conventional and unconventional participatory activities for political purposes. Citizens who prioritize democracy's intrinsic values are more likely to cast ballots, help with electoral campaigns, contact political and government agents or agencies, join a demonstration, march in a protest, or use violence for a political cause. Furthermore, the influence of popular willingness to trade off key democratic principles for instrumental gains on political participation varies significantly between societies with distinct political environments.

More specifically, in authoritarian societies, citizens' low willingness to trade off key democratic principles for instrumental gains drives them to more actively engage in electoral participation, political contacting, and unconventional political participation. In societies with improved democratic practices, the difference between citizens holding distinct conceptions of democracy regarding their propensities to engage in various conventional and unconventional participatory activities shrinks. In free societies, the difference between citizens prioritizing democracy's intrinsic versus instrumental values in terms of their engagement in electoral participation and political contacting becomes negligible and no longer statistically significant. Furthermore, in full democracies, citizens orientated toward democracy's intrinsic values are significantly less likely to engage in unconventional political participation like joining a demonstration, marching in a protest, or using violence for a political cause when compared to their fellow citizens who emphasize democracy's instrumental values.

These findings clearly show that challenging the boundaries set by authoritarian politicians and pushing for political change by engaging in various participatory activities (especially the unconventional ones) provide significant extra expressive rewards for people who prioritize democracy's intrinsic values embodied in democratic institutions, procedures, and norms. The lower the willingness to trade off key democratic principles for instrumental gains, the more active the engagement in such participatory activities. In a full democracy, exactly because of their appreciation of democracy's intrinsic values and their adherence to established democratic institutions, procedures, and norms, these citizens are more inclined to address their issues and concerns within the free society's established institutions and procedures rather than by resorting to street politics or political violence. This is highly consistent with the varying salience of expressive values associated with different modes of political participation in societies with distinct regime features. In summary, people conceptualizing democracy in distinct ways respond to the expressive values associated with various participatory activities differently depending on the features of the surrounding political environment.

Meanwhile, the influence of educational attainment varies between distinct political regimes when electoral participation and unconventional participation are under examination. Nevertheless, when political contacting is under examination, the impact of educational attainment is quite consistent between societies. More specifically, in authoritarian societies, better-educated people's enhanced political sophistication enables them to more effectively see through the flaws and hypocritical nature of manipulated electoral politics and to more rationally assess the risks and costs of joining demonstrations, protests, or civil disobedience (given the lurking threat of political oppression). Therefore, they are much less likely to channel their resources (material resources, relationships, networks, etc.) into such participatory activities. However, in societies with improved democratic practices, better-educated people's similar instrumental assessment and calculations may tilt their decisions toward more active engagement in such participatory activities. Therefore, they participate more actively in electoral politics, demonstrations, protests, or even civil disobedience thanks to their access to more resources and greater political sophistication. The dynamics are different for political contacting, which is mainly driven by personal instrumental concerns and needs and is legitimate and low risk in both democracies and autocracies. In this regard, better-educated people consistently and significantly outperform their less-educated fellow citizens by engaging in political contacting more actively. Since we have consistently accounted for the impact of educational attainment (which is mainly driven by the associated dynamics of instrumental concerns) in our models of political participation, we have more confidence in the effectiveness of identifying the associated dynamics of expressive considerations by incorporating popular understandings of democracy (proxied by the PUD instruments) in our theoretical and empirical analysis.

Our findings have critical implications for the literature on comparative public opinion and political behavior. For the former, our findings not only establish the salience of different democratic conceptions for related research but also substantiate the theoretical value of popular understandings of democracy. Popular understandings of democracy do more than just shape citizens' assessment of democratic practices; such understandings have concrete implications for how people may engage in various modes of political participation under distinct political environments. This attitude-to-behavior connection enables us to better understand why and how people engage in politics in meaningful ways and certainly merits more systematic research in the future.

For the latter, our findings establish citizens' varying sensitivity to the expressive values associated with different modes of political participation. For us, the key lies in how people conceptualize democracy, that is, the varying priorities assigned to democracy's intrinsic versus instrumental values. Existing scholarship on political participation has acknowledged the salience of expressive considerations for understanding political behavior.

However, the literature has not been very successful in identifying specific factors that merit and enable systematic comparative research. Our findings suggest that popular understandings of democracy might be a critical factor that has not received sufficient attention from the scholarship. Furthermore, examining how democratic conceptions may interact with surrounding political contexts in shaping citizens' engagement in various modes of political participation might shed more light on the micro-behavioral foundations of macro-political changes like democratic transition, consolidation, crisis, and deconsolidation.

Appendix

Table A6.1 Mixed-Effect Linear Models on Electoral Participation

	M1 Mixed OLS	M2 Mixed OLS	M3 Mixed OLS	M4 Mixed OLS	M5 Mixed OLS
Fixed effects					
Age_group	0.029 (0.001)	0.029 (0.001)		0.029 (0.001)	0.029 (0.001)
Polynomial (Age, 2)_1			13.21 (0.289)		
Polynomial (Age, 2)_2			−11.63 (0.274)		
Male	0.030 (0.002)	0.030 (0.002)	0.031 (0.002)	0.031 (0.002)	0.031 (0.002)
Education	−0.002 (0.002)	0.006 (0.001)	0.0003 (0.002)	0.005 (0.001)	−0.002 (0.002)
Political_interest	0.055 (0.001)	0.055 (0.001)	0.054 (0.001)	0.055 (0.001)	0.055 (0.001)
National_economy	0.002 (0.001)	0.002 (0.001)	0.003 (0.001)	0.003 (0.001)	0.003 (0.001)
Family_economy	0.001 (0.001)	0.001 (0.001)	0.003 (0.001)	0.001 (0.001)	0.001 (0.001)
PUD_IRT_scores	0.018 (0.004)	0.007 (0.001)	0.016 (0.004)		
PUD_LCA_Principle_holders				0.005 (0.002)	0.013 (0.007)
PUD_LCA_Fence_sitters				0.006 (0.002)	0.012 (0.007)
Economic_recession	−0.139 (0.075)	−0.134 (0.075)	−0.130 (0.075)	−0.136 (0.075)	−0.140 (0.075)
Economic_recovery	−0.024 (0.026)	−0.024 (0.026)	−0.024 (0.026)	−0.024 (0.026)	−0.024 (0.026)
GDP_per_capita (ln)	−0.055 (0.013)	−0.056 (0.013)	−0.055 (0.013)	−0.056 (0.013)	−0.055 (0.013)
Single_party_regime_history	−0.016 (0.027)	−0.015 (0.027)	−0.016 (0.027)	−0.015 (0.027)	−0.015 (0.027)
Personal_regime_history	−0.038 (0.027)	−0.037 (0.027)	−0.039 (0.027)	−0.036 (0.027)	−0.037 (0.027)
Confucian_history	0.013 (0.049)	0.014 (0.049)	0.010 (0.048)	0.011 (0.049)	0.010 (0.049)

Democratic_capital	0.001 (0.003)	0.001 (0.003)	0.001 (0.003)	0.001 (0.003)	0.001 (0.003)
Reversed_FH_rating	0.015 (0.013)	0.020 (0.013)	0.018 (0.013)	0.020 (0.013)	**0.016 (0.013)**
IRT*RFH	**−0.003 (0.0009)**		**−0.002 (0.0009)**		
LCA_PH*RFH					−0.002 (0.002)
LCA_FS*RFH					−0.001 (0.001)
Education*RFH	**0.002 (0.0004)**		**0.001 (0.0004)**		**0.002 (0.0004)**
Intercept	0.517 (0.111)	0.497 (0.110)	0.588 (0.110)	0.491 (0.110)	0.506 (0.111)
Random effects (variance)					
Intercept	0.009	0.009	0.009	0.009	0.009
Residual	0.067	0.067	0.066	0.068	0.068
# of societies	71	71	71	71	71
# of observations	93,258	93,258	93,258	88,878	88,878

Source: Global Barometer Surveys II (*N* = 104,248).

Notes:

Robust standard errors in parentheses.

Statistically significant coefficients are bolded (at the 0.05 level).

Table A6.2 Mixed-Effect Linear Models on Conventional Participation

	M1 Mixed OLS	M2 Mixed OLS	M3 Mixed OLS	M4 Mixed OLS	M5 Mixed OLS
Fixed effects					
Age_group	0.012 (0.001)	0.012 (0.001)		0.012 (0.001)	0.012 (0.001)
Polynomial (Age, 2)_1			5.532 (0.307)		
Polynomial (Age, 2)_2			−4.398 (0.291)		
Male	0.043 (0.002)	0.043 (0.002)	0.043 (0.002)	0.044 (0.002)	0.043 (0.002)
Education	0.015 (0.002)	0.016 (0.001)	0.016 (0.002)	0.016 (0.001)	0.016 (0.002)
Political_interest	0.043 (0.001)	0.043 (0.001)	0.042 (0.0009)	0.043 (0.001)	0.043 (0.001)
National_economy	0.001 (0.001)	0.001 (0.001)	0.001 (0.001)	0.001 (0.001)	0.001 (0.001)
Family_economy	0.002 (0.001)	0.002 (0.001)	0.003 (0.001)	0.001 (0.001)	0.001 (0.001)
PUD_IRT_scores	0.034 (0.005)	0.009 (0.001)	0.034 (0.005)		
PUD_LCA_Principle_holders				0.007 (0.002)	0.036 (0.008)
PUD_LCA_Fence_sitters				0.010 (0.002)	0.027 (0.007)
Economic_recession	−0.165 (0.076)	−0.164 (0.075)	−0.162 (0.075)	−0.166 (0.076)	−0.166 (0.076)
Economic_recovery	−0.017 (0.026)	−0.017 (0.026)	−0.017 (0.026)	−0.017 (0.026)	−0.017 (0.026)
GDP_per_capita (ln)	−0.003 (0.014)	−0.026 (0.014)	−0.025 (0.014)	−0.026 (0.014)	−0.026 (0.014)
Single_party_regime_history	0.003 (0.027)	0.003 (0.027)	0.002 (0.027)	0.003 (0.027)	0.002 (0.002)
Personal_regime_history	−0.019 (0.027)	−0.019 (0.027)	−0.020 (.0027)	−0.019 (0.027)	−0.019 (0.027)
Confucian_history	0.041 (0.049)	0.042 (0.049)	0.040 (0.049)	0.040 (0.049)	0.039 (0.049)
Democratic_capital	0.008 (0.003)	0.008 (0.003)	0.008 (0.003)	0.008 (0.003)	0.008 (0.003)
Reversed_FH_rating	−0.029 (0.013)	−0.028 (0.013)	−0.028 (0.013)	−0.028 (0.013)	−0.025 (0.013)

IRT*RFH	−0.006 (0.001)	−0.006 (0.001)	**−0.006 (0.002)**
LCA_PH*RFH			**−0.004 (0.002)**
LCA_FS*RFH			
Education*RFH	0.0002 (0.0005)	−0.00007 (0.0005)	−0.00007 (0.0005)
Intercept	0.029 (0.124)	0.062 (0.123)	0.010 (0.124)
		0.027 (0.123)	
		0.024 (0.123)	
Random effects (variance)			
Intercept	0.009	0.009	0.009
Residual	0.076	0.076	0.076
# of societies	71	71	71
# of observations	94,194	94,194	89,864
		94,194	89,864

Source: Global Barometer Surveys II (N = 104,248).
Notes:
Robust standard errors in parentheses.
Statistically significant coefficients are bolded (at the 0.05 level).

Table A6.3 Mixed-Effect Linear Models on Unconventional Participation

	M1 Mixed OLS	M2 Mixed OLS	M3 Mixed OLS	M4 Mixed OLS	M5 Mixed OLS
Fixed effects					
Age_group	−0.004 (0.001)	−0.004 (0.001)		−0.004 (0.001)	−0.004 (0.001)
Polynomial (Age, 2)_1			−1.968 (0.247)		
Polynomial (Age, 2)_2			−0.517 (0.234)		
Male	0.020 (0.001)	0.020 (0.001)	0.020 (0.001)	0.020 (0.001)	0.020 (0.001)
Education	0.00001 (0.002)	0.010 (0.001)	0.0001 (0.002)	0.010 (0.001)	0.002 (0.002)
Political_interest	0.025 (0.001)	0.025 (0.001)	0.025 (0.001)	0.025 (0.001)	0.025 (0.001)
National_economy	−0.0002 (0.001)	−0.0002 (0.001)	−0.0002 (0.001)	−0.0005 (0.001)	−0.0006 (0.001)
Family_economy	0.001 (0.001)	0.001 (0.001)	0.001 (0.001)	0.0003 (0.001)	0.0002 (0.001)
PUD_IRT_scores	0.021 (0.004)	0.003 (0.001)	0.021 (0.004)		
PUD_LCA_Principle_holders				0.004 (0.002)	0.014 (0.007)
PUD_LCA_Fence_sitters				0.007 (0.002)	0.002 (0.006)
Economic_recession	−0.095 (0.049)	−0.089 (0.048)	−0.094 (0.049)	−0.091 (0.049)	−0.096 (0.049)
Economic_recovery	−0.009 (0.017)	−0.009 (0.017)	−0.009 (0.017)	−0.009 (0.017)	−0.009 (0.017)
GDP_per_capita (ln)	0.0001 (0.009)	−0.0003 (0.009)	0.0002 (0.009)	−0.001 (0.009)	−0.0006 (0.009)
Single_party_regime_history	−0.015 (0.017)	−0.015 (0.017)	−0.015 (0.017)	−0.016 (0.017)	−0.016 (0.018)
Personal_regime_history	0.014 (0.017)	0.015 (0.017)	0.013 (0.018)	0.013 (0.017)	0.012 (0.018)
Confucian_history	−0.066 (0.032)	−0.064 (0.031)	−0.066 (0.032)	−0.066 (0.032)	−0.068 (0.032)
Democratic_capital	0.005 (0.002)	0.005 (0.002)	0.005 (0.002)	0.005 (0.002)	0.005 (0.002)
Reversed_FH_rating	−0.013 (0.008)	−0.007 (0.008)	−0.012 (0.008)	−0.007 (0.008)	−0.012 (0.008)

IRT*RFH	−0.004 (0.001)	−0.004 (0.001)	
LCA_PH*RFH			−0.002 (0.001)
LCA_FS*RFH			0.001 (0.001)
Education*RFH	**0.002 (0.0004)**	**0.002 (0.0004)**	**0.002 (0.0004)**
Intercept	0.009 (0.072)	−0.004 (0.072)	0.001 (0.072)
		−0.017 (0.071)	−0.011 (0.072)
Random effects (variance)			
Intercept	0.004	0.004	0.004
Residual	0.049	0.049	0.049
# of societies	71	71	71
# of observations	93,743	93,743	89,432
		93,743	89,432

Source: Global Barometer Surveys II (*N* = 104,248).

Notes:

Robust standard errors in parentheses.

Statistically significant coefficients are bolded (at the 0.05 level).

7
Conclusions

Democracy's contemporary crisis is twofold. On the one hand, in Western democracies, the rise of authoritarian populism poses critical challenges to the practice of liberal democracy (whose supremacy has been almost taken for granted since the end of World War II). These challenges have been further exacerbated by the declining popular confidence in democracy among the citizens (especially the younger cohorts) of Western democracies, which may be the harbinger of a possible deconsolidation of established democracies. On the other hand, beyond Western democracies, the long expected democratic transitions in authoritarian regimes and consolidation of new democracies (thanks to economic modernization, new information technologies, and the intentional promotion of democracy advocates, etc.) have come to a halt or even been reversed, partly due to the calculated preemptive strikes of authoritarian or populist leaders against opposition mobilization through soliciting and responding to their citizens' needs more effectively, the smart use of new information technologies, and strategic institutional engineering.

Meanwhile, democracy still enjoys its supremacy in contemporary political discourse, with limited meaningful challenges from alternatives. Authoritarian and populist politicians still have to at least pay lip service to respecting democratic principles and procedures, even though they are keener on taking advantage of or even creating institutional/procedural loopholes for political gains and maximizing their discretionary power. Among ordinary people, the desirability of democracy is widely and deeply recognized. Several rounds of large-scale public opinion surveys have established its popularity, even in societies with limited practice of democracy. Overall, democracy is still the "only game" in contemporary political discourse.

In this book, we have examined the puzzling and hotly debated crisis of democracy, given its popularity and supremacy in contemporary political discourse. Basically, we have tried to understand how democracy can be in trouble, if most people love democracy and politicians (whether they like it or not) have to live with democracy. More specifically, if people love democracy, shouldn't they despise authoritarian leaders and regimes, or even join the advocates of democracy to rebel against authoritarian leaders and regimes? Shouldn't they vote against populist leaders who have blatantly violated democratic institutions, procedures, or norms?

We have argued that in order to comprehensively address these questions, it is necessary to examine both supply-side (i.e., evolving political practices and institutional engineering led by political elites) and demand-side (i.e., transformative opinions and behaviors among the masses) dynamics. Intellectual exercises on the supply-side dynamics have received a lot of attention from students of democratization and democracy-promotion institutions. In contrast, the demand-side dynamics have been given scant attention so far. Therefore, this book focuses on key micro-dynamics that have driven related mass attitudes and behaviors, all of which are centered on how people conceptualize democracy in different ways. More specifically, we have argued that: (1) people hold distinct understandings of democracy; (2) popular conceptions of democracy are significantly shaped by socioeconomic and political contexts; (3) such varying conceptions generate different baselines for people to assess democratic practices and to establish their views of democracy; and (4) such distinct conceptions also drive political participation in different ways. Overall, popular understandings of democracy shape how citizens respond to authoritarian or populist practices in contemporary politics. As a critical but underappreciated component of the demand-side dynamics, varying democratic conceptions offer significant explanatory power for understanding why democracy is in trouble in today's world, even when most people profess to love democracy.

7.1 Key findings

Weaving comparative survey data (i.e., GBS and ABS data), survey experiments, and national statistics, using appropriate statistical modeling techniques, we have systematically examined: (1) how people assess the trade-offs between key democratic principles and instrumental gains when they conceptualize democracy; (2) individual and societal dynamics that might have shaped the varying willingness to engage in such trade-offs; (3) the influence of different understandings of democracy on how people assess democratic practices in foreign and their home societies; and (4) the influence of varying democratic conceptions on distinct modes of political participation.

New instruments for popular understandings of democracy: We adopted the new ranking instruments (PUD) designed by the GBS II to examine the patterns, origins, and consequences of varying popular understandings of democracy. Compared with the instruments adopted by existing studies to capture and measure democratic conceptions (e.g., open-ended instruments or rating scales), the PUD instruments asked people to rank different aspects of democracy. This effectively captures the critical trade-off dynamic involved in popular assessment of democracy that we are interested in. More specifically, taking advantage of the open-ended instruments used in the earlier waves of surveys, GBS II has identified four key aspects of democracy that have been widely and consistently reported as essential characteristics of democracy by ordinary people around the world, that is, (1) social equity, (2) good government, (3) norms and procedures, and (4) freedom and liberty. The first two effectively capture what we define as the substantive understanding of democracy focusing on the instrumental values of democracy in delivering quality governance; the latter two tap into what we define as the procedural understanding of democracy emphasizing the intrinsic values of democracy as a way of life that ensures people's dignity and inalienable rights. For the PUD instruments, GBS II identified four indicators for each of the four key aspects, organized four ranking sets with four different indicators (i.e., one for each of the four key aspects with randomized order), and presented the ranking sets to respondents to choose the most essential characteristic of democracy, thus capturing their respective conceptions of democracy when the trade-offs between key democratic principles and instrumental gains are highlighted.

Our empirical examination of the survey and experimental data collected from seventy-two societies (i.e., societies covered by the GBS II and the United States) shows that there is little recency or primacy effect in responses to the PUD instruments. Our survey experiment in the United States further confirms that the PUD instruments with the GBS II design closely mimic the performance of the PUD instruments with fully randomized order of answer categories. Overall, the PUD instruments do not suffer from significant design deficiencies. Meanwhile, both CFA and LCA analyses confirm that the PUD instruments effectively differentiate between distinct understandings of democracy, despite these models' different operationalization strategies, statistical modeling assumptions, and techniques in dealing with item non-response. While the CFA results reveal people's latent willingness to trade off key democratic principles for instrumental gains, which falls on a continuous spectrum; the LCA results uncover four distinct latent groups of people (i.e., Principle-Holders, Benefit-Seekers, Fence-Sitters, and Agnostics) when making choices between democracy's intrinsic and instrumental values. The CFA and LCA results align with each other quite well. This has greatly boosted our confidence in the validity and reliability of the PUD instruments in capturing the trade-off dynamic in popular understandings of democracy, which existing scholarship has generally ignored.

Significant regional and societal variation in democratic conceptions: Using the United States (i.e., a textbook case of liberal democracy with a long and rich tradition of democratic practice) as the benchmark for assessment, we pooled the GBS II data and the 2017 national survey of the United States for analysis. Following distinct operational strategies (i.e., continuous IRT latent scores versus discrete LCA latent groups of the PUR instruments), we examined democratic conceptions as both continuous latent willingness to trade off key democratic principles for instrumental gains and discrete latent groups with varying willingness to engage in such trade-offs.

Findings based on the continuous IRT latent scores of the PUD instruments suggest that, on average, citizens of the United States are more inclined to prioritize democracy's intrinsic than their counterparts in Latin America, South Asia, sub-Saharan Africa, North Africa, and East Asia. Thus, comparatively speaking, citizens of the United States are less willing to trade off key democratic principles for instrumental gains. At the same time, people living in East Asia and North Africa, on average, are more inclined to emphasize democracy's instrumental values and therefore more willing to engage in such trade-offs when necessary. Further analysis reveals substantial variation within each of the regions. For instance, citizens of the Latin American countries Ecuador, Nicaragua, Guatemala, and Paraguay are, on average, more inclined to embrace the substantive understanding of democracy, despite the fact that most of their Latin American neighbors are more attracted to the procedural understanding. Similarly, citizens of Mongolia, Cambodia, India, and the Philippines are more inclined to prioritize the intrinsic values of democracy, despite the emphasis on its instrumental values in other Asian societies. There is more heterogeneity among the citizens of African countries in terms of how they conceptualize democracy. On the one hand, those living in societies like Morocco, Swaziland, Mali, and Niger think more like their East Asian counterparts in mainland China and Singapore, emphasizing the instrumental values of democracy. On the other hand, those living in societies like Tanzania and Cameroon think more like their Latin American counterparts in Mexico or the Dominican Republic, prioritizing the intrinsic values of democracy. Meanwhile, those living in societies like Kenya, Burundi, and Mozambique hold somewhat balanced and mixed views of democracy, without systematically prioritizing its instrumental or intrinsic values.

Findings based on the discrete LCA latent groups of the PUD instruments cross-validate the significant variation in popular conceptions of democracy between regions and between societies. They further reveal nuanced compositions of citizens with distinct conceptions of democracy in each of the seventy-two societies. More specifically, Principle-Holders, Benefit-Seekers, Fence-Sitters, and Agnostics were identified as four latent groups of people showing distinct willingness to engage in the trade-offs between key democratic principles and instrumental gains. The United States and Latin America outperform other regions by boasting the largest percentage of Principle-Holders (who prioritize democracy's intrinsic values). Meanwhile, both Latin America and Asia are quite homogenous in their respective popular conceptions of democracy. In the former, most societies have a larger percentage of Principle-Holders, while in the latter, most societies have a larger percentage of Benefit-Seekers (who emphasize democracy's instrumental values). The heterogeneity among African societies in this regard is noteworthy, with some of them behaving like Asian societies and others behaving like Latin American countries. It is also important to note that, in all seventy-two societies, the presence of Fence-Sitters (whose willingness to trade off key democratic principles is not given and might be conditional upon the nature of instrumental gains under examination) is substantial. Even in the United States, around 33% of citizens are Fence-Sitters. They do not consistently prioritize democracy's instrumental or intrinsic values and so are willing to sacrifice key democratic principles when the expected return of instrumental gains is sufficiently attractive.

We further explored the longitudinal features of this critical attitude using the ABS two-wave rolling-cross-sectional surveys from thirteen East Asian societies. A high level of longitudinal stability in how East Asians, on average, conceptualize democracy has been established. With a few exceptions like Vietnam, mainland China, and Thailand, popular understandings of democracy in East Asian societies demonstrate high consistency between the two waves of surveys. Although we do not have enough information to scrutinize the significant change in the non-response rates to the PUD instruments in Vietnam, the documented changes in democratic conceptions in mainland China and Thailand are quite consistent with the two societies' macro socioeconomic and political changes between the two waves of ABS surveys. Overall, we have sufficient reason to believe in the longitudinal stability of this critical attitude. Popular understandings of democracy are unlikely to be transient and hyper-sensitive to idiosyncratic factors and more likely to be largely shaped by slow-moving dynamics and systematic transformations.

Contextualized origins of popular understandings of democracy: Like all survey instruments, the PUD instruments also suffered from non-responses among GBS II respondents. Our systematic analysis has established cognitive deficiency and lack of related information as two main drivers of non-responses to the PUD instruments. There is little evidence for the possible role of political or social desirability bias in shaping non-responses to the PUD instruments. Overall, it is fair to conclude that when confronted with the contrast between democracy's intrinsic and instrumental values, people do try to make informed choices. Thus, substantive responses to the PUD instruments provide valuable information to explore why people might be willing to trade off key democratic principles for instrumental gains.

Our detailed examination of the GBS II data reveals that, when confronted with the choice between key democratic principles and instrumental gains, males with a higher level of education and more interest in politics are significantly less inclined to trade off the former for the latter, given their deeper appreciation of democracy's intrinsic values. This pattern is consistent with the cosmopolitan communications thesis, which emphasizes the significance of cognitive capacity and self-initiative in enabling more effective engagement with cosmopolitan communication. Such engagement leads to more exposure to and embracement of self-expression or emancipative values, which are, in turn, likely to boost popular support for institutional arrangements that promote and protect such values. Accordingly, people are more inclined to prioritize democracy's intrinsic values and less willing to trade off key democratic principles for instrumental gains. Furthermore, our evidence also suggests the significant role of the surrounding socioeconomic environment in moderating the influence of education and political interest. Basically, the influence is much stronger in poorer societies than in richer ones. This finding may be related to how the better informational infrastructure, higher penetration of information technologies, and higher living standards of rich societies might produce less variation in engagement with cosmopolitan communication for people with varying cognitive capacity and self-initiative.

Nevertheless, our findings also indicate that the cosmopolitan communications thesis might have taken an oversimplified view of the influence of socioeconomic resources on popular understandings of democracy. Individuals' access to more socioeconomic resources does not necessarily increase their appreciation of democracy's intrinsic values. Our statistical modeling has established a significant interaction between self-reported family economic situation and a society's Freedom House rating in shaping democratic conceptions. More specifically, in illiberal societies, richer people are less likely to conceptualize democracy following the liberal tradition by prioritizing its intrinsic values. In addition, their willingness to trade off key democratic principles for instrumental gains is significantly higher. Conversely, in liberal societies, richer people are more likely to endorse liberal democracy as the authentic version of democracy by prioritizing its intrinsic values, and their willingness to engage in such trade-offs is much lower. This finding is consistent with the cognitive status-quo bias thesis, that is, richer people's willingness to trade off key democratic principles for instrumental gains is conditional upon surrounding political contexts, due their attachment to existing political regimes.

Societies' varying economic contexts mold their respective popular understandings of democracy in a nuanced way. Although our evidence on the influence of short-term economic dynamics like recession or crisis is not conclusive, it does suggest how such short-term economic challenges might amplify the significance of the regime's performance in delivering good governance for its citizens. This further highlights the salience and necessity of democracy's instrumental values, which, in turn, might tilt popular assessment of the trade-offs between key democratic principles and instrumental gains in the latter's favor. Meanwhile, a society's general socioeconomic development (as measured by per capita GDP) dramatically moderates the influence of education and political interest on popular democratic conceptions. Basically, a society's better economic performance and enhanced socioeconomic development not only make its people, overall, more appreciative of democracy's intrinsic values and less willing to trade off key democratic principles for instrumental gains, but also make them more homogenous in related understandings by reducing the disparities that might have been driven by their varying cognitive capacity and self-initiative.

Societies' distinct political contexts and cultural traditions also matter in terms of how their citizens conceptualize democracy. Democratic practice greatly moderates how the cognitive status-quo bias shapes popular understandings of democracy. Although our evidence on the influence of societies' accumulated democratic capital is not conclusive, it does indicate that a richer experience with liberal democratic practice enables people to learn about and appreciate the significance of democratic institutions, procedures, values, and norms in ensuring their political rights and liberties as well as their dignity as human beings. Thus, they are more likely to prioritize democracy's intrinsic values and less willing to trade off key democratic principles for instrumental gains. Furthermore, memories (individual or collective) of the chaos and calamities associated with political instability and uncertainty under personal dictatorships have made people more appreciative of the significance of institutions and procedures in politics; therefore, under the shadow of personal dictatorships, people are more likely to emphasize democracy's intrinsic values. In addition, when the trade-offs between key democratic principles and instrumental gains are highlighted, Confucian political traditions in a society significantly tilt its popular preference toward the latter. This finding seems to be associated with the paternalistic meritocracy discourse in Confucian societies, which has been sustained and promoted through cultural traditions and political socialization.

Overall, our findings have effectively established the salience of economic, political, and cultural contexts for understanding how people conceptualize democracy. Factors driven by short-term events (like economic growth or recession), mid-term evolutions (like democratic practice assessed by Freedom House ratings and economic development measured by per capita GDP), and long-term dynamics (like the history of personal dictatorships and Confucian political traditions) all play some role in shaping popular understandings of democracy. Put otherwise, incorporating contextual features into existing research to develop a more comprehensive and dynamic explanation of why people understand democracy in different ways is both fruitful and necessary. Our empirical findings not only confirm the value of various modernization theories for understanding micro-dynamics involved in democratic transition and consolidation but also echo recent calls from students of comparative politics on the importance of systematically incorporating and theorizing historical legacies (both political and cultural) for understanding contemporary politics.

Distinct benchmarks for assessing democratic practice: Theoretically, people's varying willingness to trade off key democratic principles for instrumental gains may orient them toward different aspects of democratic practice in their evaluations. For those who deeply appreciate democracy's intrinsic values, the quality of core democratic institutional settings and procedural arrangements, as well as related norms and values, in ensuring political rights, liberty, and dignity are central to their assessment of democratic practice. For those who prioritize democracy's instrumental values, the quality of delivered governance, including but not limited to improved social equity and living standards, are essential for their evaluations. As a consequence, confronted with the same regime's democratic practice (either foreign or home) for assessment, people with varying democratic conceptions are likely to draw distinct conclusions.

Our first empirical test focused on how varying understandings of democracy shape GBS II respondents' assessment of democratic practices in the United States and China. In almost all GBS II societies (including China), on average, people offer a higher rating of democratic practice in the United States than in China, which further validates the GBS II data's effectiveness in capturing popular views of democracy. Meanwhile, there is noticeable variation in related evaluations, with much more variation in how people assess China's democratic practice. Statistical modeling confirms that, regardless of how popular understandings of democracy are operationalized (i.e., as continuous IRT scores or nominal LCA groups), *ceteris paribus*, people who prioritize democracy's intrinsic values by emphasizing its institutions and procedures in protecting basic rights and liberties are more critical of China's democratic practice and hold more favorable attitudes toward US democracy. Those who are more willing to trade off key democratic principles for instrumental gains, on average, are less impressed by the performance of US democracy and show more appreciation of democratic practice with Chinese characteristics. Given the contrast between these two countries in terms of their respective ways of ruling and governance, it is reasonable to argue that the established impact of varying understandings of democracy on how people assess democratic practices in the United States and China demonstrates the salience of varying benchmarks that people adopt to assess democratic practice based on their distinct conceptions of democracy.

We further examined how such varying conceptions of democracy affected popular views of democratic practice in respondents' home societies. To ensure the robustness of our findings, we adopted two proxies (with distinct measurement strategies and scales): citizens' self-reported satisfaction with and perceived levels of democratic practice in their home society. There is a moderate but significant positive correlation between the two proxies, which provides a reassuring setting for our robustness check. Similar statistical modeling reveals that, again, people's different understandings of democracy significantly shape how they assess their home society's democratic practice. On average, people who prioritize democracy's intrinsic values (compared to their fellow citizens who are more willing to trade off key democratic principles for instrumental gains) are less satisfied with their regime's democratic practice. A nuanced but critical finding is that this impact is highly conditional upon the features of the surrounding political environment. More specifically, after accounting for other relevant features, the impact in full autocracies is twice as strong as in hybrid regimes. In democracies with minor issues, the impact further diminishes and is no longer statistically significant. In full democracies, the impact is reversed, that is, the more people appreciate democracy's intrinsic values (i.e., the lower their willingness to trade off key democratic principles for instrumental gains), the more favorable views they hold for home society's democratic practice. Put otherwise, people are highly responsive to the features of their immediate political environment when they assess their home society's democratic practice.

Our analysis also indicates that, regardless of how people differ in their conceptions of democracy, younger males with a higher level of education are generally more critical of their home society's democratic practice. Moreover, even a full democracy also needs to deliver (i.e., providing good governance through better economic and political performance) to win over its citizen's hearts and minds, therefore fostering its popular support. Furthermore, political regimes in Confucian societies might have benefited from the lasting influence of Confucian cultural traditions and enjoyed some premium in popular assessments of democracy.

Varying sensitivity to expressive values associated with political participation: Besides the critical role of shaping the benchmarks people use for democratic assessment, different democratic conceptions also have significant implications for how people respond to the expressive values associated with political participation, thus shaping their incentives to engage in various modes of political participation. Following best practice in political behavior research, we examined the influence of popular understandings of democracy on both conventional and unconventional political participation. Furthermore, given the salience and indispensability of electoral politics for democracies, as well as the adoption of manipulated or rigged elections in many autocracies and hybrid regimes, we also examined electoral participation separately from political contacting (although both are conceptualized as critical components of conventional political participation).

Overall, we found that, compared to their fellow citizens who emphasize the instrumental values of democracy in delivering good governance, people who prioritize democracy's intrinsic values in ensuring individual dignity and basic rights and liberties through appropriate institutions and procedures are significantly more likely to engage in a range of conventional and unconventional participatory activities for political purposes. The latter are more likely to cast ballots, help with electoral campaigns, contact political and government agents or agencies, join a demonstration, march in a protest, or use violence for a political cause. However, the influence of popular willingness to trade off key democratic principles for instrumental gains on political participation varies significantly between societies with different regime types.

More specifically, in authoritarian societies, citizens' low willingness to trade off key democratic principles for instrumental gains drives them to more actively engage in electoral participation, political contacting, and unconventional political participation. In societies with improved democratic practices, the difference between citizens holding distinct conceptions of democracy regarding their propensity to engage in various conventional and unconventional participatory activities shrinks. In free societies, the difference between citizens prioritizing democracy's intrinsic versus instrumental values in terms of their propensity to engage in electoral participation and political contacting becomes negligible and no longer statistically significant. Furthermore, in full democracies, citizens orientated toward democracy's intrinsic values are significantly less likely to engage in unconventional political participation like joining a demonstration, marching in a protest, or using violence for a political cause when compared to their fellow citizens who emphasize democracy's instrumental values.

These findings clearly show that challenging the boundaries set by authoritarian politicians and pushing for political change by engaging in various participatory activities (especially the unconventional ones) provide significant extra expressive rewards for people who prioritize democracy's intrinsic values embodied in democratic institutions, procedures, and norms. The lower the willingness to trade off key democratic principles for instrumental gains, the more active the engagement in such participatory activities. In a full democracy, exactly because of their appreciation of democracy's intrinsic values and their adherence to established democratic institutions, procedures, and norms, these citizens are more inclined to address their issues and concerns within the free society's established institutions and procedures rather than by resorting to street politics or political violence. This is highly consistent with the varying salience of expressive values associated with different modes of political participation in societies with distinct regime features. In summary, people conceptualizing democracy in distinct ways respond differently to the expressive values associated with various participatory activities depending on the features of the surrounding political environment.

Meanwhile, the influence of educational attainment varies between distinct political regimes when electoral participation and unconventional participation are under examination. Nevertheless, when political contacting is under examination, the impact of educational attainment is quite consistent between societies. More specifically, in authoritarian societies, better-educated people's enhanced political sophistication enables them to more effectively see through the flaws and hypocritical nature of manipulated electoral politics and to more rationally assess the risks and costs of joining demonstrations, protests, or civil disobedience (given the lurking threat of political oppression). Therefore, they are much less likely to channel their resources (material resources, relationships, networks, etc.) into such participatory activities. However, in societies with improved democratic practices, better-educated people's similar instrumental assessment and calculations may tilt their decisions toward more active engagement in such participatory activities. Therefore, they participate more actively in electoral politics, demonstrations, protests, or even civil disobedience thanks to their access to more resources and greater political sophistication. The dynamics are different for political contacting, which is mainly driven by personal instrumental concerns and needs and is legitimate and low risk in both democracies and autocracies. In this regard, better-educated people consistently and significantly outperform their less-educated fellow citizens by engaging in political contacting more actively. Since we have consistently accounted for the impact of educational attainment (which is mainly driven by the associated dynamics of instrumental concerns) in our models of political participation, we have more confidence in the effectiveness of identifying the associated dynamics of expressive considerations by incorporating popular understandings of democracy (proxied by the PUD instruments) in our theoretical and empirical analysis.

7.2 Scholarly contributions

Overall, this book contributes to three lines of research in comparative politics: (1) democracy's contemporary crisis, (2) popular conceptions of democracy, and (3) attitude-behavior connections.

A coherent framework for understanding democracy's contemporary crisis: This book offers a coherent framework to bridge a noticeable division in the literature on democracy's contemporary crisis. Conversations between students of democratic deconsolidation in established democracies and scholars who are interested in the stagnation or recession of democratic transitions in authoritarian regimes are limited. The former are more interested in macro socioeconomic, political, and technological changes (including resulting cultural backlashes); while the latter are more oriented toward authoritarian leaders' strategic institutional engineering. However, as we try to understand the prospects for democracy in today's world, both sides are crucial and should not be treated as isolated research domains. This book tries to shed light on a crucial but frequently ignored micro-foundation for understanding the crisis of democracy in various political regimes, that is, different conceptions of democracy. More specifically, we focus on popular views of the trade-offs between democracy's instrumental and intrinsic values.

In established democracies, when confronted with socioeconomic difficulties triggered by, for instance, globalization and technical innovations and given their resentment against deteriorating living standards and decreasing employment opportunities, people prioritizing the instrumental values of democracy in delivering quality governance might be more responsive to populist politicians' mobilization. Furthermore, these citizens are also more likely to be manipulated by populist politicians (thanks to new technologies like social media) into blaming existing democratic institutions and procedures for their difficulties and grievances. As the percentage of citizens embracing such views grows, the danger of democratic deconsolidation rises. Meanwhile, few authoritarian leaders publicly denounce democracy, and most have made enormous efforts to present their regimes as various forms of democracy (of course, generally stripped of genuine democratic procedures and institutions). With their control of the mass media and education systems and the assistance of new information technologies, authoritarian leaders also are keen on indoctrinating their citizens with certain understandings of democracy that favor their political practices. In such political contexts, people prioritizing the instrumental values of democracy may sincerely believe in the democratic nature of their authoritarian regimes, as long as their regimes can satisfy their socioeconomic needs. Therefore, democracy advocates' mobilization for political changes may fall on deaf ears, weakening future prospects for democratic transition. Despite the distinct syndromes associated with democracy's contemporary crisis in democracies and autocracies, they may share some common micro-dynamics centered around how people assess the trade-offs between key democratic principles and instrumental gains.

Important but ignored trade-off dynamics in democratic conceptions: This book also defends and examines new survey instruments for measuring popular conceptions of democracy and scrutinizes this critical political attitude in a much broader geographical context. Different from existing instruments for varying democratic conceptions, our new ranking instruments were intentionally designed to capture popular responses when confronted with salient trade-offs between key democratic principles and instrumental gains in any society. The recent rise of populism in Europe and North America and populist politicians' blatant violations of key democratic principles and norms without being punished or even being rewarded by their electorates are glaring reminders that key democratic institutions and norms are under sustained attack and might be sacrificed when conditions are ripe. In short, people do recognize and evaluate potential trade-offs and, thus, make meaningful and consequential choices between key democratic principles/institutions and something else, depending on their respective understandings of democracy. Therefore, instead of assuming that "all good things go together" in democracies, our theorization of popular conceptions of democracy focuses on the trade-offs between desirable socioeconomic outcomes, on the one hand, and political institutional and procedural arrangements, on the other hand, that both are conventionally assumed to be associated with democracy. Furthermore, we place such trade-offs at the central of our theorization, operationalization, and measurement. Empirically, we have used distinct types of data (i.e., survey experiments and large-scale comparative surveys) and applied various psychometric models (i.e., IRT and

LCA models) to test and establish the validity of the new survey instruments. Compared to existing research on popular conceptions of democracy, our empirical exercise has a much broader coverage of societies with varying socioeconomic, political, and cultural characteristics. This much broader geographical coverage effectively tests the scope conditions of existing theories of popular conceptions of democracy and significantly improves our understanding of how this critical political attitude works under distinct environments.

Altogether, this book's exercise has demonstrated the futility of hunting the "holy grail" that might provide the "best instruments" for measuring popular understandings of democracy. All instruments have their unique values and may serve distinct functions for specific theoretical arguments. To effectively examine democratic conceptions, researchers have to specify their research questions first, and, accordingly, craft or select the most appropriate instruments tailored to their theoretical concerns. The trade-off dynamics are central to our theoretical concerns but are not the only possible approach for scholarship on popular understandings of democracy. For some research questions, open-ended instruments or rating scales might be a much better choice. Therefore, for more fruitful academic dialogue and discussions in the future, scholars should be more sensitive to the extent to which their empirical instruments match their theoretical models and be more transparent in their operationalization and instrument selection.

More solid attitude-behavior connections: By examining the attitudinal and behavioral consequences of popular understandings of democracy, this book also contributes to existing comparative research on public opinion and political behavior, especially the connections between political attitudes and behaviors. Simply demonstrating the existence of varying understandings of democracy (as most pertinent research has done), as well as how democratic conceptions shape popular assessment of democratic practice (as some other studies have done), is far from satisfying. To more effectively demonstrate the value of this critical political attitude for understanding democracy's contemporary crisis, we need to present concrete evidence regarding the influence of democratic conceptions on political behavior. More specifically, we examined how varying understandings of democracy might shape popular engagement in participatory activities like electoral participation, contacting politicians, petitions, strikes, and protests, or even more radical forms of participation like political violence, as well as how this influence has been moderated by surrounding socioeconomic, political, and cultural contexts.

This has rarely been done in the literature on popular understandings of democracy. More broadly, there is an unfortunate dearth of similar large-scale empirical research on attitude-behavior connections in comparative politics.

Our findings substantiate the theoretical value of this critical variable. Popular understandings of democracy do more than just shape citizens' assessment of democratic practices, they have concrete implications for how people engage in various modes of political participation under distinct political contexts. More specifically, people's varying willingness to trade off key democratic principles for instrumental gains might make them respond to the expressive values associated with different modes of political participation in different ways. People prioritizing democracy's intrinsic values are far more sensitive to associated expressive values than their counterparts emphasizing democracy's instrumental values when they engage in political participation. Existing scholarship of political participation has acknowledged the salience of expressive considerations for understanding political behavior. However, the literature has not been very successful at identifying concrete factors that merit and enable systematic comparative research in this regard. Our findings suggest that popular understandings of democracy might be a critical factor that has not received sufficient attention from the scholarship. Furthermore, examining how democratic conceptions interact with surrounding political contexts in shaping citizens' engagement in various modes of political participation sheds more light on the micro-behavioral foundations of macro-political changes like democratic transition, consolidation, crisis, and deconsolidation.

7.3 Implications for the future of democracy

As we were completing this book, the world was haunted and attacked by a highly contagious, deadly, and mysterious virus, later identified as COVID-19. Despite its lower mortality rate, COVID-19 is more contagious than SARS and is expected to be around for much longer. It was first reported in Wuhan, China, and later identified in every continent, including Antarctica. Globally, the World Health Organization had recorded over 187 million confirmed cases of COVID-19, including more than 4 million deaths, as of July 13, 2021.[1] This is not just a public health crisis; it also has severe implications for the world's socioeconomic and political outlook. The socioeconomic impact of the COVID-19 pandemic might be more grievous than that of the

2008–2009 global financial crisis (which set the key background for our research presented in this book).

To contain the spread of COVID-19, governments have taken stringent but necessary measures. Travel via public transportation systems has been restricted. Public gatherings have been banned. Schools, parks, offices, department stores, government agencies, and even entire cities have been closed down. Given the highly contagious and deadly nature of the virus, as well as rising infections, voluntary social distancing has been widely adopted around the world. As a consequence, socioeconomic activities have been greatly constrained and significantly reduced. According to the World Economic Outlook Report issued by the IMF in October 2020, although there were some optimistic signs of the global economy recovering from the Great Lockdown in April 2020 (especially thanks to the swift recovery in China), "the global economy's long ascent back to pre-pandemic levels of activity remains prone to setbacks."[2] More specifically, the projected real GDP growth rate for the world in 2020 is −4.4%, a considerable decrease from the estimated growth rate of 2.8% in 2019. The Euro area is expected to witness the most serious economic recession (−8.3%) in 2020, followed by Latin America and the Caribbean (−8.1%), the United States (−4.3%), Middle East and Central Asia (−4.1%), sub-Saharan Africa (−3.0%), and Emerging and Developing Asia (−1.7%). According to the IMF, mainland China, where the first COVID-19 cases were reported, is likely to be the only economy in the world to show positive growth in 2020 (with a projected growth rate of 2%).

As discussed earlier, when people perceive rising existential and socioeconomic insecurity (like the one triggered by the 2008–2009 financial crisis and the ongoing COVID-19 pandemic), their evaluations of the trade-offs between key democratic principles and instrumental gains are very likely to be tilted in favor of the latter. In other words, when people are overwhelmed with securing basic necessities, finding new sources of incomes to cover the shortfalls because of shrinking employment opportunities, or paying off growing medical bills, their adherence to democracy's intrinsic values embodied in institutions, procedures, and norms might be challenged and shaken. As the discussion in this book suggests, this shift in prioritizing democracy's instrumental values over its intrinsic values has significant implications for the future of democracy in the world.

In some liberal democracies, this growing priority assigned to democracy's instrumental values in popular understandings of democracy might offer additional leeway for shrewd, populist, and even authoritarian politicians.

These politicians are more than happy to mobilize support by playing to these grievances and make attractive promises to secure voters' support simply to serve their political ambitions. With a higher willingness to trade off key democratic principles for instrumental gains, these people might be less sensitive to politicians' abuse of power and violation of key democratic principles. As a consequence, democracy's deconsolidation and even backsliding to authoritarianism might be accelerated in these societies.

In some non-democracies, the ongoing COVID-19 pandemic might, at least for a short period, have cast some positive light on authoritarian regimes, especially in terms of their responses to the pandemic. Given their capacity in resource and personnel mobilization and ability to enforce stringent but necessary measures (in some cases, intruding on personal privacy and compromising freedom and liberty), their performance in containing the spread of COVID-19 and restoring socioeconomic order and activities might have impressed a significant portion of their citizens, especially in contrast to the piling up of infections and deaths and ongoing lockdowns in Western democracies. Furthermore, with the growing priority assigned to democracy's instrumental values in popular conceptions of democracy, advocates of democracy are likely to face an even more challenging uphill battle in winning over people's hearts and minds. As a consequence, democratic transition might face more uncertainty and resistance, and even come to a halt, in these societies.

Liberal democracy has long been under stress, with a glaring income inequality brought about by hyper-globalization, the rise of homegrown populist and nationalist movements, and external geopolitical threats from resilient authoritarian actors. But COVID-19 created a new kind of stress test, bringing into question the ability of the democratic system to cope with an existential challenge, i.e., protecting the citizens from a menacing public health crisis and society from a devastating economic catastrophe.

We are very concerned that democracy's contemporary crisis might be further exacerbated and prolonged because of events like the 2008–2009 global financial crisis and the COVID-19 pandemic. Furthermore, catastrophic events like these are likely to strike the world again in the future. However, one might find some solace in the observation that the evidence so far suggests that political regimes are not good predictors of performance in pandemic management. Some democracies, among them Australia, New Zealand, Taiwan, and South Korea, have been fairly successful in containing the virus and limiting deaths. Others, like the United States, most Western

European countries, Brazil, Mexico, and India have not performed as well. Amongst authoritarian regimes, China, Cambodia, and Vietnam contained the spread of COVID-19, while Turkey and Russia have largely failed to do so.

Democracy defenders might also find some comfort in the explanation offered by Fukuyama (2020) that the factors responsible for successful pandemic responses have been state capacity, social trust, and leadership, rather than regime type. Countries with all three—a competent state apparatus, a government that citizens trust and listen to, and effective leaders—have performed impressively, limiting the damage they have suffered. Countries, notably the United States, the United Kingdom, and Brazil, with populist incumbents, dysfunctional states, polarized societies, and a leadership that ignores science and defies the advice of experts have done badly, leaving their citizens and economies exposed and vulnerable. But we need to probe deeper by asking why so many Western democracies have experienced the protracted problems of worsening political polarization, dwindling of social capital, depletion of institutional trust, and growing cynicism. As Micklethwait and Wooldridge (2014, p. i) pointed out, "In most of the states of the West, disillusion with government has become endemic. Gridlock in America; anger in much of Europe; cynicism in Britain; decreasing legitimacy everywhere."

Evidently, in most Western societies, the dominance of neo-liberal ideology since the 1980s and the hyper-globalization of the last three decades have led to a chronic lack of investment in the state. In contrast, most East Asian political systems, both democratic and non-democratic, have developed adequate state capacity to cope with all sorts of social or natural contingencies. The political elites in these societies were not swayed by the prevailing ethos of neo-liberal ideology, which enshrines the free market while demonizing the state. Over the last few decades, East Asian countries have been continuously upgrading and investing in the state's capacity in tackling their countries' long-term socioeconomic challenges as well as short-term shocks such as financial crises, earthquakes, typhoons, or epidemics.

For Western democracies, it is imperative to re-invest in and re-invent the state; otherwise, their political systems will not be able to address the pressing needs of the bereaved families, struggling communities, and fractured economies, much less restore public trust in political institutions. Building a sustainable and resilient economy and society requires a wide range of public-sector investments with long-term objectives in mind. To reverse the decline in Western democracy, it may be necessary for the political elites in the West to learn something from the East, where the public for centuries have tended to view an effective state as a "necessary good" rather than a "necessary evil."

To defend democracy against the corrosive influence of such devastating events, to restore democracy's intrinsic values, and to reestablish the priority of key democratic principles in popular evaluations of the trade-offs between them and instrumental gains, democracy needs to do more than just defending and promoting its supremacy in discourse. Democracy needs to perform, deliver, and satisfy its citizens with both material and spiritual rewards.

Notes

Chapter 1

1. For different interpretations and debates on related findings, see, among others, Inglehart (2016) and Brunkert et al. (2019).
2. As we revised this book, the Russian referendum on constitutional changes ended on July 1, 2020. The referendum allows Putin to seek two more six-year terms after 2024.
3. Contemporary scholarly debates and discussions on the merits and deficiencies of different democratic governments, as well as how to effectively reform existing democratic institutions for more effective and better governance, involve both empirical and normative concerns (Rotberg 2014; Achen and Bartels 2016; Leemann and Wasserfallen 2016). This book focuses on the former.
4. In the existing literature, researchers have used "understandings of democracy," "conceptions of democracy," and "democratic conceptions" interchangeably. We follow this conventional practice in this book and do not differentiate between these terms.
5. Although the aforementioned studies on the crisis of democracy have significant implications for underlying micro-foundations, few studies have engaged in systematic research in this regard. The evolutionary modernization theory proposed by Inglehart (2018), Welzel (2013), and their collaborators also has specific implications for mass opinion and political behaviors. Nevertheless, most of their empirical work focuses on societal-level correlations rather than individual-level dynamics. Furthermore, with a few exceptions (Welzel and Deutsch 2012; Dalton et al. 2009), most of this empirical work does not address related behavioral dynamics in a cross-society context.
6. For comprehensive media coverage on related issues, see *The Economist*'s special report on "What's Gone Wrong with Democracy?" in 2014.
7. An outstanding example is the infamous Muammar Gaddafi who ruled Libya between 1969 and 2011 and declared Libya a directly democratic state (*jamahiriya*) in 1977. Donald Trump is another interesting case here, especially his comments during the 2016 presidential campaign regarding his political opponents (Inglehart and Norris 2017).
8. It is noteworthy that the significance of electoral politics for democracy is widely acknowledged among Europeans (Ferrin and Kriesi 2016). This finding is based on the 2020-2014 WVS rating instruments, which cannot effectively capture the trade-off dynamics we are interested in. Detailed discussions on the advantages and disadvantages of distinct survey instruments for popular understandings of democracy are provided in Chapter 2.
9. Singapore, China, and Vietnam are prominent examples here. For related discussions, see, among others, Chen (2013), Chu (2013), Shi (2015), and Dickson (2016).

10. Alberto Fujimori in Chile and Hugo Chavez in Venezuela are prominent examples here. For related discussions, see, among others, Mainwaring and Pérez-Liñán (2013), Slater et al. (2014), Levitsky and Ziblatt (2018), and Tomini and Wagemann (2018).
11. This resonates with the conclusion of some recent research on how political polarization makes Americans willing to trade off democratic principles for partisan interests (Graham and Svolik 2020; Svolik 2019). However, there is little comparative research on the trade-off dynamics in the literature of popular conceptions of democracy.
12. For a recent review on related issues, see Shin and Kim (2018).
13. In this book, we identify the former (i.e., conceptualizing democracy as a way of governance) as an instrumental understanding of democracy and the latter (i.e., conceptualizing democracy as a way of life) as an intrinsic understanding of democracy. In the literature, scholars also use the contrast between substantive vs. procedural understandings to describe similar phenomena. Thus, in this book, we also use the two pairs of terms interchangeably.
14. The contrast between the so-called Washington Consensus (primarily based on the US model of governance) and the so-called Beijing Consensus (mainly based on the Chinese model of governance) has attracted the attention of many developing societies and triggered heated debates and discussions (Malesky and London 2014; Ortmann and Thompson 2016; Bell 2015; Nathan 2015).
15. For detailed information, visit https://info.kpmg.us/content/dam/info/en/innovation-enterprise-solutions/pdf/2019/technology-innovation-hubs-2019.pdf#page=2. Accessed on 07/29/2019.
16. For detailed information, see *Global Wage Growth Falls to Its Lowest Level in Four Years*, a public release of the International Labor Organization in 2016.
17. For related information, visit https://www.project-syndicate.org/onpoint/china-one-belt-one-road-strategy-by-francis-fukuyama-2016-01?barrier=accesspaylog. Accessed on 10/10/2019.
18. Thanks to the growing regional comparative survey industries, there are an increasing number of comparative studies on popular understandings of democracy in single societies (Lu and Shi 2015; Crow 2010; Gillman 2018) or multiple societies in one specific region like East Asia (Lu 2013; Shin 2013), Africa (Bratton et al. 2005; Mattes and Bratton 2007), Latin America (Canache 2012; Baviskar and Malone 2004), or Europe (Ferrin and Kriesi 2016; Heyne 2019; Quaranta 2018).
19. Detailed information about the new survey instruments is provided in Chapter 2. Detailed information about the GBS II seventy-one societies is provided in Table A1.1.
20. The Principal Investigators of GBS did explore the possibility of collaboration with the European Barometer Survey around 2005 but this attempt was not successful. Therefore, we ran a national survey in the United States in 2017 using the GBS module to ensure a meaningful comparative analysis by including of one of the textbook cases of liberal democracy.
21. We also have coverage of more Latin American societies. However, the difference is not as significant as for the coverage of Asian and African societies.

Chapter 2

1. For a recent review on related issues, see Shin and Kim (2018).
2. Topic models built upon the natural language processing (NLP) algorithms of machine learning (supervised or automated) might offer some help here (Roberts et al. 2014). Nevertheless, such models are quite sensitive to the dictionaries used for language tokenization (especially for languages other than English) and face even more serious challenges when dealing with comparative research that covers multiple languages. Furthermore, the fragmented nature of people's generally short answers to the open-ended survey question, which offers limited text corpora for exploring the relations between meaningful key words (i.e., the key to topic models), also compromises the application of such models in the scholarship.
3. The conventional open-ended survey question is: "Many people talk about democracy. What does democracy mean to you?" Usually, interviewers are required to probe respondents multiple times and record their responses.
4. In the 2010–2014 WVS, a series of rating instruments were used to measure varying understandings of democracy (Kirsch and Welzel 2019; Kruse et al. 2019). Besides the aforementioned issues with rating instruments, some key aspects identified by the 2010–2014 WVS for ratings are not of equal salience for people in different societies, such as the role of religious authorities in politics. It should be reasonable to argue that the four aspects that GBS II focused should be able to secure a higher level of equal salience for most people in any society when they assess democracy.
5. Although we did not run the experiment using respondents from the GBS II societies due to logistic and technical constraints, we do believe that American voters' responses to the PUD instruments can be legitimately used to assess the influence of possible recency or primacy effect, given the similar psychological and cognitive processes involved in surveys.
6. There are two types of factor analysis: exploratory versus confirmatory. The former lets the data itself reveal the structure of the latent construct without imposing theoretically informed constraints, while the latter tests whether the theoretically deduced structure of the latent construct fits the data. In our case, we do have clearly specified theoretical conjectures on the structure of the latent construct (i.e., willingness to trade off key democratic principles for instrumental gains). Thus, the CFA model is more appropriate here for theory testing.
7. We can also interpret this as a kind of sensitivity test. Basically, the extent to which our conclusions might be driven by specific assumptions regarding the nature of the latent construct of interest (i.e., popular conceptions of democracy).
8. To further assess the validity of this one-factor CFA model, we ran the same CFA model for each of the seventy-two societies and plotted the histograms of their key model-fit statistics in Figure A2.1. The dotted lines in Figure A2.1 show the critical thresholds for RMSEA, CFI, and TLI respectively. As shown in Figures A2.1a and A2.1b, the majority of the CFA models report RMSEAs less than 0.08 or CFIs larger than 0.9. Although the percentage of CFA models reporting TLIs larger than 0.9 is not

as encouraging as the percentages reporting satisfying RMSEAs or CFIs, the highest density in Figure A2.1c still is found between 0.9 and 1.0.

9. Social desirability bias might be another factor of concern here. As demonstrated in the literature of survey methodology (Atkeson et al. 2014; Tourangeau and Yan 2007), this bias cannot be completely ruled out in any survey. Compared to asking for respondents' assessment of their regime or support for democracy (especially in an authoritarian context) (Panel 2019), asking for their ranking of different aspects of democracy is politically much less sensitive and much more conducive for offering meaningful and truthful answers. The GBS has enforced strict and standardized protocols for survey administration to minimize such influence.

10. As acknowledged among methodologists, the number of latent classes should not be identified exclusively based on statistical criteria, given the complexities in related model assessment. Different statistical criteria might offer distinct suggestions for model selection. Thus, theories are highly relevant in LCA modeling (Collins and Lanza 2010; McCutcheon 1987). In our case, the trade-off dynamics between key democratic principles and instrumental gains are central. Therefore, we focus on the comparisons between two-, three-, and four-class LCA models.

11. We strongly believe that the LCA's identification of Agnostics and Fence-Sitters as distinct latent types offers critical evidence for the validity of the PUD instruments. In many cases, people may not have a strong and consistent preference when presented with the trade-offs between democracy's intrinsic and instrumental values. Thus, their responses might be contingent upon the context or specific indicators presented for evaluation; or, they might have difficulty in making up their minds. If the PUD instruments cannot pick up the two groups of people, we should seriously question their validity. It is exactly because of the identification of such contingency or difficulty in reported choices that we believe our findings are not artificial and have effectively captured the underlying dynamics.

12. For statistical identification purposes, the variance of the latent propensities in the CFA has been fixed to one.

13. The Agnostics are either dropped (with non-response to all four ranking sets) or filled with extrapolated information based on other similar observations (using the full information maximum likelihood method) in the CFA model. It is further reassuring to find that all dropped cases in the CFA are indeed classified as Agnostics in the LCA.

Chapter 3

1. We have provided the raw scores of the PUD instruments in Figures A3.1–A.3.4 for readers who might be interested.
2. The median IRT scores in the United States and Latin America are 0.56 and 0.48, respectively.
3. The median IRT scores in East Asia and North Africa are identical, −0.39.
4. The median IRT scores in South Asia and sub-Saharan Africa are −0.13 and 0.01, respectively.

NOTES 193

5. This does not contradict some recent findings on Americans' willingness to trade off key democratic principles for partisan interests (Graham and Svolik 2020; Svolik 2019). As shown in Figure 3.1, there is notable variation in Americans' willingness to engage in such trade-offs. We simply argue that, compared with their Latin American, African, and Asian counterparts, Americans, on average, are less likely to do so. Joe Biden's victory against Donald Trump in the 2020 presidential election confirms our interpretation here.
6. Societies that we do not have survey data for are left blank simply to ensure an appropriate presentation of the world map.
7. The mean IRT scores in the remaining Latin American societies are greater than 0.30. Panama, Honduras, Colombia, Costa Rica, Argentina, Brazil, and Peru show a mean IRT score similar to the US score (i.e., around 0.40).
8. The mean IRT scores in Japan, South Korea, and Taiwan (i.e., the three East Asian democracies) are −0.41, −0.21, and −0.32, respectively.
9. Mean IRT scores are reported in parentheses.
10. Again, societies wherein we do not have related survey data are left in blank, simply to ensure an appropriate presentation of the world map.
11. It is quite interesting to find that Japan and Taiwan fall in the same group as Vietnam and China when it comes to the prevalence of the Principle-Holders among their citizens. We will come back to this point in later chapters with further analyses.
12. Paradata refers to the process-related information collected during survey administration (Kreuter 2013). It includes respondents' behavior related information, like the time they spent thinking, reading, and clicking and interviewers' behavior related information, like the records of their keystrokes, pace of reading questions, and skill levels.
13. An increasing number of studies use a similar research design to examine longitudinal dynamics in attitudes and behaviors (Yang 2008; Bartels and Jackman 2014; Tilley and Evans 2014; Dinas and Stoker 2014).
14. Myanmar has only one wave of survey in ABS IV. Thus, we dropped it from subsequent analysis.
15. We dropped Vietnam from subsequent correlation analyses due to this wild change in its non-response rate to the PUD instruments between the two waves of ABS surveys.
16. Again, Vietnam and Thailand are the outliers, showing substantive changes in the presence of Fence-Sitters and Agnostics among their citizens. It is worth noting that Singapore witnessed a substantial growth of Agnostics between the two ways of ABS Surveys (rising from around 2% to 14%).

Chapter 4

1. Some recent studies engaging in cross-national analysis of how people understand democracy and including an extensive list of individual features primarily use data from the World Values Survey, including dozens of European countries with well-established infrastructure for survey research and data collection (Cho 2015; Kirsch

and Welzel 2019; Zagrebina 2020; Ceka and Magalhães 2020). The GBS II includes seventy-one societies exclusively from Asia, Africa, and Latin America, covering most of the world's developing societies. The infrastructure for survey research and data collection is underdeveloped in most GBS societies (mainly due to technical and economic reasons). In some cases, the political environment is not friendly and even hostile for survey research.

2. Causal analysis relies on the validity of identification strategies like regression discontinuity, instrumental variables, or difference-in-differences. Alternatively, researchers can introduce fully controlled exogenous stimuli as we did in the survey experiments reported in Chapter 2. However, for comparative survey projects like the GBS, it is quite challenging to engage in similar research designs.

3. There are two types of non-response in surveys, that is, item and unit non-response. Unit non-response (i.e., sampled respondents cannot be located or refuse to participate) is a more serious issue that compromises the quality of representation. Item non-response (i.e., respondents cannot make a choice from the given answer categories for a closed-ended instrument or provide meaningful answers to an open-ended instrument) reduces the useful information in survey data. Here we focus on the latter.

4. The conventional measure of political interest asks respondents: "How interested would you say you are in politics?" The answer categories are: "Not at all interested," "Not very interested," "Somewhat interested," and "Very interested."

5. To account for possible curvilinear relationship between age and the outcome variable, we have tried both age and its quadratic form in estimations. Detailed results can be found in Table A4.1.

6. The cases of non-response coded using the IRT scores is roughly half of the cases coded using the LCA groups.

7. Table A4.1 shows all the regression results in detail; lme4 and MCMCglmm packages were used for the estimations in R 4.0.2.

8. A zero-order mixed-effect OLS model of the IRT scores (including all GBS II seventy-one societies) decomposes the total variance in the IRT scores into two parts: one attributed to individual-level dynamics and the other attributed to societal-level dynamics. The former accounts for 83.6% of total variance in the IRT scores and the latter accounts for the remaining 16.4%. We also ran a similar zero-order mixed-effect logistic model for the LCA outcomes (i.e., dichotomizing the outcomes as Principle-Holders versus Others) and got an almost identical result, that is, individual-level dynamics account for around 84% of the total variance in popular understandings of democracy.

9. Theoretically, scholars still debate about the specific mechanisms that drive the effect of age (e.g., the well-known conundrum of the age-period-cohort complex or the distinction between life-cycle and generation effects) and gender (e.g., socialization effects, genetic differences, etc.). Again, to account for possible curvilinear relationship between age and the outcome variable, we tried both age and its quadratic form in estimations. Detailed regression results can be found in Table A4.2.

10. This is similar to the logic of relative-deprivation arguments that explain protests, revolutions, and other radical political activities (Davis 1962; Gurr 1970).
11. Multiple indicators can be used to gauge a society's democratic features, besides the Freedom House rating (e.g., Polity IV, V-Dem, etc.). We have chosen this indicator exactly because of its focus on a society's political rights and civil liberties, which are directly related to democracy's intrinsic values and key principles. Using this indicator also facilitates our dialogue with the existing literature on popular understandings of democracy.
12. More specifically, we coded each GBS II society for each year starting from 1972 until the year of its GBS II survey as 1 (Free), 0.5 (Partly free), or 0 (Not free) using the Freedom House's criteria. Gerring et al. (2012) followed the same logic in creating their democracy stock variable, though unlike our study, they used Polity2 data since 1900 and a discount factor of 0.99. We tried different discount factors, but the results are quite stable. Although our choice of the starting year is primarily determined by the availability of the Freedom House data, using 1972 as the beginning of our assessment of accumulated democratic capital also effectively aligns this measure with the beginning of the third wave of democratization (Huntington 1991; Diamond 1997; Møller and Skaaning 2013; Haggard and Kaufman 2016).
13. Accordingly, we dropped missing values of the IRT scores or the "Agnostics" of LCA groups from the analysis. Detailed regressions results can be found in Table A4.2. Mixed-effect discrete choice models were run for the LCA groups.
14. The estimated average marginal effect of political interest in these societies is negative, with the upper boundary of its 95% confidence interval extending above zero.

Chapter 5

1. To ease interpretation, we reversed the order of the original seven-point scale adopted by Freedom House as we did in previous chapters.
2. The Pearson's correlation coefficient is 0.27, with an associated p-value of 0.02.
3. Such questions were not asked in the five South Asian countries (i.e., Bangladesh, India, Nepal, Pakistan, and Sri Lanka). We dropped the observations from mainland China when we examined how people assessed democratic practice in mainland China to ensure a similar level of objectivity in related evaluations.
4. Using anchoring vignettes to impose the same and objective baseline for effective comparisons across societies (King and Wand 2007; Wand 2013; King et al. 2004) does not work effectively here due to the nature of our theoretical arguments. For anchoring vignettes to work, researchers must assume that people share the same understanding of the construct of interest (e.g., political efficacy) but assess the construct in different ways. It is similar to the scenario wherein people try to gauge the length of the same object but using rulers with different measurement units (e.g., inches or centimeters). The use of anchoring vignettes then can effectively align the measurement units of all the rulers, thus ensuring effective

comparisons. However, we argue that people actually use different criteria for assessing democratic practices; and such criteria are primarily shaped by their respective democratic conceptions. Thus, for us, the key issue is that people do not share the same understanding of the construct of interest (i.e., democracy). This is similar to the scenario wherein some people try to assess the length of an object using rulers; while others try to evaluate the weight of the same object using scales. It is impossible to align the measurement units of rulers (e.g., inches) and scales (e.g., ounces) by simply using anchoring vignettes.

5. For the IRT scores, missing values were dropped. For the LCA groups, the group of "Agnostics" was dropped.
6. Detailed regression results are provided in Table A5.1.
7. Most people are able to assess the level of democracy in major foreign countries such as the United States and China, given their exposure to relevant information. However, it is inappropriate to ask for their satisfaction with the practice of democracy in most other foreign countries due to the lack of any meaningful personal stakes or experiences of democracy in those countries. Conversely, it is meaningful to ask respondents for both their perceived levels of and satisfaction with the practice of democracy in their home societies.
8. The twenty-four societies are (in ascending order): Egypt, Swaziland, Sudan, Togo, Nigeria, Madagascar, Mali, Tunisia, Bangladesh, Zimbabwe, Uganda, Nepal, Guinea, Ivory Coast, Cameroon, Kenya, Mongolia, Lesotho, Guatemala, Pakistan, India, El Salvador, Morocco, and Mexico.
9. The twenty-two societies are (in ascending order): Indonesia, Taiwan, Ecuador, Zambia, Mozambique, Mauritius, Cambodia, Namibia, Benin, Botswana, Argentina, Burundi, Algeria, Cape Verde, Malaysia, Singapore, Venezuela, Liberia, Ethiopia, Uruguay, China, and Vietnam.
10. Detailed regression results are provided in Tables A5.2 and A5.3.
11. M2 in Tables A5.2 and A5.3 show the regression results without the interaction.
12. With a reversed Freedom House rating of 6 or 6.5 at the time of the survey.
13. With a reversed Freedom House rating of 1, 1.5, or 2 at the time of the survey.
14. With a reversed Freedom House rating of 4, 4.5, or 5 at the time of the survey.
15. With a reversed Freedom House rating of 1 at the time of the survey.
16. With a reversed Freedom House rating of 5.5 or 6 at the time of the survey.
17. There are different interpretations of these findings, see Inglehart (2016).

Chapter 6

1. There are debates on how to reform electoral institutions in established democracies. For instance, in the United States, there are ongoing debates on the Electoral College system, voter registration laws, gerrymandering, and campaign finance. However, regarding the one-person-one-vote system, as well as the regularity and competitiveness of elections, there is little challenge or disagreement.

2. In country-specific studies or comparative studies of democracies, voting has been examined as a solo independent variable. However, for comparative projects like the GBS covering different political regimes, the meaning of voting varies on many dimensions (e.g., national vs. local, competitive vs. semi-competitive, presidential vs. parliamentary, etc.), thus making it very challenging to focus just on voting for related analysis. We have taken a compromise approach by using the summary index to gauge people's general propensity to engage in election-related activities (including both voting and campaigning activities) to ensure a higher level of comparability.
3. The three instruments adopted the same dichotomous scale: zero for "No" and one for "Yes." The associated Cronbach's alpha reliability coefficient is 0.48. Given the dichotomous nature of the scales, the relatively low reliability coefficient is not surprising.
4. It is reasonable to argue that for people to enjoy expressive values associated with defending democracy's intrinsic values via electoral participation, they should, at least, be able to attach some meanings to the D-word.
5. We also specified mixed-effect model with a quadratic form of people's age to capture possible curvilinear relationships. Detailed regression results are provided in Table A6.1.
6. M3 in Table A6.1 shows that the relationship between electoral participation and age might be curvilinear, more specifically, an inverted-U shaped relationship. Middle-aged citizens, *ceteris paribus*, reported the highest rate of participation in electoral politics. This specification does not change any other result and related conclusions.
7. M2 and M4 in Table A6.1 show the regression results without interactions.
8. All the research adopts the WVS module (i.e., using rating scales) to measure different democratic ideals or conceptions. We discussed related issues and problems in Chapter 2. The PUD instruments focus on how people might trade off key democratic principles for instrumental gains as they conceptualize democracy. Therefore, compared to the WVS module, the PUD instruments are more effective in capturing the dynamics of expressive considerations in political participation.
9. The three instruments used the same trichotomous scale: zero for "Never," one for "Once," and two for "More than once." Due to the very small percentage of respondents choosing "More than once," we combined that category with the "Once" category for subsequent analyses. The Cronbach's alpha reliability coefficient for the three instruments is 0.71.
10. Detailed regression results are provided in Table A6.2.
11. There is a high level of uncertainty associated with the estimate of this coefficient, due to the limited number of societies witnessing economic recession at the time of the GBS II survey. Therefore, we shall not over-interpret this finding.
12. M2 and M4 in Table A6.2 show the regression results without interactions.
13. The regression coefficient of education is positive and statistically significant.
14. The two instruments used the same trichotomous scale: zero for "Never," one for "Once," and two for "More than once." Due to the very small percentages of respondents choosing "More than once," we combined that category with the "Once" category for subsequent analyses. The Cronbach's alpha reliability coefficient for the two instruments is 0.41.

198 NOTES

15. Detailed regression results are provided in Table A6.3.

Chapter 7

1. Accessed on December 20, 2020. Detailed information can be found at https://covid19.who.int.
2. Accessed on November 11, 2020. Detailed information can be found at https://www.imf.org/en/Publications/WEO/Issues/2020/09/30/world-economic-outlook-october-2020#Full%20Report%20and%20Executive%20Summary.

References

Acemoglu, Daron, and James A. Robinson. 2006. *Economic Origins of Dictatorship and Democracy*. New York: Cambridge University Press.

Achen, Christopher, and Larry M. Bartels. 2016. *Democracy for Realists: Why Elections Do Not Produce Responsive Government*. Princeton, NJ: Princeton University Press.

Aldrich, John. 1993. "Rational Choice and Turnout." *American Journal of Political Science* 37 (1):246–78.

Aldrich, John, Jacob Montgomery, and Wendy Wood. 2011. "Turnout as a Habit." *Political Behavior* 33 (4):535–63.

Alwin, Duane F., and Jon A. Krosnick. 1985. "The Measurement of Values in Surveys: A Comparison of Ratings and Rankings." *Public Opinion Quarterly* 49 (4):535–52.

Ananda, Aurelia, and Damien Bol. Forthcoming. "Does Knowing Democracy Affect Answers to Democratic Support Questions? A Survey Experiment in Indonesia." *International Journal of Public Opinion Research*.

Anderson, Christopher J. 2007. "The End of Economic Voting? Contingency Dillemas and the Limits of Demcoratic Accountability." *Annual Review of Political Science* 10:271–96.

Anderson, Christopher J. 2002. "Good Questions, Dubious Inferences, and Bad Solutions: Some Further Thoughts on Satisfaction with Democracy." Working Paper No. 116. Center on Democratic Performance, Department of Political Science, Binghamton University.

Ansolabehere, Stephen, Marc Meredith, and Erik Snowberg. 2012. "Sociotropic Voting and the Media." In *Improving Public Opinion Surveys: Interdisciplinary Innovation and the American National Election Studies*, ed. J. Aldrich and K. M. McGraw. Princeton, NJ: Princeton University Press.

Atkeson, Lonna Rae, Alex N. Adams, and R. Michael Alvarez. 2014. "Nonresponse and Mode Effects in Self- and Interviewer-Administered Surveys." *Political Analysis* 22 (3):304–20.

Bakule, Jakub. Forthcoming. "The Good, the Bad and the Ugly: Linking Democratic Values and Participation in the Czech Republic." *Democratization*:1–19.

Barnes, Samuel H., and Max Kasse. 1979. *Political Action: Mass Participation in Five Western Democracies*. Beverly Hills, CA: Sage Publications.

Barro, Robert J. 1999. "Determinants of Democracy." *Journal of Political Economy* 107 (6):158–83.

Bartels, Larry M., and Simon Jackman. 2014. "A Generational Model of Political Learning." *Electoral Studies* 33:7–18.

Baviskar, Siddhartha, and Mary Fran T. Malone. 2004. "What Democracy Means to Citizens—and Why It Matters." *European Review of Latin American and Caribbean Studies* 76:3–23.

Beaulieu, Emily, and Susan D. Hyde. 2009. "In the Shadow of Democracy Promotion: Strategic Manipulation, International Observers, and Election Boycotts." *Comparative Political Studies* 42 (3):392–415.

Beissinger, Mark R., and Stephen Kotkin, eds. 2014. *Historical Legacies of Communism in Russia and Eastern Europe.* New York: Cambridge University Press.

Bell, Daniel A. 2015. *The China Model: Political Meritocracy and the Limits of Democracy.* Princeton, NJ: Princeton University Press.

Bell, Daniel A., and Ruiping Fan, eds. 2012. *A Confucian Constitutional Order: How China's Ancient Past Can Shape Its Political Future.* Princeton, NJ: Princeton University Press.

Bell, Daniel A., and Chenyang Li, eds. 2013. *The East Asian Challenge for Democracy: Political Meritocracy in Comparative Perspective.* New York: Cambridge University Press.

Bentler, Peter M. 2000. "Rites, Wrongs, and Gold in Model Testing." *Structural Equation Modeling* 7 (1):82–91.

Berinsky, Adam J., and Joshua A. Tucker. 2006. "'Don't Knows' and Public Opinion towards Economic Reform: Evidence from Russia." *Communist and Post-Communist Studies* 39 (1):73–99.

Bishop, George F. 1987. "Experiments with the Middle Response Alternative in Survey Questions." *Public Opinion Quarterly* 51 (2):220–32.

Brennan, Geoffrey, and Alan Hamlin. 1998. "Expressive Voting and Electoral Equilibrium." *Public Choice* 95 (1):149–75.

Boix, Carles. 2003. *Democracy and Redistribution.* New York: Cambridge University Press.

Boix, Carles. 2011. "Democracy, Development, and the International System." *American Political Science Review* 105 (04):809–28.

Boix, Carles, and Susan C. Stokes. 2003. "Endogenous Democratization." *World Politics* 55 (July):517–49.

Boix, Carles, and Milan M. Svolik. 2013. "The Foundations of Limited Authoritarian Government: Institutions, Commitment, and Power-Sharing in Dictatorships." *Journal of Politics* 75 (2):300–16.

Bonikowski, Bart, and Noam Gidron. 2016. "The Populist Style in American Politics: Presidential Campaign Rhetoric, 1952–1996." *Social Forces* 94 (4):1593–621.

Bratton, Michael, and Robert Mattes. 2001. "Support for Democracy in Africa: Intrinsic or Instrumental?" *British Journal of Political Science* 31 (3):447–74.

Bratton, Michael, Robert Mattes, and E. Gyimah-Boadi. 2005. *Public Opinion, Democracy, and Market Reform in Africa.* New York: Cambridge University Press.

Browne, Michael W., and Robert Cudeck. 1993. "Alternative Ways of Assessing Model Fit." In *Testing Structural Equation Models*, ed. K. A. Bollen and J. S. Long. Newbury Park, CA: Sage Publication.

Brunkert, Lennart, Stefan Kruse, and Christian Welzel. 2019. "A Tale of Culture-Bound Regime Evolution: The Centennial Democratic Trend and Its Recent Reversal." *Democratization* 26 (3):422–43.

Bunce, Valerie J., and Sharon L. Wolchik. 2010. "Defeating Dictators: Electoral Change and Stability in Competitive Authoritarian Regimes." *World Politics* 62 (1):43–86.

Burns, Nancy, K. Lehman Schlozman, and Sidney Verba. 2001. *The Private Roots of Public Action: Gender, Equality, and Political Participation.* Cambridge, MA: Harvard University Press.

Camp, Ai Roderic, ed. 2001. *Citizen Views of Democracy in Latin America.* Pittsburgh, PA: University of Pittsburgh Press.

Canache, Damarys. 2012. "Citizens' Conceptualization of Democracy: Structural Complexity, Substantive Content, and Political Significance." *Comparative Political Studies* 45 (9):1132–58.

Canache, Damarys, Jeffery J. Mondak, and Mitchell A. Seligson. 2001. "Meaning and Measurement in Cross-National Research on Satisfaction with Democracy." *Public Opinion Quarterly* 65 (4):506–28.

Carey, John M., Gretchen Helmke, Brendan Nyhan, Mitchell Sanders, and Susan Stokes. 2019. "Searching for Bright Lines in the Trump Presidency." *Perspectives on Politics* 17 (3):699–718.

Carnaghan, Ellen. 1996. "Alienation, Apathy, or Ambivalence? "Don't Knows" and Democracy in Russia." *Slavic Review* 55 (2):325–63.

Carothers, Thomas. 2015. "Democracy Aid at 25: Time to Choose." *Journal of Democracy* 20 (1):59–73.

Ceka, Besir, and Pedro C. Magalhães. 2020. "Do the Rich and the Poor Have Different Conceptions of Democracy? Socioeconomic Status, Inequality, and the Political Status Quo." *Comparative Politics* 52 (3):383–412.

Chan, Joseph. 2007. "Democracy and Meritocracy: Toward a Confucian Perspective." *Journal of Chinese Philosophy* 34 (2):179–93.

Chan, Joseph. 2014. *Confucian Perfectionism: A Political Philosophy for Modern Times*. Princeton, NJ: Princeton University Press.

Chan, Joseph. 2013. "Political Meritocracy and Meritorious Rule: A Confucian Perspective." In *The East Asian Challenge for Democracy: Political Meritocracy in Comparative Perspective*, ed. D. Bell and C. Li, 31–54. New York: Cambridge University Press.

Chen, Jidong, Jennifer Pan, and Yiqing Xu. 2016. "Sources of Authoritarian Responsiveness: A Field Experiment in China." *American Journal of Political Science* 60 (2):383–400.

Chen, Jie. 2013. *A Middle Class without Democracy: Economic Growth and the Prospects for Democracy in China*. New York: Oxford University Press.

Chen, Xi. 2012. *Social Protest and Contentious Authoritarianism in China*. New York: Cambridge University Press.

Cho, Youngho. 2014. "To Know Democracy Is to Love It: A Cross-National Analysis of Democratic Understanding and Political Support for Democracy." *Political Research Quarterly* 67 (3):478–88.

Cho, Youngho. 2015. "How Well are Global Citizenries Informed about Democracy? Ascertaining the Breadth and Distribution of Their Democratic Enlightenment and Its Sources." *Political Studies* 63 (1):240–58.

Choi, Incheol, and Richard E. Nisbett. 1998. "Situational Salience and Cultural Differences in the Correspondence Bias and Actor-Observer Bias." *Personality and Social Psychology Bulletin* 24 (9):949–60.

Chu, Yun-han. 2013. "Sources of Regime Legitimacy and the Debate over the Chinese Model." *China Review* 13 (1):1–42.

Collier, David, and James Mahoney. 1993. "Conceptual 'Stretching' Revisited: Adapting Categories in Comparative Analysis." *American Political Science Review* 87 (4):845–55.

Collins, Linda M., and Stephanie T. Lanza. 2010. *Latent Class and Latent Transition Analysis: With Applications in the Social, Behavioral, and Health Sciences*. Hoboken, NJ: John Wiley & Sons, Inc.

Comşa, Mircea, and Camil Postelnicu. 2013. "Measuring Social Desirability Effects on Self-Reported Turnout Using the Item Count Technique." *International Journal of Public Opinion Research* 25 (2):153–72.

Converse, Philip E. 2006. "The Nature of Belief System in Mass Publics (1964)." *Critical Review* 18 (1–3):1–74.

Croke, Kevin, G. U. Y. Grossman, Horacio A. Larreguy, and John Marshall. 2016. "Deliberate Disengagement: How Education Can Decrease Political Participation in Electoral Authoritarian Regimes." *American Political Science Review* 110 (3):579–600.

Crow, David. 2010. "The Party's Over: Citizens' Conceptions of Democracy and Political Dissatisfaction in Mexico." *Comparative Politics* 43 (1):41–62.

Dahl, Robert A. 1956. *A Preface to Democratic Theory*. Chicago, IL: University of Chicago Press.

Dahl, Robert A. 1989. *Democracy and Its Critics*. New Haven, CT: Yale University Press.

Dahlberg, Stefan, and Sören Holmberg. 2014. "Democracy and Bureaucracy: How their Quality Matters for Popular Satisfaction." *West European Politics* 37 (3):515–37.

Dalton, Russell, Doh Chull Shin, and Willy Jou. 2007. "Understanding Democracy: Data from Unlikely Places." *Journal of Democracy* 18 (4):142–56.

Dalton, Russell, Alix Van Sickle, and Steven Weldon. 2009. "The Individual–Institutional Nexus of Protest Behaviour." *British Journal of Political Science* 40 (1):51–73.

Davis, James C. 1962. "Toward a Theory of Revolution." *American Sociological Review* 27 (1):5–19.

Deacon, Robert T. 2009. "Public Good Provision under Dictatorship and Democracy." *Public Choice* 139 (1/2):241–62.

Diamond, Larry. 1997. *Consolidating the Third Wave Democracies*. Baltimore, MD: Johns Hopkins University Press.

Diamond, Larry. 2019. *Ill Winds: Saving Democracy from Russian Rage, Chinese Ambition, and American Complacency*. New York: Penguin Press.

Diamond, Larry, and Leonardo Morlino. 2005. *Assessing the Quality of Democracy*. Baltimore, MD: Johns Hopkins University Press.

Diamond, Larry, and Marc F. Plattner, eds. 2015. *Democracy in Decline?* Baltimore, MD: Johns Hopkins University Press.

Dickson, Bruce J. 2016. *The Dictator's Dilemma: The Chinese Communist Party's Strategy for Survival*. New York: Oxford University Press.

Dinas, Elias, and Laura Stoker. 2014. "Age-Period-Cohort Analysis: A Design-Based Approach." *Electoral Studies* 33:28–40.

Distelhorst, Greg, and Yue Hou. 2017. "Constituency Service under Nondemocratic Rule: Evidence from China." *Journal of Politics* 79 (3):1024–40.

Drinkwater, Stephen, and Colin Jennings. 2007. "Who Are the Expressive Voters?" *Public Choice* 132 (1/2):179–89.

Druckman, James N. 2004. "Political Preference Formation: Competition, Deliberation, and the (Ir)relevance of Framing Effects." *American Political Science Review* 98 (4):671–86.

Druckman, James N., Erik Peterson, and Rune Slothuus. 2013. "How Elite Partisan Polarization Affects Public Opinion Formation." *American Political Science Review* 107 (1):57–79.

Easton, David. 1965. *A Systems Analysis of Political Life*. New York: John Wiley & Sons, Inc.

Easton, David. 1975. "A Re-Assessment of the Concept of Political Support." *British Journal of Political Science* 5 (4):435–57.

Eckstein, Harry. 1975. "Case Study and Theory in Political Science." In *Handbook of Political Science, Vol. 7: Strategies of Inquiry*, ed. F. Greenstein and N. Polsby. Reading, MA: Addison-Wesley Publishing Company.

Eisenstadt, Shmuel N. 1966. *Modernization: Protest and Change*. Englewood Cliffs, NJ: Prentice-Hall.

Erikson, Robert S. 2015. "Income Inequality and Policy Responsiveness." *Annual Review of Political Science* 18:11–29.

Feng, Y., and P. Zak. 1999. "The Determinants of Democratic Transition." *Journal of Conflict Resolution* 43 (2):162–77.

Ferrin, Monica, and Hanspeter Kriesi, eds. 2016. *How Europeans View and Evaluate Democracy*. New York: Oxford University Press.

Ferrin, Monica, and Hanspeter Kriesi. 2016. "Introduction: Democracy—The European Verdict." In *How Europeans View and Evaluate Democracy*, ed. M. Ferrin and H. Kriesi. New York, NY: Oxford University Press.

Fewsmith, Joseph. 2013. *The Logic and Limits of Political Reform in China*. New York: Cambridge University Press.

Flanagan, Constance A., Leslie S. Gallay, Sukhdeep Gill, Erin Gallay, and Naana Nti. 2005. "What Does Democracy Mean? Correlates of Adolescents' Views." *Journal of Adolescent Research* 20 (2):193–218.

Foa, Roberto Stefan, and Yascha Mounk. 2016. "The Danger of Deconsolidation: The Democratic Disconnect." *Journal of Democracy* 27 (3):5–17.

Foa, Roberto Stefan, and Yascha Mounk. 2017. "The Signs of Deconsolidation." *Journal of Democracy* 28 (1):5–15.

Fuchs-Schündeln, Nicola, and Matthias Schündeln. 2015. "On the Endogeneity of Political Preferences: Evidence from Individual Experience with Democracy." *Science* 347 (6226):1145–8.

Fukuyama, Francis. 1992. *The End of History and the Last Man*. New York: Free Press.

Fukuyama, Francis. 1995a. "Confucianism and Democracy." *Journal of Democracy* 6 (2):20–33.

Fukuyama, Francis. 1995b. "The Primacy of Culture." *Journal of Democracy* 6 (1):7–14.

Fukuyama, Francis. 2006. *America at the Crossroads: Democracy, Power, and the Neoconservative Legacy*. New Haven, CT: Yale University Press.

Fukuyama, Francis. 2014. *Political Order and Political Decay: From the Industrial Revolution to the Globalization of Democracy*. New York: Farrar, Straus and Giroux.

Fukuyama, Francis. 2016. "Governance: What Do We Know, and How Do We Know It?" *Annual Review of Political Science* 19 (1):89–105.

Fukuyama, Francis. 2020. "The Pandemic and Political Order: It Takes a State." *Foreign Affairs* July/August:26–32.

Gandhi, Jennifer. 2008. *Political Institutions under Dictatorship*. New York: Cambridge University Press.

Gandhi, Jennifer, and Ellen Lust-Okar. 2009. "Elections Under Authoritarianism." *Annual Review of Political Science* 12:403–22.

Geddes, Barbara, Joseph Wright, and Erica Frantz. 2014. "Autocratic Breakdown and Regime Transitions: A New Data Set." *Perspectives on Politics* 12 (02):313–31.

Geddes, Barbara, Joseph Wright, and Erica Frantz. 2018. *How Dictatorships Work: Power, Personalization, and Collapse*. New York: Cambridge University Press.

Geddes, Barbara, and John Zaller. 1989. "Sources of Popular Support for Authoritarian Regimes." *American Journal of Political Science* 33 (2):319–47.

Gelman, Andrew, and Jennifer Hill. 2007. *Data Analysis Using Regression and Multilevel/Hierarchical Models*. New York: Cambridge University Press.

Gerring, John. 2007. "Is There a (Viable) Crucial-Case Method?" *Comparative Political Studies* 40 (3):231–53.

Gerring, John. 2012. *Social Science Methodology: A Unified Framework*. 2nd. ed. New York: Cambridge University Press.

Gerring, John, Strom C. Thacker, and Rodrigo Alfaro. 2012. "Democracy and Human Development." *The Journal of Politics* 74 (1):1–17.

Gilens, Martin. 2005. "Inequality and Democratic Responsiveness." *Public Opinion Quarterly* 69 (5):778–96.

Gilens, Martin. 2012. *Affluence and Influence: Economic Inequality and Political Power in America*. Princeton, NJ: Princeton University Press.

Gillman, Anne. 2018. "Ideals Without Institutions: Understandings of Democracy and Democratic Participation among Ecuadorian Youth." *Studies in Comparative International Development* 53 (4):428–48.

Gimpel, J. G., Irwin L. Morris, and David R. Armstrong. 2004. "Turnout and the Local Age Distribution: Examining Political Participation Across Space and Time." *Political Geography* 23 (1):71–95.

Goodwin, Jeff. 2001. *No Other Way Out: States and Revolutionary Movements, 1945–1991*. New York: Cambridge University Press.

Graham, Matthew H., and Milan W. Svolik. 2020. "Democracy in America? Partisanship, Polarization, and the Robustness of Support for Democracy in the United States." *American Political Science Review* 114 (2):392–409.

Grasso, Maria T. 2014. "Age, Period and Cohort Analysis in a Comparative Context: Political Generations and Political Participation Repertoires in Western Europe." *Electoral Studies* 33:63–76.

Groves, Robert M., Floyd J. Fowler Jr., Mick P. Couper, James M. Lepkowski, Eleanor Singer, and Roger Tourangeau. 2009. *Survey Methodology*. 2nd ed. Hoboken, NJ: Wiley.

Gurr, Ted. 1970. *Why Men Rebel*. Princeton, NJ: Princeton University Press.

Haggard, Stephan, and Robert R. Kaufman. 2016. "Democratization During the Third Wave." *Annual Review of Political Science* 19:125–44.

Hainmueller, Jens, Daniel J. Hopkins, and Teppei Yamamoto. 2014. "Causal Inference in Conjoint Analysis: Understanding Multidimensional Choices via Stated Preference Experiments." *Political Analysis* 22 (1):1–30.

Hardin, Russell. 1995. *One for All: The Logic of Group Conflict*. Princeton, NJ: Princeton University Press.

Hayes, Andrew F., Carroll J. Glynn, and James Shanahan. 2005. "Willingness to Self-Censor: A Construct and Measurement Tool for Public Opinion Research." *International Journal of Public Opinion Research* 17 (3):298–323.

Hayes, Andrew F., Brian Uldall, and Carroll J. Glynn. 2010. "Validating the Willingness to Self-Censor Scale II: Inhibition of Opinion Expression in a Conversational Setting." *Communication Methods and Measures* 4 (3):256–72.

Heyne, Lea. 2019. "The Making of Democratic Citizens: How Regime-Specific Socialization Shapes Europeans' Expectations of Democracy." *Swiss Political Science Review* 25 (1):40–63.

Hough, Jerry F. 1976. "Political participation in the Soviet Union AU." *Soviet Studies* 28 (1):3–20.

Houle, Christian. 2009. "Inequality and Democracy: Why Inequality Harms Consolidation but Does Not Affect Demcoratization." *World Politics* 61 (4):589–622.

Howe, Paul. 2017. "Eroding Norms and Democratic Deconsolidation." *Journal of Democracy* 28 (4):15–29.

Hoyle, Rick H. 1995. *Structural Equation Modeling: Concepts, Issues, and Applications.* Thousand Oaks, CA: Sage Publications.

Hu, Yue. 2020. "Refocusing Democracy: The Chinese Government's Framing Strategy in Political Language." *Democratization* 27 (2):302–20.

Huang, Min-Hua, Yun-han Chu, and Yu-tzung Chang. 2013. "Popular Understandings of Democracy and Regime Legitimacy in East Asia." *Taiwan Journal of Democracy* 9 (1):147–71.

Huntington, Samuel P. 1991. *The Third Wave: Democratization in the Late Twentieth Century.* Norman: University of Oklahoma Press.

Inglehart, Ronald. 1990. *Culture Shift in Advanced Industrial Society.* Princeton, NJ: Princeton University Press.

Inglehart, Ronald. 1997a. *Modernization and Postmodernization: Cultural, Economic, and Political Change in 43 Societies.* Princeton, NJ: Princeton University Press.

Inglehart, Ronald. 1997b. "Postmaterialist Values and the Erosion of Institutional Authority." In *Why People Don't Trust Government*, ed. J. S. Nye, P. Zelikow, and D. C. King, 217–36. Cambridge, MA: Harvard University Press.

Inglehart, Ronald. 2016. "How Much Should We Worry?" *Journal of Democracy* 27 (3):18–23.

Inglehart, Ronald. 2018. *Cultural Evolution: People's Motivations Are Changing and Reshaping the World.* New York: Cambridge University Press.

Inglehart, Ronald, and Pippa Norris. 2017. "Trump and the Populist Authoritarian Parties: The Silent Revolution in Reverse." *Perspectives on Politics* 15 (2):443–54.

Inglehart, Ronald, and Christian Welzel. 2005. *Modernization, Cultural Change, and Democracy: The Human Development Sequence.* New York: Cambridge University Press.

Inglehart, Ronald, and Christian Welzel. 2010. "Changing Mass Priorities: The Link between Modernization and Democracy." *Perspectives on Politics* 8 (2):551–67.

Jennings, M. Kent. 1998. "Gender and Political Participation in the Chinese Countryside." *Journal of Politics* 60 (4):954–73.

Jessee, Stephen A. 2017. "'Don't Know' Responses, Personality, and the Measurement of Political Knowledge." *Political Science Research and Methods* 5 (4):711–31.

Kagan, Robert. 2015. "The Weight of Geopolitics." *Journal of Democracy* 26 (1):21–31.

Karklins, Rasma. 1986. "Soviet Elections Revisited: Voter Abstention in Noncompetitive Voting." *American Political Science Review* 80 (2):449–69.

Kelley, Judith. 2011. "Do International Election Monitors Increase or Decrease Opposition Boycotts?" *Comparative Political Studies* 44 (11):1527–56.

Kelley, Judith. 2012. *Monitoring Democracy: When International Election Monitoring Works and Why It Often Fails.* Princeton, NJ: Princeton University Press.

Kiewiet de Jonge, Chad P. 2016. "Should Researchers Abandon Questions about 'Democracy'? Evidence from Latin America." *Public Opinion Quarterly* 80 (3):694–716.

Kim, Wonik, and Jennifer Gandhi. 2010. "Coopting Workers under Dictatorship." *Journal of Politics* 72 (3):646–58.

Kinder, Donald R., and Nathan P. Kalmoe. 2017. *Neither Liberal nor Conservative: Ideological Innocence in the American Public.* Chicago, IL: University of Chicago Press.

King, Gary, Christopher J. L. Murray, Joshua A. Salomon, and Ajay Tandon. 2004. "Enhancing the Validity and Cross-Cultural Comparability of Measurement in Survey Research." *American Political Science Review* 98 (1):191–207.

King, Gary, Jennifer Pan, and Margaret E. Roberts. 2013. "How Censorship in China Allows Government Criticism but Silences Collective Expression." *American Political Science Review* 107 (2):326–43.

King, Gary, Jennifer Pan, and Margaret E. Roberts. 2017. "How the Chinese Government Fabricates Social Media Posts for Strategic Distraction, Not Engaged Argument." *American Political Science Review* 111 (3):484–501.

King, Gary, and Jonathan Wand. 2007. "Comparing Incomparable Survey Responses: Evaluating and Selecting Anchoring Vignettes." *Political Analysis* 15 (1):46–66.

Kirsch, Helen, and Christian Welzel. 2019. "Democracy Misunderstood: Authoritarian Notions of Democracy around the Globe." *Social Forces* 98 (1):59–92.

Koss, Daniel. 2018. *Where the Party Rules: The Rank and File of China's Communist State*. New York: Cambridge University Press.

Kreuter, Frauke, ed. 2013. Improving Surveys with Paradata: Analytic Use of Process Information. Hoboken, NJ: John Wiley & Sons, Inc.

Kriesi, Hanspeter, and Leonardo Morlino. 2016. "Conclusion: What Have We Learnt, and Where Do We Go from Here?" In *How Europeans View and Evaluate Democracy*, ed. M. Ferrin and H. Kriesi. New York: Oxford University Press.

Kruse, Stefan, Maria Ravlik, and Christian Welzel. 2019. "Democracy Confused: When People Mistake the Absence of Democracy for Its Presence." *Journal of Cross-Cultural Psychology* 50 (3):315–35.

Kumlin, Staffan, and Peter Esaiasson. 2011. "Scandal Fatigue? Scandal Elections and Satisfaction with Democracy in Western Europe, 1977–2007." *British Journal of Political Science* 42 (2):263–82.

Kung, James Kai-sing, and Chicheng Ma. 2014. "Can Cultural Norms Reduce Conflicts? Confucianism and Peasant Rebellions in Qing China." *Journal of Developmental Economics* 111:132–49.

Kuran, Timur. 1995. *Private Truths, Public Lies: The Social Consequences of Preference Falsification*. Cambridge, MA: Harvard University Press.

Leemann, Lucas, and Fabio Wasserfallen. 2016. "The Democratic Effect of Direct Democracy." *American Political Science Review* 110 (4):750–62.

Lei, Xuchuan, and Jie Lu. 2017. "Revisiting Political Wariness in China's Public Opinion Surveys: Experimental Evidence on Responses to Politically Sensitive Questions." *Journal of Contemporary China* 26 (104):213–32.

Leighley, Jan E., and Jonathan Nagler. 2014. *Who Votes Now? Demographics, Issues, Inequality, and Turnout in the United States*. Princeton, NJ: Princeton University Press.

Leighley, Jan E., and Arnold Vedlitz. 1999. "Race, Ethnicity, and Political Participation: Competing Models and Contrasting Explanations." *Journal of Politics* 61 (4):1092–114.

Levitsky, Steven, and Lucan Way. 2010. *Competitive Authoritarianism: The Emergence and Dynamics of Hybrid Regimes in the Post-Cold War Era*. New York: Cambridge University Press.

Levitsky, Steven, and Daniel Ziblatt. 2018. *How Democracies Die*. New York: Crown Publishing.

Li, Cheng. 2012. "The End of the CCP's Resilient Authoritarianism? A Tripartite Assessment of Shifting Power in China." *China Quarterly* 211:595–623.

Lichbach, Mark Irving. 1995. *The Rebel's Dilemma*. Ann Arbor: University of Michigan Press.

Lipset, Seymour Martin. 1959. "Some Social Requisites for Democracy: Economic Development and Political Legitimacy." *American Political Science Review* 53 (1):69–105.

Long, J. S. 1983. *Confirmatory Factor Analysis: A Preface to LISREL*. Beverly Hills, CA: Sage Publications.

Lorenzo, David J. 2013. *Conceptions of Chinese Democracy: Reading Sun Yat-sen, Chiang Kai-shek, and Chiang Ching-kuo*. Baltimore, MD: Johns Hopkins University Press.

Lu, Jie. 2013. "Democratic Conceptions in East Asian Societies: A Contextualized Analysis." *Taiwan Journal of Democracy* 9 (1):117–45.

Lu, Jie, John Aldrich, and Tianjian Shi. 2014. "Revisiting Media Effects in Authoritarian Societies: Democratic Conceptions, Collectivistic Norms, and Media Access in Urban China." *Politics & Society* 42 (2):253–83.

Lu, Jie, and Tianjian Shi. 2015. "The Battle of Ideas and Discourses before Democratic Transition: Different Democratic Conceptions in Authoritarian China." *International Political Science Review* 36 (1):20–41.

Luke, Douglas A. 2004. *Multilevel Modeling*. Thousand Oaks, CA: Sage Publications.

Luskin, Robert C., and John G. Bullock. 2011. "'Don't Know' Means 'Don't Know': DK Responses and the Public's Level of Political Knowledge." *Journal of Politics* 73 (2):547–57.

Magaloni, Beatriz. 2008. "Credible Power-Sharing and the Longevity of Authoritarian Rule." *Comparative Political Studies* 41 (4/5):715–41.

Mainwaring, Scott, and Aníbal Pérez-Liñán. 2013. "Democratic Breakdown and Survival." *Journal of Democracy* 24 (4):123–37.

Malesky, Edmund, and Jonathan London. 2014. "The Political Economy of Development in China and Vietnam." *Annual Review of Political Science* 17:395–419.

Manion, Melanie. 2016. *Information for Autocrats: Representation in Chinese Local Congresses*. New York: Cambridge University Press.

Markowski, Radoslaw. 2016. "Determinants of Democratic Legitimacy: Liberal Democracy and Social Justice." In *How Europeans View and Evaluate Democracy*, ed. M. Ferrin and H. Kriesi. New York: Oxford University Press.

Mattes, Robert, and M. Bratton. 2007. "Learning about Democracy in Africa: Awareness, Performance, and Experience." *American Journal of Political Science* 51 (1):192–217.

McAdam, Doug, John D. McCarthy, and Mayer N. Zald. 1996. *Comparative Perspectives on Social Movements: Political Opportunities, Mobilizing Structures, and Cultural Framings*. New York: Cambridge University Press.

McAdam, Doug, Sidney G. Tarrow, and Charles Tilly. 2001. *Dynamics of Contention*. New York: Cambridge University Press.

McCutcheon, Allan. 1987. *Latent Class Analysis*. Thousand Oaks, CA: Sage Publications.

Micklethwait, John, and Adrian Wooldridge. 2014. *The Fourth Revolution: The Global Rrace to Reinvent the State*. New York: Penguin Press.

Miller, Joan G. 2001. "The Cultural Grounding of Social Psychological Theory." In *Blackwell Handbook of Social Psychology: Intraindividual Processes*, ed. A. Tesser and N. Schwarz. Malden, MA: Blackwell Publishers Inc.

Miller, Warren E., and J. Merrill Shanks. 1996. *The New American Voter*. Cambridge, MA: Harvard University Press.

Moffitt, Benjamin. 2016. *The Global Rise of Populism: Performance, Political Style, and Representation*. Stanford, CA: Stanford University Press.

Møller, Jørgen, and Svend-Erik Skaaning. 2013. "The Third Wave: Inside the Numbers." *Journal of Democracy* 24 (4):97–109.

Morse, Yonatan L. 2012. "The Era of Electoral Authoritarianism." *World Politics* 64 (1): 161–98.

Mounk, Yascha. 2018. *The People vs. Democracy*. Cambridge, MA: Harvard University Press.

Mudde, Cas, and Cristóbal Rovira Kaltwasser, eds. 2012. *Populism in Europe and the Americas: Threat or Corrective for Democracy?* New York: Cambridge University Press.

Nathan, Andrew J. 2003. "Authoritarian Resilience." *Journal of Democracy* 14 (1):6–17.

Nathan, Andrew J. 2015. *Beijing Bull: The Bogus China Model*. The National Interest [cited October 23 2015].

Naughton, Barry J. 2007. *The Chinese Economy: Transition and Growth*. Cambridge, MA: MIT Press.

Norris, Pippa, and Ronald Inglehart. 2009. *Cosmopolitan Communications*. New York: Cambridge University Press.

Norris, Pippa, and Ronald Inglehart. 2018. *Cultural Backlash: Trump, Brexit and the Rise of Authoritarian Populism*. New York: Cambridge University Press.

Ober, Josiah. 1989. *Mass and Elite in Democratic Athens: Rhetoric, Ideology, and the Power of the People*. Princeton, NJ: Princeton University Press.

Olken, Benjamin A. 2010. "Direct Democracy and Local Public Goods: Evidence from a Field Experiment in Indonesia." *American Political Science Review* 104 (2):243–67.

Olson, M. 1971. *The Logic of Collective Action: Public Goods and the Theory of Groups*. Cambridge, MA: Harvard University Press.

Öniş, Ziya. 2017. "The Age of Anxiety: The Crisis of Liberal Democracy in a Post-Hegemonic Global Order." *The International Spectator* 52 (3):18–35.

Ortmann, Stephan, and Mark R. Thompson. 2016. "China and the 'Singapore Model.'" *Journal of Democracy* 27 (1):39–48.

Oser, Jennifer, and Marc Hooghe. 2018. "Democratic Ideals and Levels of Political Participation: The Role of Political and Social Conceptualisations of Democracy." *British Journal of Politics and International Relations* 20 (3):711–30.

Park, Jong H. 2002. "The East Asian Model of Economic Development and Developing Countries." *Journal of Developing Societies* 18 (4):330–53.

Panel, Sophie. 2019. "Is Popular Support for Democracy Underreported? Evidence From 32 African Countries." *International Journal of Public Opinion Research* 31 (4):753–66.

Pepinsky, Thomas B. 2013. "The Institutional Turn in Comparative Authoritarianism." *British Journal of Political Science* 44 (3):631–53.

Persson, T., and G. Tabellini. 2009. "Democratic Capital: The Nexus of Political and Economic Change." *American Economic Journal: Macroeconomics* 1 (2):88–126.

Plattner, Marc F. 2017. "Liberal Democracy's Fading Allure." *Journal of Democracy* 28 (4):5–14.

Pop-Eleches, Grigore, and Joshua A. Tucker. 2014. "Communist Socialization and Post-Sommunist Economic and Political Attitudes." *Electoral Studies* 33:77–89.

Pop-Eleches, Grigore, and Joshua A. Tucker. 2017. *Communism's Shadow: Historical Legacies and Contemporary Political Attitudes*. Princeton, NJ: Princeton University Press.

Preuss, Ulrich K. 2006. "The Significance of Cognitive and Moral Learning for Democratic Institutions." In *Rethinking Political Institutions: The Art of the State*, ed. I. Shapiro, S. Skowronek, and D. Galvin, 303–21. New York: New York University Press.

Przeworski, Adam, Michael E. Alvarez, Jose A. Cheibub, and Fernando Limongi. 2000. *Democracy and Development: Political Institutions and Well-Being in the World, 1950–1990*. New York: Cambridge University Press.

Przeworski, Adam, Susan C. Stokes, and Bernard Manin. 1999. *Democracy, Accountability, and Representation*. New York: Cambridge University Press.

Quaranta, Mario. 2018. "How Citizens Evaluate Democracy: An Assessment Using the European Social Survey." *European Political Science Review* 10 (2):191–217.

Raudenbush, Stephen W., and Anthony S. Bryk. 2002. *Hierarchical Linear Models: Applications and Data Analysis Methods*. Thousand Oaks, CA: Sage Publications.

Reilly, Jonathan J., and L. J. Zigerell. 2012. "Don't Know Much about Democracy: Reporting Survey Data with Nonsubstantive Responses." *PS: Political Science & Politics* 45 (3):462–7.

Reise, Steven P., Keith F. Widaman, and Robin H. Pugh. 1993. "Confirmatory Factor Analysis and Item Response Theory: Two Approaches for Exploring Measurement Invariance." *Psychological Bulletin* 114:552–66.

Reuter, Ora John, and David Szakonyi. 2015. "Online Social Media and Political Awareness in Authoritarian Regimes." *British Journal of Political Science* 45 (1):29–51.

Rotberg, Robert I. 2014. "Good Governance Means Performance and Results." *Governance* 27 (3):511–8.

Roberts, Margaret E., Brandon M. Stewart, Dustin Tingley, Christopher Lucas, Jetson Leder-Luis, Shana Kushner Gadarian, Bethany Albertson, and David G. Rand. 2014. "Structural Topic Models for Open-Ended Survey Responses." *American Journal of Political Science* 58 (4):1064–82.

Sartori, Giovanni. 1970. "Concept Misformation in Comparative Politics." *American Political Science Review* 64 (4):1033–53.

Schaffer, Frederic C. 1998. *Democracy in Translation: Understanding Politics in an Unfamiliar Culture*. Ithaca, NY: Cornell University Press.

Schaffer, Frederic C. 2014. "Thin Descriptions: The Limits of Survey Research on the Meaning of Democracy." *Polity* 46 (3):303–30.

Schedler, Andreas. 2013. *The Politics of Uncertainty: Sustaining and Subverting Electoral Authoritarianism*. New York: Oxford University Press.

Schedler, Andreas, and Rodolfo Sarsfield. 2007. "Democrats with Adjectives: Linking Direct and Indirect Measures of Democratic Support." *European Journal of Political Research* 46 (5):637–59.

Schelling, Thomas C. 1960. *The Strategy of Conflict*. Cambridge, MA: Harvard University Press.

Schlozman, K. L., S. Verba, and D. Bradley. 2010. "Weapon of the Strong? Participatory Inequality and the Internet." *Perspectives on Politics* 8 (2):487–509.

Schmitter, Philippe C., and Terry L. Karl. 1991. "What Democracy Is and Is Not." *Journal of Democracy* 2 (3):75–88.

Shambaugh, David. 2008. *China's Communist Party: Atrophy and Adaptation*. Berkeley: University of California Press.

Shambaugh, David. 2016. *China's Future*. Malden, MA: Polity Press.

Shen, Xiaoxiao, and Rory Truex. Forthcoming. "In Search of Self-Censorship." *British Journal of Political Science*:1–13.
Shi, Tianjian. 1997. *Political Participation in Beijing*. Cambridge, MA: Harvard University Press.
Shi, Tianjian. 1999. *Generational Differences in Political Attitudes and Political Behaviour in China*. Singapore: Singapore University Press.
Shi, Tianjian. 1999. "Voting and Non-voting in China." *Journal of Politics* 61 (4):1115–39.
Shi, Tianjian. 2008. "China: Democratic Values Supporting an Authoritarian System." In *How East Asians View Democracy*, ed. Y.-h. Chu, L. Diamond, A. J. Nathan, and D. C. Shin, 209–31. New York: Columbia University Press.
Shi, Tianjian. 2015. *The Cultural Logic of Politics in Mainland China and Taiwan*. New York: Cambridge University Press.
Shi, Tianjian, and Jie Lu. 2010. "The Shadow of Confucianism." *Journal of Democracy* 21 (4):123–30.
Shin, Doh Chull. 2012. *Confucianism and Democratization in East Asia*. New York: Cambridge University Press.
Shin, Doh Chull. 2013. "Cultural Origins of Diffuse Regime Support among East Asians: Exploring Alternative to the Theory of Critical Citizens." *Taiwan Journal of Democracy* 9 (2):1–32.
Shin, Doh Chull. 2013. "How East Asians View Meritocracy: A Confucian Perspective." In *The East Asian Challenge for Democracy: Political Meritocracy in Comparative Perspective*, ed. D. Bell and C. Li. New York: Cambridge University Press.
Shin, Doh Chull. 2017. "Popular Understanding of Democracy." In *Oxford Research Encyclopedias: Politics*, ed. W. R. Thompson. New York: Oxford University Press.
Shin, Doh Chull, and Hannah June Kim. 2018. "How Global Citizenries Think about Democracy: An Evaluation and Synthesis of Recent Public Opinion Research." *Japanese Journal of Political Science* 19 (2):222–49.
Shirk, Susan L. 2007. *China: Fragile Superpower*. New York: Oxford University Press.
Simpser, Alberto, Dan Slater, and Jason Wittenberg. 2018. "Dead but Not Gone: Contemporary Legacies of Communism, Imperialism, and Authoritarianism." *Annual Review of Political Science* 21 (1):419–39.
Slater, Dan, Benjamin Smith, and Gautam Nair. 2014. "Economic Origins of Democratic Breakdown? The Redistributive Model and the Postcolonial State." *Perspectives on Politics* 12 (02):353–74.
Sniderman, Paul M. 2018. "Some Advances in the Design of Survey Experiments." *Annual Review of Political Science* 21 (1):259–75.
Snijders, Tom, and Roel Bosker. 2012. *Multilevel Analysis: An Introduction to Basic and Advanced Multilevel Modeling*. 2nd ed. London: Sage Publications.
Sondheimer, Rachel Milstein, and Donald P. Green. 2010. "Using Experiments to Estimate the Effects of Education on Voter Turnout." *American Journal of Political Science* 54 (1):174–89.
Steenbergen, Marco R., and B. S. Jones. 2002. "Modeling Multilevel Data Structures." *American Journal of Political Science* 46 (1):218–37.
Stegmueller, Daniel. 2013. "How Many Countries for Multilevel Modeling? A Comparison of Frequentist and Bayesian Approaches." *American Journal of Political Science* 57 (3):748–61.
Stockmann, Daniela. 2013. *Media Commercialization and Authoritarian Rule in China*. New York: Cambridge University Press.

Svolik, Milan M. 2012. *The Politics of Authoritarian Rule*. New York: Cambridge University Press.
Svolik, Milan M. 2019. "Polarization versus Democracy." *Journal of Democracy* 30 (3): 20–32.
Tang, Wenfang. 2016. *Populist Authoritarianism: Chinese Political Culture and Regime Sustainability*. New York: Oxford University Press.
Tenn, Steven. 2007. "The Effect of Education on Voter Turnout." *Political Analysis* 15 (4):446–64.
Tilley, James, and Geoffrey Evans. 2014. "Ageing and Generational Effects on Vote Choice: Combining Cross-Sectional and Panel Data to Estimate APC effects." *Electoral Studies* 33:19–27.
Tilly, Charles. 2008. *Contentious Performance*. New York: Cambridge University Press.
Tipps, Dean C. 1973. "Modernization Theory and the Comparative Study of Societies: A Critical Perspective." *Comparative Studies in Society and History* 15 (2):199–226.
Tomini, Luca, and Claudius Wagemann. 2018. "Varieties of Contemporary Democratic Breakdown and Regression: A Comparative Analysis." *European Journal of Political Research* 57 (3):687–716.
Tourangeau, Roger, Lance J. Rips, and Kenneth A. Rasinski. 2000. *The Psychology of Survey Response*. New York: Cambridge University Press.
Tourangeau, Roger, and Ting Yan. 2007. "Sensitive Questions in Surveys." *Psychological Bulletin* 133 (5):859–83.
Treier, Shawn, and Simon Jackman. 2008. "Democracy as a Latent Variable." *American Journal of Political Science* 52 (1):201–17.
Treisman, Daniel. 2000. "The Causes of Corruption: A Cross-national Study." *Journal of Public Economics* 76 (3):399–457.
Truex, Rory. 2016. *Making Autocracy Work: Representation and Responsiveness in Modern China*. New York: Cambridge University Press.
Tsai, Lily L. 2015. "Constructive Noncompliance." *Comparative Politics* 47 (3):253–79.
Tsai, Lily L., and Yiqing Xu. 2018. "Outspoken Insiders: Political Connections and Citizen Participation in Authoritarian China." *Political Behavior* 40 (3):629–57.
Ulbig, Stacy, and Carolyn Funk. 1999. "Conflict Avoidance and Political Participation." *Political Behavior* 21 (3):265–82.
Verba, Sidney, Norman H. Nie, and Jae-on Kim. 1971. *The Modes of Democratic Participation: A Cross-National Comparison*. Beverly Hills, CA: Sage Publications.
Verba, Sidney, Norman H. Nie, and Jae-on Kim. 1978. *Participation and Political Equality: A Seven-Nation Comparison*. New York: Cambridge University Press.
Verba, Sidney, and Gary R. Orren. 1985. *Equality in America: The View from the Top*. Cambridge, MA: Harvard University Press.
Verba, Sidney, Kay L. Schlozman, and Henry E. Brady. 1995. *Voice and Equality: Civic Voluntarism in American Politics*. Cambridge, MA: Harvard University Press.
Vermunt, Jeroen K., and Jay Magidson. 2002. "Latent Class Cluster Analysis." In *Applied Latent Class Analysis*, ed. J. A. Hagenaars and A. McCutcheon. New York: Cambridge University Press.
Wand, Jonathan. 2013. "Credible Comparisons Using Interpersonally Incomparable Data: Nonparametric Scales with Anchoring Vignettes." *American Journal of Political Science* 57 (1):249–62.
Wang, Shaoguang. 2006. "Historical Transition in China: from Economic Policy to Soical Policy." Hong Kong: Department of Government and Public Administration, Chinese University of Hong Kong.

Wang, Shaoguang. 2008. "Changing Models of China's Policy Agenda Setting." *Modern China* 34 (1):56–87.
Webb, Paul. 2013. "Who Is Willing to Participate? Dissatisfied Democrats, Stealth Democrats and Populists in the United Kingdom." *European Journal of Political Research* 52 (6):747–72.
Welzel, Christian. 2011. "The Asian Values Thesis Revisited: Evidence from the World Values Surveys." *Japanese Journal of Political Science* 12 (1):1–31.
Welzel, Christian. 2013. *Freedom Rising: Human Empowerment and the Quest for Emancipation.* New York: Cambridge University Press.
Welzel, Christian, and Franziska Deutsch. 2012. "Emancipative Values and Non-Violent Protest: The Importance of 'Ecological' Effects." *British Journal of Political Science* 42 (02):465–79.
Welzel, Christian, and Alejandro Moreno Alvarez. 2014. "Enlightening People: The Spark of Emancipative Values." In The Civic Culture Transformed: From Allegiant to Assetive Citizens, ed. R. Dalton and C. Welzel. New York: Cambridge University Press.
Whitehead, Laurence. 2001. *The International Dimensions of Democratization: Europe and the Americas.* New York: Oxford University Press.
Wolf, Martin. 2017. "Seven Charts That Show How the Developed World Is Lossing Its Edge." *Financial Times*, July 20.
Wolf, Martin. 2019. "Why Rigged Capitalism Is Damaging Liberal Democracy." *Financial Times*, September 18.
Yan, Jie. 2008. "Distribution of Non-response in Chinese Political Survey Research." *Wuhan University Journal (Philosophy & Social Sciences)* 61 (2):225–31.
Yang, Yang. 2008. "Social Inequalities in Happiness in the United States, 1972 to 2004: An Age-Period-Cohort Analysis." *American Sociological Review* 73 (2):204–26.
Zagrebina, Anna. 2020. "Concepts of Democracy in Democratic and Nondemocratic Countries." *International Political Science Review* 41 (2):174–91.
Zaller, John. 1992. *The Nature and Origins of Mass Opinion.* New York: Cambridge University Press.
Zavadskaya, Margarita, and Christian Welzel. 2015. "Subverting Autocracy: Emancipative Mass Values in Competitive Authoritarian Regimes." *Democratization* 22 (6):1105–30.
Zhu, Jian-Hua. 1996. "'I Don't Know' in Public Opinion Surveys in China: Individual and Contextual Causes of Item Non-Response." *Journal of Contemporary China* 5 (12):223–44.

Index

For the benefit of digital users, indexed terms that span two pages (e.g., 52–53) may, on occasion, appear on only one of those pages.

Note: Tables and figures are indicated by *t* and *f* following the page number

Africa, 15–16, 51
   North Africa, 7, 49–50, 55, 58, 172–73
   South Africa, 105, 122–23
   sub-Saharan Africa, 49–50, 55, 58, 172–73
Agnostics, 41–42, 57–58, 64–65, 67, 173, 192n.11, 192n.13
anchoring vignettes, 195–96n.4
ancient Greek political thought, 134
answer categories (CATs), 31–34, 32*f*, 33*f*, 43–44, 75, 171–72
Argentina, 55–56, 105, 121–22, 140–41, 154–55
Asia. *See also specific Asian countries*
   East Asia, 15–16, 17, 49–51, 52, 55, 64–65, 172–74
   South Asia, 15–16, 17, 49–50, 55
   Southeast Asia, 15–16, 17
Asian Barometer Survey (ABS), 47–48, 62–64, 63*f*
attitude-behavior connections, 183–84
authoritarian regimes
   democracy impact on, 1–2, 3–5, 6–8
   electoral participation, 134–35, 136–37, 140–42, 179–80
   notions of democracy, 15
   people's assessments of their, 43
   people's indoctrination by, 86
   resilience against democracy, 17
   transition to democracy, 11, 25–26

Bangladesh, 55–56
Benefit-Seekers, 40–42, 54, 56–57, 64–65, 67, 111–14, 173
Benin, 105
Bolivia, 57–58, 154–55

Botswana, 118
Brazil, 52–53, 55–56, 105, 118, 121–22, 140–41, 154–55, 186–87
Burkina Faso, 122–23, 140–41
Burundi, 52, 66–67, 85, 172–73

Cambodia, 52, 55–56, 60–62, 66–67, 118, 172–73, 186–87
Cameroon, 52, 55–56, 66–67
capacity building in government, 2
Cape Verde, 55–56, 87–88, 121–23, 156
Central America, 15–16
Chile, 58, 87–88, 121–23, 140–41, 156
China
   Confucianism, 13–14, 50–51, 87, 93–94, 110, 115, 123–24, 153–54, 176
   COVID-19 containment, 186–87
   democratic assessment in, 105–16, 109*f*, 111*f*, 124–27
   democratic practice in, 19–20
   economic growth, 13–14, 60–61, 106–7, 108, 113, 124–25
   as "great democracy," 12, 26–27
   LCA models of, 66–67
   market-oriented reforms, 13
   one-party regime, 13–14
   politics and democracy in, 12
   popular understanding of democracy, 106–7
   Principle-Holders in, 55–56
   rivalry with US, 14
   understanding of democracy, 60–61
Chinese Communist Party (CCP), 13–14, 113, 115
civil disobedience, 159–60, 180–81

civil liberties, 77, 87–88, 92, 110, 120–21, 137–38, 145–47, 153–54
closed-ended survey instruments, 24–25, 27, 43–44
cognitive capacity effects, 90, 91f
cognitive features of democracy, 19, 98, 103
Cold War, 12–13
collective action, 150–51
collective welfare, 6
Colombia, 55–56, 118
Color Revolutions, 136–37, 150
Communism, 13–14
confirmatory factor analysis (CFA), 34–43, 36t, 44–45, 45f, 47, 59–68, 192n.13
Confucianism, 13–14, 50–51, 87, 93–94, 110, 115, 123–24, 153–54, 176
consolidation of democracies, 1, 10, 11, 17, 25–26, 97, 126–27, 133, 150, 160–61, 169, 176, 184
contemporary popular understanding of democracy (PUD)
 confirmatory factor analysis, 47, 59–68
 as continuous latent spectrum, 48–53
 introduction to, 47–48, 50f
 latent class analysis, 47, 52–68, 54f
 longitudinal stability in, 59–66, 61f, 63f, 65f, 69f, 70f, 71f, 72f
conventional participation in democracy, 143–50, 146f, 148f, 164f
cosmopolitan communications, 82, 89–90, 95–96, 174–75
Costa Rica, 121–23
country-unique features constant, 106
COVID-19 pandemic, 184–87
crisis of democracy
 coherent framework for understanding, 181–82
 critical missing dynamics, 9–14
 demand-side dynamics, 2–3, 170
 democratic constructions in understanding of, 3–6
 importance of understanding, 6–9, 17–18
 introduction to, 1–3
 key findings on, 170–81
 overview of, 17–20, 18f, 21t
 research design and data, 14–17, 16t
 summary of, 169–70
 supply-side dynamics, 2, 170
cultural features of democracy
 democratic assessment in, 110
 introduction to, 5–6, 14–15
 in popular understandings of democracy, 24, 25, 52, 86–98

deconsolidation in democracies, 1, 3, 7–8, 25–26, 123, 126–27, 133, 160–61, 169, 181–82, 184, 185–86
demand-side dynamics, 2–3, 170
democracy/democracies. *See also* contemporary popular understanding of democracy; crisis of democracy; cultural features of democracy; political participation in democracy; politics and democracy; popular understanding of democracy; socioeconomic features of democracy; trade-offs with democracy
 apathy toward, 7–8
 attitude-behavior connections, 183–84
 authoritarian notions of, 15
 authoritarian resilience against, 17
 cognitive features of, 19, 98, 103
 consolidation of, 1, 10, 11, 17, 25–26, 97, 126–27, 133, 150, 160–61, 169, 176, 184
 conventional participation in, 143–50, 146f, 148f, 164f
 COVID-19 pandemic and, 184–87
 declining confidence in, 1
 deconsolidation in, 1, 3, 7–8, 25–26, 123, 126–27, 133, 160–61, 169, 181–82, 184, 185–86
 defining features of, 7, 8–9
 electoral participation in, 134–43, 138f, 140f, 162f
 empirical analysis of, 6–7
 freedom-and-liberty-centered democracy, 28, 35, 44, 49, 53
 global popular support for, 75–76
 good-government-centered understanding of, 28, 38, 44, 49, 53
 "great democracies," 12, 26–27
 impact on authoritarian regimes, 1–2, 3–5, 6–8
 implications for future of, 184–88
 industrial democracies, 3, 10, 12–13, 139

institutional features of, 5–6
instrumental values of, 158, 176, 177, 179, 192n.11
intrinsic values of, 10–11, 136–37, 151–52, 175–76, 177–78, 179, 184
key aspects of, 27–28
liberal democracy, 1, 12–13, 82, 95–96, 176
mature democracies, 10
media criticism of, 28
norms-and-procedures-based democracy, 28, 35, 44, 49, 53
operationalization of democracy conceptions, 9–10
procedural understandings of, 26–27, 34–37, 44, 48–52, 53–54, 58, 60–61, 66–67, 171–73
psychological features of, 19, 98
public opinion research on, 1–2, 7, 105, 183–84
scholarly contributions to research on, 181–84
social-equity-based understanding of, 28, 44, 49
socioeconomic features of, 2–3, 5–6, 10–12, 14–15
substantive understandings of, 26–27
theorization on democracy conceptions, 9–10
Third Wave democracy, 6, 17
trade-offs with, 10, 11–12, 15, 17–18, 81, 86, 182–83
unconventional participation in, 150–57, 153f, 155f, 166f
violations of fundamental democratic principles, 10, 11
visible vs. invisible attributes of, 15
democracy-promoting institutions, 2
democratic assessment
   benefits of, 177–78
   in China, 105–16, 109f, 111f, 124–27
   Global Barometer Surveys (GBS II) data, 103–5, 104f, 108–10, 113–14, 116–27
   in home countries, 116–24, 117f, 120f, 122f, 130t, 131t
   introduction to, 103–5, 104f
   summary of, 124–27
   in US, 105–16, 109f, 112f, 124–27

democratic transition, 10, 11, 25–26, 43, 97, 126–27, 133, 150, 160–61, 176, 181–82, 184, 186
democratization, 2, 8
demographic features of democracy, 19
demonstrations, 20, 28, 150, 151–52, 157, 159–60, 180–81
dictatorships, 19, 86–88, 93–94, 96–97, 110, 137–38, 176
Dominican Republic, 52, 66–67, 172–73
Duterte, Rodrigo, 1–2

East Asia, 15–16, 17, 49–51, 52, 55, 64–65, 172–74
economic growth
   of autocracies, 118–19
   in China, 13–14, 60–61, 106–7, 108, 113, 124–25
   democracy and, 5, 13–14, 17
   economic recessions and, 85–86
   in industrial societies, 84–85
economic insecurity, 10, 185
economic modernization, 1, 169
economic prosperity, 4, 115
economic recessions, 85, 110, 137–38, 145–47, 185
economic recovery, 12–13
economic stagnation, 3
Ecuador, 52, 66–67, 172–73
educational attainment, 89–90, 110, 156–57, 159–60, 180–81
education systems, 8–9, 11, 181–82
Egypt, 55–56, 118
electoral integrity, 2
electoral participation in democracy, 134–43, 138f, 140f, 162f
elite-dynamics, 4
employment opportunities, 181–82, 185
entitlement programs, 10
Ethiopia, 118, 121–22
ethnic intolerance, 17
European Barometer Survey, 190n.20
evolutionary modernization theory, 84–85, 189n.5

Fence-Sitters, 40–42, 53, 55, 64–65, 67, 113–14, 173, 192n.11
forced-choice questions, 24

four-point Likert scale, 116–18, 119–20
freedom-and-liberty-centered democracy, 28, 35, 44, 49, 53
Freedom House ratings, 14–15, 19, 80–81, 92, 93, 97, 103–5, 110, 120–23, 137, 139, 148–49, 154
   political participation, 137, 139, 148–49, 154
   reasons for choosing, 195n.11
freedom of expression, 28
free elections, 7

generational replacement concerns, 5–6
Ghana, 55–56, 87–88, 118, 121–22, 140–41, 156
Global Barometer Surveys (GBS II) data
   democratic assessment, 103–5, 104f, 108–10, 113–14, 116–27, 177
   European Barometer Survey and, 190n.20
   introduction to, 15–16, 18–20
   new ranking instruments in, 27–30, 29t, 171–72
   political participation, 142–44, 145, 152–53
   popular understanding of democracy, 27–45, 29t, 47–48, 73–74, 85–86, 87–88
   question order effect, 31–34, 32f, 33f
global financial crisis (2008-2009), 12–13, 25–26, 110, 113
globalization, 10, 181–82, 186, 187
good-government-centered understanding of democracy, 28, 38, 44, 49, 53
governance hypothesis, 119
"great democracies," 12, 26–27
Great Depression, 25–26
Great Recession, 10, 13
gross domestic product (GDP), 12–13, 83, 85, 90, 92–93
G20 countries, 13
Guatemala, 52, 66–67, 172–73

higher living standards, 95
Honduras, 118, 121–23, 140–41
Hong Kong, 60–61
hybrid regimes, 121–23, 140–42, 148–49, 154–55, 158, 177–79
hyper-globalization, 186, 187

illiberal societies, 82, 95–96, 175
inalienable rights and liberty, 10–11, 12–13, 26, 44, 47, 49–50, 113, 171
India
   COVID-19 containment, 186–87
   democracy in, 52, 122–23
   global technology innovation, 13
   intrinsic values of democracy, 66–67, 172–73
   IRT scores, 61–62
   political violence in, 154–55
individual-level macro-mechanisms, 73, 110, 137–38
indoctrination tactics, 11
Indonesia, 60–62, 122–23, 154–55
industrial democracies, 3, 10, 12–13, 139
information technologies, 1, 3–4, 95
Inglehart, Ronald, 84–85
institutional features of democracy, 5–6
institutionalization, 8, 86–87, 105, 143–45
instrumental values of democracy, 158, 176, 177, 179, 192n.11
international organizations, 14–15, 134
intrinsic values of democracy, 10–11, 136–37, 151–52, 175–76, 177–78, 179, 184, 192n.11
item non-response, 194n.3
Item Response Theory (IRT) model
   political participation, 139, 145–48
   popular understanding of democracy, 41, 49, 50f, 51, 52–53, 59–66, 74–81, 88–89, 120–21, 172–73
   zero-order mixed-effect OLS model of, 194n.8
Ivory Coast, 55–56

Japan
   global technology innovation, 13
   Principle-Holders in, 55–56
   understanding of democracy, 60–61, 121–22, 140–41, 156

Kenya, 52, 66–67, 172–73

latent class analysis (LCA)
   democratic assessment, 110–11
   political participation, 145–47

popular understanding of democracy, 34–43, 40f, 42f, 44–45, 47, 52–68, 54f, 74–75, 173, 192n.11
Latin America, 7, 49–50, 51, 52, 55–58, 172–73. *See also individual Latin American countries*
legislative oversight, 28
liberal democracy, 1, 12–13, 82, 95–96, 176
Liberia, 85
living standards, 4, 85–86, 95, 124, 174–75, 177, 181–82
longitudinal stability in PUD, 59–66, 61f, 63f, 65f, 69f, 70f, 71f, 72f

Madagascar, 55–56, 85, 118
Malawi, 85
Malaysia, 60–61, 118, 121–23, 140–41
Mali, 55–56, 66–67, 121–22, 140–41, 172–73
market-oriented reforms, 13
mass-dynamics, 4
mass media, 8–9, 11
mature democracies, 10
Mauritius, 118, 156
media criticism of democracy, 28
"Me Too" movement, 150
Mexico, 66–67, 118, 154–55, 172–73, 186–87
Middle East, 15–16, 150, 185
minorities' rights, 2
mixed-effect models
  democratic assessment, 110, 120f
  introduction to, 19–20
  political participation, 137, 138f, 138–39, 145–47, 146f, 152–53
  popular understanding of democracy, 74, 78f, 78–79, 89f, 99t
modernization theory, 5, 84–85, 97, 176, 189n.5
Mongolia, 52, 60–61, 66–67, 105, 122–23, 154–55, 172–73
Morocco, 55–56, 66–67, 172–73
Mozambique, 52, 66–67, 172–73

Namibia, 105, 122–23, 154–55
neo-liberal ideology, 187
Nepal, 121–23, 140–41
Nicaragua, 52, 66–67, 172–73
Niger, 55–56, 66–67, 85, 172–73
Nigeria, 121–23, 140–41

NIMBY (Not-In-My-Back-Yard) movement, 150
non-democracies, 6–7, 8, 37, 43, 126–27, 142–44, 149–50, 186, 187
non-governmental organizations (NGOs), 134
non-response rates, 38–41, 40f, 76–78, 99t, 194n.3
norms-and-procedures-based democracy, 28, 35, 44, 49, 53
North Africa, 7, 49–50, 55, 58, 172–73
North America, 10, 51, 58, 182–83. *See also* United States

one-party regime, 13–14, 106–7, 124–25
open-ended survey questions, 27–28, 43–44
operationalization of democracy conceptions, 9–10
operationalization strategies for PUD, 34–45, 36t, 39f, 40f, 42f

Pakistan, 55–56, 121–22
Panama, 55–56, 105, 122–23
Paraguay, 51–52, 66–67, 118, 172–73
personal dictatorships, 19, 86–88, 93–94, 96–97, 110, 137–38, 176
Peru, 52–53, 55–56, 118, 122–23
Philippines, 1–2, 52, 60–62, 66–67, 154–55, 172–73
pocketbook economic evaluations, 119, 137–38
political fig leaf, 6–7
political interest coefficients, 89–90
political oppression, 105, 107, 156–57, 159–60, 180–81
political participation in democracy
  conventional participation, 143–50, 146f, 148f, 164f
  electoral participation, 134–43, 138f, 140f, 162f
  expressive values associated with, 178–81
  introduction to, 133–34
  summary of, 158–61
  unconventional participation, 150–57, 153f, 155f, 166f
political polarization, 3, 4–5, 107–8, 187, 190n.11

political rights, 7, 77, 87–88, 92, 96–97, 105, 110, 118–19, 120–21, 124, 137–38, 144–47, 153–54, 176–77
political sophistication, 114, 123, 141–42, 149–50, 156–57, 159–60, 180–81
political violence, 150–51, 153–56, 159, 179–80, 183–84
politics and democracy
  democratic assessment, 103–5, 104f, 110, 119
  effects of political interest, 80f
  features of, 14–15
  popular understandings of democracy, 20, 24, 25–26, 52, 86–98
  supremacy of, 1–2, 4
  trade-offs with democracy, 11–12
popular sovereignty principle, 10–11, 26
popular understanding of democracy (PUD). *See also* contemporary popular understanding of democracy; democratic assessment
  in China, 106–7, 110
  comparative research on, 24
  conceptual understanding, 23–27
  confirmatory factor analysis, 34–43, 36t, 44–45, 45f
  contextualized origins, 174
  GBS II ranking instruments, 27–30, 29t, 171–72
  instruments to measure, 17–19, 28–43
  introduction to, 14–15, 18–19, 23
  Item Response Theory (IRT) model, 41, 49, 50f, 51, 52–53, 59–66, 74–81, 88–89, 120–21, 172–73
  latent class analysis, 34–43, 40f, 42f, 44–45, 173
  operationalization strategies, 34–45, 36t, 39f, 40f, 42f
  political participation and, 152–53
  question order effect, 31–34, 32f, 33f
  summary of, 43–45, 45f, 66–68
  in US, 106–7, 110
popular understanding of democracy (PUD), origins
  cosmopolitan communications, 82, 89–90, 95–96
  cultural contexts impact on, 24, 25, 52, 86–98
  economic contexts impact on, 84–86
  Global Barometer Surveys (GBS II) data, 73–74, 85–86, 87–88
  individual features impact on, 82–84
  introduction to, 73–74
  latent class analysis, 74–75
  multilevel dynamics driving, 81–94
  non-response to PUD instruments, 74–81
  political contexts impact on, 86–94
  summary of, 94–98
populism, 4–5, 57, 181–83
Principle-Holders, 40–42, 53–54, 55–56, 64–65, 67, 113–14, 118–19, 173
procedural understandings of democracy, 26–27, 34–37, 44, 48–52, 53–54, 58, 60–61, 66–67, 171–73
propaganda tactics, 6–7, 11, 43, 118–19, 126–27, 141–42
protests, 20, 28, 150, 151–52, 157, 159–60, 180–81
psychological features of democracy, 19, 98
public opinion research, 1–2, 7, 105

quality governance, 4–5, 7–8, 44, 113, 114, 123, 171, 181–82
quality public services, 28
question order effect, 31–34, 32f, 33f

radical political activities, 4–5
regional barometer survey projects, 15
regional variation in democratic conceptions, 172–74
rule of law, 2, 8, 12–13

self-initiative effects, 90, 91f
self-report measures, 76–77, 82–83, 95–96, 107–8, 125–26, 133, 175, 177–78
Senegal, 105, 118, 121–22
Sierra Leone, 154–55
Singapore, 13, 60–61, 66–67, 118, 121–22, 172–73
social desirability bias, 76, 77, 192n.9

social-equity-based understanding of democracy, 28, 44, 49
social mobility, 12–13
social science research, 103
societal-level macro-mechanisms, 14–15, 73
societal variation in democratic conceptions, 172–74
socioeconomic features of democracy
  democratic assessment, 103–5, 104f, 110, 115, 119
  higher living standards, 95
  introduction to, 2–3, 5–6, 10–12, 14–15
  political participation, 137, 145–47
  popular understandings of democracy, 24, 25–26, 52, 82, 83–84, 91–92, 93f, 94–98
sociotropic economic evaluations, 119, 137–38
South Africa, 105, 122–23
South America, 15–16, 51
South Asia, 15–16, 17, 49–50, 55
Southeast Asia, 15–16, 17
South Korea, 60–62, 87–88, 121–22, 140–41, 156
strategic institutional engineering, 1, 3–4, 181
subprime mortgage market crisis, 12–13
sub-Saharan Africa, 49–50, 55, 58, 172–73
substantive understandings of democracy, 26–27
Sudan, 121–23, 140–41
supply-side dynamics, 2, 170
Swaziland, 66–67, 105, 121–22, 172–73

Taiwan, 55–56, 60–61, 118, 156
Tanzania, 52, 55–56, 118, 172–73
Thailand, 55–56, 60–62, 118
theorization on democracy conceptions, 9–10
Third Wave democracy, 6, 17
Togo, 118
trade-offs with democracy
  ignoring of, 182–83
  for instrumental gains, 175, 179–80
  intrinsic *vs.* instrumental values, 135–36, 192n.11

introduction to, 10, 11–12, 15, 17–18
  in political participation, 135–36
  in popular understanding of democracy, 81, 86
transition to democracy, 10, 11, 25–26, 43, 97, 126–27, 133, 150, 160–61, 176, 181–82, 184, 186
transparency concerns, 2
Tunisia, 55–56
Turkey, 186–87
Twitter, 1–2

ultra-nationalistic populist movement, 10
unconventional participation in democracy, 150–57, 153f, 155f, 166f
United States (US)
  COVID-19 containment, 187
  democratic assessment in, 105–16, 109f, 112f, 124–27
  democratic practice in, 19–20, 49–50, 51–52
  economic recovery, 12–13
  as "great democracy," 12, 26–27
  liberal democracy in, 12–13
  political polarization in, 190n.11
  politics and democracy in, 12
  popular understanding of democracy, 53
  populism rise in, 57
  rivalry with China, 14
Uruguay, 87–88, 118, 121–23, 140–41, 156

Venezuela, 121–22
Vietnam, 55–56, 60–62, 118, 121–22, 140–41, 173–74, 186–87
violations of fundamental democratic principles, 10, 11

within-society variation, 106
World Values Survey (WVS), 15, 62–64, 192n.3, 192n.4, 193–94n.1, 197n.8

Zambia, 55–56
zero-order mixed-effect OLS model, 194n.8
Zimbabwe, 121–22, 140–41